I0820326

WHAT WE CALL MASALA

I live and write on Wadandi Boodja and pay respects to elders past and present. As a current householder in a long line of Kashmiri women who trace their ancestry to the Seven Rishi Saints and the constellation Pleiades, I similarly pay my respects to the family who have come before. I am proud to carry forward our legacy.

murdoch books
Sydney | London

A cook's practical guide to the poetry of Indian spices

74 spices, 85 recipes

Photography Patricia Niven
Styling Kirsten Jenkins
Design Pfisterer + Freeman

KA 03 HH 2012
CNG
KA 03 JS 3854

ಸುಧಾಕರ್
Thums Up

CONTENTS

THE GANJU FAMILY TREE

The key to recurring names throughout this book

The cradle of masala is family, which means mine appears rather a lot in this book. For the sake of not having to repeat the relationship every time I mention a name, here is a brief Ganju family tree mentioning only those who form part of the story here.

Badi Ammi
Chandramohini Gamkhar:
my paternal great-grandmother, Ammi's mum

Papa .... **Ammi**

Papa
Shyam Nath Ganju
my paternal grandfather

Ammi
Kamini Kamala Ganju (née Gamkhar)
my paternal grandmother

Bui
Nirupma Raina (née Ganju)
my paternal aunt, Dad's sister

Bapu .... **Chachi**

Bapu
Munishwar Nath Ashish Ganju
my paternal uncle, Dad's elder brother

Chachi
Neelima Ganju (née Dhar)
my paternal aunt, Dad's elder brother's wife

Chachu
Alok Nath Ganju
my paternal uncle, Dad's younger brother

Dad .... **Mum**

Dad
Anup Ganju

Mum
Jennifer Suzanne Ganju (née Godkin)

Shivani
Shivani Raina
my cousin-sister, Bui's daughter

Eeshan
Eeshan Nath Ganju
my elder brother

Me .... **Scott**

Me
Sarina Kamini Lewis (née Ganju)

Scott
Scott William Lewis
my husband

Shyam
Shyam Nath Ganju
my younger brother

Kaira
Kaira Raina Ghosh
Shivani's daughter

Cailean
Cailean Lewis
our eldest son

Ash
Ashok Alexander Lewis
our youngest son

Introduction

THE MAGIC OF MASALA

I was invited to run a spice class a few years back by a group of ten women who were part of a book club that had set themselves the lofty goal of reading Salman Rushdie's *Midnight's Children*. A few chapters in and there was a general consensus they'd overstretched their literary interest. But the appeal of *India* still resonated. It seemed I'd be the easier option: a two-hour masala masterclass where they could sip wine, possibly learn a thing or two about 'Indian spices' and snag a Kashmiri feast into the bargain.

The host's beautiful house was in Yallingup, near my own town, Margaret River on Wadandi Boodja. In this area of raw beauty in south-west Western Australia, at the bottom left corner of Australia on a map, I run private events at a lot of bush blocks – down red-gravel tracks, kangaroos on the lawn, the coastline hiding over the next ridge. This time we set up on the low table in the dining room so everyone could be comfortable: a lot of the class is focused on tasting raw spices and fats from the bottle, so we don't need to be in the kitchen. There's always laughing, and back and forth. I love watching the faces, knowing that at some point I'll get to witness each individual's aha moment.

Maybe the only real difference with this group was that one of the women was really quiet. Reading faces in a class can be difficult because there's lots of *them* and only one of me, so I've developed a habit of verbally checking in when I teach. Like a touch to your elbow. Have I gone on too long? Not been simple enough? Every time I put out feelers, the other women in the group responded with resounding cries of 'We're great!' But this one woman wasn't showing me anything. At least not until the end of the class, when she approached me to let me know she'd lost her sense of taste after a sudden illness. In the six years since she had experienced almost no recovery. Her distress was so close to the surface. But equal to that distress was more than a tiny bit of hope: through our class she'd been able to connect to the raw spice she was tasting by being aware of what was happening in her mouth. The gingery-earthy primary qualities of turmeric had eluded her, but she could feel the weight of it on her palate floor, like clay drying out. She couldn't detect the licorice salt of fennel seeds, but their sticky quality when she chewed them was something she'd been able to hold onto. She could barely discern the sweetness and smoke of Kashmiri chilli powder, but the tingling sensation of her top palate implied heat and light.

Her aha moment didn't arrive until the meal. When she took her first few bites I saw her face just kind of explode – her eyes were wide with the experience of sharing food with her friends in a way she'd thought had been lost to her. She was all joy. It was as if her very *frequency* had changed. She cornered me in the kitchen, wanting to know if I was magic. 'Not magic,' I laughed, blushing. I hadn't given her back her sense of taste. I'd given her something Indians call masala. Masala is deeper and wider than flavour. It is shape, weight, texture, feeling. It's a whole different way of experiencing food.

I arrived at teaching masala in a way that was neither easy nor natural. I grew up in a Kashmiri Hindu family steeped in masala, but I wanted to write, not to cook. Kashmir is a region of mountains and valleys in the far north of India bordering Pakistan and China. To the outside world, it is recognised as a land of saffron, and a disputed territory that has ignited three wars between Pakistan and India since partition in 1947. (That's if Kashmir is known at all – the Western world's general knowledge of regional Indian geography doesn't usually stretch beyond the big cities and southern beach resorts.) To be a Kashmiri Hindu is to be part of a small ethnic minority of Shaivites (a particular sect of Hindus) and a Pandit. And to call Kashmir your ancestral home.

'Ancestral' because *our* family moved south and out of the valley in the seventeenth century, when the Mughlai ruler Aurangzeb introduced Sharia law in Kashmir, resulting in forced conversion of Hindus to Islam or death by beheading. In the four centuries since, our connection to our kitchens and our *pujas* (our household temples) has kept our culture relevant and present. But the cooking has always been personal, not for public consumption – traditionally, as Brahmans, the Pandits were considered scholars. As part of the nomenclature of India's now outlawed caste system, the words 'Brahman' and 'Pandit' carry a taint, but that scholarly notion has persisted as part of our Ganju family character, even as it relates to masala. Maybe especially as it relates to masala. Our food, the way we eat, our choices, our spices, our dishes – they're built into our identity. Teaching it to someone else felt as foreign an idea to me as showing a stranger how to do their own laundry.

When I moved to Margaret River in 2015 with my husband Scott, and my sons Cailean and Ash, my perspective changed. I'd quit journalism to write my first book, a memoir, *Spirits in a Spice Jar*, working part-time in a popular local deli while I finished it and sold the manuscript. People didn't know me but wanted to, and so the explanations started. How Mum and Dad met and married in New Delhi before moving to Australia. How as a family we lived the bulk of the year in a quiet coastal town around an hour from Melbourne on Australia's eastern seaboard, before spending our summer holidays back home with Ammi and our extended Ganju family in New Delhi. The high school years in Bengaluru. The back and forth between cultures. But that the beauty of knowing who we were – a Kashmiri Hindu family – was a constant because we ate that reminder every day.

Repeatedly telling the story helped me to see the specialness of my family legacy. And the sadness, too: I let go of masala from my very late teens, through my twenties and into the cusp of my thirties because it reminded me too much of what I thought I'd lost. I was about thirteen when Mum was diagnosed with early onset Parkinson's disease, and it changed our family. Incurable degenerative neurological conditions like hers are the kinds of diagnoses that can create corrosion in families over time. I didn't handle it well as the years went on. Gradually it felt easier to seal off some of the tough bits. Our family food – masala – burrows into the deepest parts of us and that hurt too much, so I just stopped.

I only picked masala back up after Cailean and Ash were born, because I needed to retrieve those pieces of myself so that I could pass our traditions on to them. So I pulled out Ammi's recipes, the ones Dad had written down while watching her cook back in the 1980s, set up my kitchen and started out on my own journey as an Indian householder.

The pertinent information here is that I stepped away and came back. Masala is so woven into Indians that it's a feat to be able to articulate the warren of meaning it holds. The reason I can do that is my re-entry – once we leave something behind, any future relationship to that thing has to begin anew. And that meant finding new ways to experience past meaning through masala. Or, to put it another way, I closed the door on the way out and found a way back in through a side window. And in the process, masala performed its magic on me; not just bringing me home and transforming my life, but undercutting my own prejudice that the domestic isn't worth examination.

That experience of leaving, coming home and then teaching has given me an understanding of what those who are new to masala perhaps don't know, and developed my ability to give them what they need.

As kids we ate dinner cross-legged on the floor, rolling out our eating mat – our *chatai* – when Mum and Dad yelled at us from the kitchen. My brothers shoved each other forward to cook chapatis on the tawa – a concave cast-iron griddle that pretty much never left the stovetop. I had to make the raita. Mum and Dad would be arguing over who'd timed the rice. Years later, Scott laughed that we needed to immortalise that question on a T-shirt: *Who's Timing the Rice?!*

Coded into that nightly scene in our Desi (culturally Indian) household was all kinds of information that doesn't seem obvious. Eating cross-legged on the floor is about improving digestion – and traditional Indian medicine, Ayurveda, sees a healthy digestive system as *the* central tenet of a healthy life. Perfecting raita meant trying, trying, trying – watching Mum when she corrected me and learning how to taste. The nightly flatbreads were connection to Kashmir for a Kashmiri Hindu family living a small-town Australian coastal life – in Kashmir, breads are literally *everything*. It didn't matter if the flatbreads in our family were Dad's special Saturday-lunch parathas or the easy midweek option of supermarket pita bread slathered in ghee and cooked on the tawa. This was dinner, not dogma. The meal and everything around it connected us to tradition and to each other. And the food was so *gooood*. All of that together equals masala.

Back in that Yallingup living room, the women and I sat together on the floor around the coffee table and I opened my six masala dabbas – my stainless steel spice tins, each one holding seven katoris: small silver bowls for individual spices. The aroma of forty-two different spices hit the air. We played guessing games, trying to identify what was what. One woman pointed curiously at fenugreek powder. For another, ajwain seeds unlocked memories of a trip to India. The smoky smell of black cardamom elicited a little thrill. We tasted raw spices, pinching and licking each one off our fingers. But we didn't stop with spices. We also swallowed fats from teaspoons in oily mouthfuls. Tasted this way, aromatics and fats have a feeling, a weight. Ghee can feel claustrophobic. Cumin seeds calming. Mustard oil hot and heavy. Everyone has a different perspective. But the togetherness – spice and everything around it – is what my special student tasted that night. Not a magic trick but a re-creation of what masala means to an Indian.

Spices, India and the geography of taste

Spices have been used in India since at least 2000 BC, and the Indian subcontinent lay at the heart of the ancient spice trade. For me, though, the geography of spice relates to the visceral way that spice categories and individual spices connect with very specific aspects of nature. Sometimes a spice will evoke landscape, sometimes it's elemental expression. Like the movement of chilli and that of flames.

In this book, I've divided spices into eleven categories. I developed these divisions over years of teaching as a way to help people create their own relationship to masala outside of its cultural context. Some of the categories take their name directly from the elements they resemble – earth spices, for example, are the seeds and powders possessed of grounding qualities and soil-like tastes and textures. Forest-floor spices recall the way winds shift leaves across the forest floor – an analogy for the way the dried and fresh leaf spices in this category move the weight of masala across the palate in gusts.

Although I developed these categories for other people to come to grips with masala, I persist with them because they have also helped me. These kinds of connections establish a natural logic to flavour-making decisions. If I want to tamp down heat – flame – in a masala, then I can use more earth spices to throw dirt on that fire. If I want to create brightness, I can apply acids to masala and enjoy the frisson, the way lemon juice sharpens the pain of a cut. Having these references on hand at once simplifies masala and creates a unique poetry that can help to modernise and personalise traditional spice storytelling while also honouring the treasure chest of ancestry.

This approach also offers a portal into traditional Ayurvedic practice via a gentler sensory pathway: like any ancient and traditional practice, classical Ayurvedic teaching is austere, and bracketed by a complex cultural frame of Indian language, perspective and philosophy. The valuable contemporary applications of its traditional teachings can get lost in rules and rigour. Learning to use our own sensory body as a guide to connect with the deeper meaning of spices through how they taste, what their tastes evoke and how these evocative sensations make us feel, is a way to connect directly with masala, no matter our food and cooking experience or background.

Choose your own adventure

Read from cover to cover, *What We Call Masala* is a lesson in masala, an in-depth version of the one I gave that night in Yallingup. We'll start with concepts everyone, no matter their background, can absorb easily, then build on them over the course of the book until you will not only have a thorough understanding of what masala is, but you will have developed your own relationship with masala. We'll examine each spice in detail, and learn about its impact on taste and emotion through its accompanying recipes. If you read the book in this way, your commitment will be rewarded with a deeper understanding of what masala could become to you.

But I do understand that my readers all approach books differently, so these pages are structured so that you can dip in and out and experiment with different recipes, thoughts and approaches.

***What We Call Masala* is divided into three parts:**

—

In Part 1: FOUNDATIONS, we'll gather on the living-room floor and explore fats, salts and the spices that provide a *spine* for masala.

—

In Part 2: TEXTURE, we'll head to the kitchen bench and work with the spices that give masala its *shape* and *form.*

—

In Part 3: MOVEMENT, we'll pull out the pots and pans and delve a little deeper into the spices and techniques that offer a *next-level relationship* to masala.

However you approach this book, its comprehensiveness will allow learning over time. There is no fast track to getting inside masala. No single answer to any one question. The reward for uncertainty is the pleasure of finding constant new perspectives. The ability to accept being caught off guard in this way is part of masala's message. It seems an obvious thing to say, but not knowing something is an imperative for developing understanding. This doesn't always feel comforting, especially given certainty feels so nice. What I will say is that uncertainty works both ways. What you think you know about spice and masala now might unravel as we move through the book. But you might also find that what you think you *don't* know about spice, you actually understand pretty well already.

The more I learn about masala and its magic, the less I feel I know. And in a world of thirty-second reels and at-your-fingertips online solutions, that mystery has very real beauty.

'The more I learn about masala and its magic, the less I feel I know.'

The QR codes throughout this book offer quick access to additional video content – use your smartphone camera to open the link.

FAQs

These questions come up in every class, so I'll address them first. Then we can move on to the *really* fun stuff. But you can't build a house without good foundations. Learning the ins and outs of how to buy and keep spice is the starting point for masala.

'Where do you buy your spices?'

I have a few sources. I sell my own organic blends to retailers, so I order my spices in small bulk quantity through an Australian importer. The ones I don't order myself I buy from Seven Seas Tea near where I live. At Seven Seas Tea you can take your own jars to fill up, or buy 100 gram (3½ oz) pouches if you just want a little of something. Cathy, the founder of Seven Seas, was the impetus behind me both beginning classes and creating my own blends. In 2017 she organised the first class and made me teach, and the next year she became my partner in the masala blend business. Though we are no longer in business together, I know Cathy buys spice thoughtfully, stores it well and has high turnover.

Otherwise I buy from Blue Ginger in my own town. Not everything stocked there is organic, but I do know they have high turnover. The owner, Bridget, and her manager, Susie, are longtime friends. Working at the Blue Ginger deli was the first job I had when I moved to Margaret River with my family in 2015. They buy spices in small quantities, then seal them in small bags and date them. It's a super busy little spot so they run through them quickly.

Obviously most of you aren't going to be in Margaret River or Western Australia or even perhaps Australia, but my point is you really *do* need to know your spice purveyor. Think of your spice retailer as you would a butcher, baker or grocer. The quality of your spices will categorically impact your dish. Older spices near the end of their life will have less flavour. They'll be blunter. With chilli, for example, you'll get heat, but not the floral and smoky aspects that make chillies so beautiful. Your food will be less delicious because old spice has no subtlety.

If you don't have this kind of retailer close and you have to default to a supermarket, buy organic. It makes a huge difference and is generally pretty affordable because of the small quantities. The other option is to buy online from reliable web-based spice stores.

'How long do you keep your spices?'
For me within three months is the sweet spot, but up to six months is workable. If you're not someone who uses a lot of spice, then I'd say twelve months, maximum. I think the record for keeping spice among those I've encountered went to one woman who hadn't updated her spice cupboard for twenty-five years. Generally the less confident someone is with spice, the less likely that they are to refresh them. But it's these very people who will get the most out of making sure their spices are 'fresh'. Fresh dried spices will be more forgiving when you're learning and making mistakes with ratios or combinations, because the spices are beautiful enough to soften your blunders. (Speaking of dried spices as fresh sounds like an oxymoron, but I promise it isn't.)

'How do you store your spices?'
I store most of my spices in masala dabbas (see page 28). These are traditional round tins with smaller containers called katoris (see page 28) inside. This makes it easier to cart them around to my spice classes, but it also makes it more pleasurable to cook – popping the lids and laying the dabbas on the kitchen bench feels like prepping paints for a canvas. I love it. It's also practical: I'll empty each little katori of spice through usage before refilling so that I know they're fresh. This might not be the solution for everyone. Dad kept his spices in small jars in a top drawer by the stovetop. He wrote the names on white labels on the lids. Dad was slower and more methodical with his cooking than I am, so taking the time to open and shuffle and replace his jars in between sips of red wine or tokes on a joint was part of his masala practice.

Work out a system that feels easy and best fits you and your kitchen. If your spices are easy to get to, you'll use them more, which means they'll stay fresher, so it's a win-win.

'Do the spices contaminate each other in a spice tin?'
The short answer is yes. The longer one is that it doesn't matter. On the journey to masala, purity isn't necessary. Masala ultimately teaches us to work with what we have in order to make something real. Keeping your cumin seeds in a dabba next to your ginger powder is just what happens in a kitchen. The important thing is that the spice is fresh and of good quality.

'How can you tell when spices are old?'
Taste them. It won't mean much to you at first. But if you buy a few really good-quality dried spices and then try them side by side with the old ones in your cupboard – comparing like with like – that will give you a baseline. You'll notice the blunt and bitter aspect of old spices in comparison with the 'flounce' of fresh dried spice. If you keep tasting each spice every time you buy it, you'll build a sensory reference library. This sensory library will allow you to blend intuitively, get to know new ingredients without coaching, and create your own personal version of masala.

'There's no ideal action that will make my relationship to spice more true.'

'What do you do with your old spices?'
I tip them out in the garden. Dad would never let us throw food in the bin. It always had to be thrown out the kitchen window for the birds. In all regional Indian traditions food is *prasad* – an edible blessing from God. We make it an offering by giving it back to nature. This is part of masala, too.

'Do you grind your own spices?'
Short answer? Not always. I'd rather buy good-quality coriander powder than get out a mini-blitzer and my dried coriander seeds every time I cook. I prefer to spend that time on cooking itself. I'll happily stand at the stovetop and brown lamb for Salan walah chawal (page 286) for 90 minutes, but I hate cleaning out those blitzer things afterwards. Nor do I grow my own spices. We live in a rental property, so I'm not keen to invest time and money in a transient edible garden.

Just like you, I have myriad competing demands on my time. Partner. Kids. Work. Older parents. Community work. Friends. Pets. On the odd occasion I have freshly ground my coriander seeds I *do* notice the difference. But a bit of convenience in a family kitchen is normal, just like that supermarket pita bread we cooked when we were kids. There's no ideal action that will make my relationship to spice more true. Paying attention to quality, storing your spices with care, and using them with feeling and flexibility is what matters. And – you guessed it – distinguishing between what actually matters to you and dogma is also masala.

This goes with that
Before I started running masala classes for kids, I had a pretty significant list of do and don't matches in my mind – aromatic combos I thought couldn't/wouldn't gel. Black mustard seeds and fennel seeds, perhaps? I'm struggling to recall my old edicts and provide examples.

After introducing kids to the idea of spice, I would give them free rein to build whatever masala they wanted from the forty-two spices in front of them. I used to cringe sometimes, but I actually never tasted a bad outcome. The kids worked with colour and texture and intuitively reached for the spices whose stories resonated with them – the excitement of chillies, or the windy, unsettling quality of something like nigella seeds. And because *they* put the masala together, it worked. Sometimes it needed a bit of adjustment. Sometimes I might have warned about too much of a particular spice. I tried to keep my nose out of it, though. They were curious, unafraid, and their curiosity tasted good.

It can be hard as an adult to drop into that zone. In this book I need to create frameworks to promote understanding, but please don't construe this as regulation. If you ever feel that way, or feel yourself double-guessing your choices, remind yourself that you doing you is the key. In getting to know masala with this book, you'll need to swing back and forth between information-gathering and intuitive action.

SPICE CATEGORIES

I've found that spice categories are a concise way to climb inside masala. Here is a broad overview of the eleven categories I commonly work with and – where it matters – the relationships between those categories. We'll go deeper into each category and spice as we move through.

Salts

Salts clarify flavour by making the aromatic contribution of every single ingredient both clearer and louder. As a category, it's responsible for *drive*. As an entrance point into masala it's pivotal. Try tasting three or four different salts and you will notice the wild difference between, say, an Italian sea salt and an Australian pink lake salt. You will also see that not even the simplest element can be taken for granted. According to the ancient Indian medical practice of Ayurveda, each type of salt has different health impacts. Unlike other salts, for example, kala namak, Indian black salt, is considered to be cooling. Tasting salts side by side is a great way to see how much potential for experimentation we have in the simplest of ingredients.

Fats & other masala carriers

Fats and other masala carriers – such as yoghurt, milk and water – are included under the banner of 'spice' because masala is broader in Indian cooking than conventional Western cooking ideas might make you think. The masala carriers in this category work not just as vehicles for spice but as *filters* on flavour. Ghee, for example, makes an aromatic classically beautiful by pulling out its sweetest and softest character. Mustard oil, on the other hand, draws out the hot, floral and blunt qualities. Salts and fats are deeply entwined. Simply understanding how to use salt and fat with flair and complexity will make your food exponentially more delicious and completely alter your approach to cooking.

Bitter spices

For Indian householders, bitter spices serve as the *spine* of both the kitchen and the medicine cabinet, much to our chagrin as kids. Swallowing *chyawanprash*, a bitter Ayurvedic medicine, always felt worse than the actual illness. In the kitchen, bitter aromatics create structural support for prettier spices, satiate the appetite, allow for darker emotive flavour expression and, according to Ayurvedic medicine, support the health of the gut. Bitter spices generally require the most sophisticated handling because they're not naturally delicious. Examples include turmeric and fenugreek powders.

Hot spices

Spices in this category introduce *persistence* and *height* to masala. Persistence comes from peppercorn-based spices – these are the aromatics that anchor flavour in the back of the mouth and hold it firmly. Chilli-derived spices give height – they work like a hot wind and draft flavour up and through the top of the mouth. Hot spices can make dark masala feel brighter, or drive energy into flavour that feels flat and heavy. They also work as stimulants.

Sweet spices

Sweet spices are ground zero for the human experience of taste. The breastmilk or formula that is our first mouthful establishes sweetness as a primal experience of *nourishment* and *safety*. Our familiarity with sweetness means we can detect its traces wherever they appear – as a shadow hiding behind the wood of cinnamon powder, for example. Including sweet spice in masala provides a point of safety amid the contrast.

Earth spices
Earth spices are dried seeds, either whole or powdered. Some have a soil-like aroma and taste. Earth spices are responsible for *texture*. They're generally the first spices – other than chillies – that people who haven't grown up with masala already use. A spice like cumin seeds is a really important touchstone, like a familiar face in a strange crowd. Spices from this category contribute this feeling of home or recognition to every dish: these flavours are settling.

Warm spices
The relationships between spices in the warm and earth categories are much like those between fats and salts – they're intrinsically entwined. Where earth spices bring familiarity and texture to masala, warm spices contribute *pleasure* and *density*. These spices are all powdered forms of whole spices – cinnamon stick, cassia bark, cloves, nutmeg, green cardamom pods, and so on. The dense nature of these powdered aromatics gives masala depth, warmth and weight. Warm spices are also aromatically pretty. Together, earth and warm spices create simply delicious flavour within the complex world of masala.

Acidic spices
Acidic spices are the third wheel to the earth and warm spices – not always essential, occasionally disruptive, but also capable of contributing another dimension of obvious *deliciousness* to masala. Tamarind in a traditional tamarind eggplant sabji (page 188), for example, zings up the pungent combo of mustard oil, fennel powder and ginger powder. Used in the right quantities at the right moments, acidic spices contribute to pleasure. Ayurveda sees pleasure as a part of wellness, and masala takes this into account.

Astringent–sulphurous spices
This is the first of two 'second-tier' categories. They are aromatics that alter the overall shape or movement of masala. Do I want to take the dish deeper? Make the flavour darker? In these cases, astringent–sulphurous aromatics create a sensation of *opening* – just as cutting fresh onion clears the sinuses. Opening up the mouth allows us to jam more flavour into a dish without feeling overwhelmed. Overwhelming flavour isn't just harder to enjoy, it also impacts our bodily systems. Masala links sensory experience to our digestion – flavours that feel good to us are easier to digest.

Forest-floor spices
The other second-tier category is forest-floor spices, the leafy aromatics we use either fresh or dried to move flavour along. They're like the ultimate English bobby – nothing to see here! These spices bring *levity* by shifting dense, dark and pungent aromatic qualities in a dish. 'Forest-floor' here refers to the way leaves are moved across the landscape by wind. It's how spices in this category behave.

Structural spices
Aromatics in this category are used whole – think star anise, black cardamom pods, cassia bark – and create both exclamation marks of flavour *and* structural support for other aromatics across the entire palate. Think of these spices as like verandah posts.

THE PALATE

Dividing the palate into nine regions helps us taste and understand masala. As with the spice categories, this is an easy introduction to concepts that will unfold throughout the book. It's worth noting that the palate as it relates to masala encompasses more than the mouth.

The palate floor | Bitter spices | Pungent
For masala, stimulation of the palate floor is about creating a base reference point: you cannot know where you've been or where you're going unless you know where you are. The palate floor broadly refers to the tongue surface, but also encompasses an imaginary floor that stands in for the tongue itself. In a flavour sense, stimulating the palate floor tells you where you are. I make masala from here. Generally bitter and pungent spices will do the job – anything heavy, structural and stable. Turmeric powder from the bitter spices is my go-to.

The lateral palate | Salts
The lateral palate starts at the centre of the mouth bow and then drives out laterally through the cheeks in both directions with even intensity. Lateral drive is created by salts and works as a volume dial on flavour, driving it out and through the mouth so that spice won't feel muffled, echoey or stifled. When you get this aspect of masala right, aroma is articulated, and everything tastes *more*.

The top palate | Hot spices
The top palate extends beyond the top of the mouth and up into the sinus cavity behind the eyes. Hot spices activate this part of the mouth and stretch flavour out long. Long flavour is elegant. It also works as a counterweight to deeper and darker flavour tones. Because masala is complex, these contrasting bright and light aspects are invaluable.

The mouth interior | Earth spices
I know, I know – technically every part of the palate is the interior of the mouth. But here I mean the negative space between the tongue and the top palate. It's the empty bit stimulated by the textural spices from the earth category. Working with this part of the mouth increases sensations of satiety – texture and weight here help us *feel* like we're eating. When this aspect is missing, masala loses its persistence: flavour disappears into the mid-palate like a planet into a blackhole.

The back palate | Pepper family hot spices
If the palate floor is about creating a base reference, then masala uses the back palate as a flavour anchor. Pepper family hot spices sit here and hook into the back molars, holding in the lighter aromatics. Without this element of masala, prettier spices are quick to dissipate out the front of the face. Clever masala work can extend and hold flavour through the back palate behind the molars.

The front palate | Warm spices
More than just the tip of the tongue, the front palate encompasses the whole area around the mouth and nose outside the mouth. Warm spices bloom out from the mouth to fill this space. Stimulation of the front palate aids masala by creating density and beauty: think of the pleasure and sensation of burying your nose in a fragrant rose. Masala that activates the front palate brings this kind of pleasure.

The gullet | Astringent–sulphurous spices
The gullet takes in the external area from beneath the chin to the base of the throat. It's a pocket of space stimulated by astringent–sulphurous spices – including elements such as mustard oil (page 93) and

hing or asafoetida (page 248). Opening this space is like opening a trapdoor in the palate floor; it allows heavier flavours to disperse downwards.

The inner cheek | Acidic spices

The inner cheek is that section of the mouth that typically puckers when we suck on a lemon. Activation of this part of the palate is a pleasure indicator for masala – it's attention-grabbing and kind of thrilling. It's worth noting that masala doesn't need activation of the inner cheek to feel complete, but knowing how to use acidity brings flair and excitement to the eating experience.

The central palate

The central palate is the straight line that runs from the bow of the lips to the back of the tongue, and its activation is pivotal to clear communication of masala. Unlike the other areas of the palate, the central palate is stimulated not by a particular category of spice, but by overall well-executed flavour construction. This aspect of masala is a must.

Iterating masala

Learning about masala involves looking at the same things in different ways, circling back again and again. Not just so you remember or because different people learn in different ways, but because as individuals we're concentric. Each day we circle the same patterns as new versions of ourselves, going over things, repeating behaviours and thoughts, but each repetition finds us in a slightly different place from before. Circling back lets us retrace similar ground with slightly different understanding. This is also my gentle way of writing – expect to read the same thing more than once. Or to find concepts re-cloaked as we move through the book.

THE SENSORY BODY

Before we dive in to the book proper, let's connect the spice categories and palate stimulation to our sensory body. I've developed the phrase 'sensory body' as a way to pay attention to sensation and how it affects us. It's how a traditional Indian householder teaches their kids about health *and* about taste. It's how I learned.

Some of the things I learned as a child were really small and apparently innocuous, like Dad telling us it wasn't healthy to drink water with our meals. Water's cold, you see, and so it tamps down the heat our body needs and generates through digestion. Dad was making us aware of what cold feels like – the slowing effect cold has on our body, and the impact this has on our digestive function. He told us this mattered because a healthy digestive system is the key to good overall health, at least from the point of view of a traditional Indian householder.

The sequence of explanations below is deliberate: to the best of my ability, they reflect my own thought process.

Bitter spices | The palate floor | The deep gut

An Indian householder views deep gut health as the prerequisite for everything – emotional, physical and spiritual stability. It's why I'm specific about the term. The gut is a physical space. But the notion of the *deep* gut is metaphysical as much as physical – I explain it as the cradle from beneath our pelvis, between our hips and into the base of our physical gut. It is our metaphysical centre of gravity and contains the sum of who we are. In masala, when we stimulate the palate floor, we activate the deep gut. Think of bitter spices as the spark that flicks this connection to life.

Salts | The lateral palate | The mouth
Salt doesn't just clarify flavour, it wakes the mouth up to the experience of taste. When the mouth is properly awake, the body can instantly access information from the deep gut, and thus make the connection between taste and digestion.

Fats and other spice carriers | The entire body

Fats work outside masala by providing both a vessel and a filter for the message. A well-chosen fat will hold masala in the palate space for longer, allowing the sensory body to extract maximum information and experience from each mouthful. This allows for full-body engagement with masala.

Hot spices | The top palate | Metabolism
A little heat is essential stimulation for the body's systems – particularly as it relates to digestive efficiency. Hot spices light up the top palate and fire the body into digestive mode. Too much can lead to inflammation, but in just the right amount it triggers metabolism and a powerful sensation of alertness.

Sweet spices | The heart | Safety
Sweet spices are the bolthole for feelings of love and safety. As our first taste, they stimulate not the mouth but the heart. Their use in masala opens a doorway to our own internal secure space, allowing our sensory body to find greater ease in the experience of eating when our system feels tired or overwhelmed – or if masala is particularly challenging.

Earth spices | The mouth interior | Settling
Earth spices act like a cosy quilt for the sensory body: these are the seedy spices that fill the mouth interior and signal comfort. This aspect of masala ensures a familiar touchstone. It always reminds me of walking in the front door from school and smelling cumin seeds and ghee, and knowing Mum or Dad was in the kitchen. I knew where I was. I knew I was home. Waking up the mouth interior with earth spice has the same effect on our sensory body.

Warm spices | The front palate | Memory
Masala relies on sensory memory to create beautiful food. Warm spices are the prettiest and connect to our most treasured recollections: those moments we wrap in metaphorical tissue paper, like eating Grandma's cinnamon buns at her kitchen table. Sparking these connections is the family storytelling element, and it's vital to the meaning of masala.

Acidic spices | The inner cheeks | Adrenal glands

Adrenal stimulation gets a bad rap, but in the right context (and quantity), masala loves it. Acidic spices that wake up the inner cheeks signal a taste of excitement – an adrenaline rush of flavour. This sensation of alertness anchors us to the experience of eating. It's a focal point for our attention.

Structural spices | The whole palate | Fascial system

The aromatic strength of structural spices creates a whole-palate frame for masala, like scaffolding around a building site. These spices work in the same way with the sensory body, so we can use them to activate full-body connection to the experience of masala.

Masala and the imaginative experience

The deeper we move into these pages, the more imaginative and storied some of the information will become. Because masala is more than flavour, we have to be more than cooks. Dad gave us imagination by domesticating Hindu mythology. He told us stories like Ganeshji losing his head in a battle with his father Shivji so many times that they became part of our real-life family tapestry. After that, it was pretty straightforward to see *spice* as family.

I'm going to keep asking you to believe in your own ability to mine flavour for meaning by presenting and re-presenting aromatics as food, function, pharmacy and fantasy. Imagining how your body connects with aspects of masala is just the beginning.

AYURVEDIC DOSHAS AT A GLANCE

Ayurveda is the ancient system of Indian medicine, but like most things Indian it goes far deeper than the English definition can convey.

Writing about the formal aspects of Ayurveda is a little tricky for me. Practitioners spend a lifetime studying the Ayurvedic doshas, or body types, and how they present in individuals, but I don't have that wisdom. My understandings are the same as others who, like me and my brothers, grew up in relatively traditional homes where conversations about Ayurvedic concepts formed part of parenting. Which means that I, like Indian householders everywhere, keep this aspect of masala really conversational and anecdotal.

Broadly speaking, the concept of doshas in Ayurveda refers to body constitutions or body types. Our individual body type takes in our physical construction, our internal functions, our temperament and the workings of our intellect. There are three doshas, and we're generally thought to be made up of more than one, though one dosha will usually dominate.

- **Vata:** associated with air and space, vata is described as cool, light and dry. Vata-dominant folk are said to be very thin and either small or tall, with a sensitive digestive system, quick movements and creative spark. Vata types will find connection to windier, lighter or drier spices; stimulation in bright, energetic and exciting aromatics; and counterbalance in rounded, dense and soothing masala.
- **Pitta:** associated with fire and water, pitta is described as driving, heating and energetic. Pitta-dominant folk are said to be of medium height and ruddy, with a well-developed athletic figure, and a charismatic, fiery and tenacious nature. Pitta types will find connection to hot, astringent and acidic spices; stimulation in windy, lighter or drier spices; and counterbalance in earthy masalas with a pattern of subtle cooling and soft warmth.
- **Kapha:** associated with water and earth, kapha is described as steady, consistent and heavy. Kapha-dominant folk are said to be physically solid, with lustrous hair and shining eyes, and to be mentally strong, reliable, protective, thoughtful and calm. Kapha types will find connection to rich fats, dairy and earthy spices; stimulation in hot and pungent spices; and counterbalance in masala with lighter elements of forest-floor spices and wet aromatics that promote light and bright movement – fresh turmeric and fresh ginger among them.

Doshas and masala

The idea of the dosha serves as a baseline for understanding our own responses to masala. Getting inside masala is a personal endeavour. Everyone's journey will look different, which means that we have to become our own point of reference, and knowing our dosha is one way to establish an individual framework of understanding.

The doshas and masala work well in combination because they encompass the same compartments. They both reference the physical, the emotional and the metaphysical or conceptual. And just as masala is about more than flavour, doshas are about more than the physical body.

Doshas play into deliciousness, allowing us to tailor tastes to our own bodily needs. When you know what you love – and what doesn't just *feel* good for the sum of you, but *is* good for the sum of you – then it's easier to feed yourself better. And to enjoy what's on your plate more.

NOT JUST POTS & PANS

Like everything with masala, your cookware matters. If you want to replicate the authentic tastes of India, the extra step is the right cookware. Having said that, you'll see in the recipes that I always suggest alternative cookware you're likely to have already.

Kadai

A kadai is a heavy, rounded, wok-like vessel, normally made from cast-iron, that suits the Indian penchant for high heat, oil-based cooking. A lot of recipes throughout this book will call for a kadai. A kadai cultivates a deep and even heat that allows for browning or cooking at high temperatures over prolonged periods. A thin South-East Asian–style wok won't be up to the task – it's designed to cook high and fast. If you don't have an Indian grocer nearby, you can find relatively inexpensive but heavy cast-iron woks (make sure it has a stable base for safe cooking) in cooking or camping stores. Seasoned well and treated with care, they last a lifetime.

Pressure cooker

Flavour-wise, a pressure cooker will win over a slow cooker or ordinary saucepan any day of the week. The technique of cooking under pressure and steam softens produce while retaining its form. Slow-cooking, however, breaks down produce, and when the structure of produce collapses, so does masala's clarity.

When I talk about pressure cookers, I mean the flameproof, non-electric version – a saucepan-like vessel with a lid that locks, allowing the pressure to build. These are what I use to cook, but I do realise that many people have an electric pressure cooker or a multicooker that allows for pressure cooking. Obviously you can't put these on the stovetop, which with the recipes in this book will often mean transferring things from one cooking vessel to another, and learning the cues to determine when things are sufficiently cooked in your own pressure cooker. If you get deep enough into masala that this becomes tiresome, you may find yourself investing in a flameproof non-electric pressure cooker like mine.

Whenever I cook with a pressure cooker, I allow time for the depressurisation process to happen on its own. This can add an extra 25 minutes to the cooking time, but it's worth it. Give it the same importance you would to resting meat after grilling or roasting. Force-releasing the pressure valve and letting the steam escape brings the pressure down quickly, but all that steam jetting out contains aroma. When we let the pressure cooker depressurise on its own, the steam will be reintegrated into the dish. This creates additional tenderness in proteins, and greater subtlety and clarity in masala.

If you're really pressed for time and you're using a flameproof non-electric pressure cooker, you can use Dad's trick – he would stick the pressure cooker under the kitchen tap and run cold water over the pot until he heard the click of release. You will lose some of the resting time, but this way the steam is at least contained.

Tawa

A tawa is a great piece of kitchen equipment. Traditionally used to cook regional Indian flatbreads (paratha, roti, chapati, etc.), it's a thin and slightly concave plate/pan made from iron, cast iron, aluminium or carbon steel. It can have a handle, but often doesn't. A tawa is designed to sit on a gas or open flame and conduct and hold heat well at high temperatures. I use mine to fry a fast egg, and it's also great for frying up caramelised onion, the kind you might use to top a steak or a hamburger.

Not non-stick

I'm not a fan of non-stick cooking vessels. There's a tension created by heat and a cast-iron pan surface that allows masala to communicate at full volume. Think of non-stick surfaces as slack guitar strings – they produce flabby, out-of-tune and muted sound. In a dish where tensile flavour is part of the story, using the right cookware becomes especially important.

Katoris and thalis

As kids, we used plates and bowls for Western food and thalis and katoris for Indian food. Thalis are plates, katoris are small bowls, and they are both made (these days) from stainless steel. Thalis and katoris are worth talking about because they are symbolic of the way regional Indian food is 1. thought of, 2. served, and 3. eaten:

1. The word *thali* refers to the style of plate, but also to a complete meal – a non-veg North Indian thali bought at any neighbourhood restaurant across India's regions would include rice, some kind of naan or paratha, a North Indian-style dal, raita, pickle or achaar, maybe gobi sabji, and a mutton curry.

2. A thali is designed to hold small tastes of a range of dishes (see above) that appeal to different aspects of appetite and reflect a traditional approach to nourishment.

3. The combination of thali and katori reflects traditional food lore as it relates to the serving of food: while rice and the major sabji or curry might be served upon the thali itself, condiments, dals and non-solid chutneys are served in katoris.

Dabbas

In this book, I refer to dabbas in general as the spice tins Indian householders use to keep commonly used spices. Though not essential, they are great tools to make spices attractive and easily accessible when learning. They are available at Indian or Asian grocers, and some spice specialty stores. A dabba can also refer to a lidded container used to keep leftovers, or the carrier that stores packed lunches – also known as a tiffin. These dabbas or tiffins are usually made from stainless steel.

1

FOUNDATIONS

THE LIVING-ROOM FLOOR

When we ate dinner every night on the living-room floor on our *chatai*, our eating mat, it was as a line of three in front of the quiz show *Sale of the Century* on TV – Eeshan in the middle, me on his left and Shyam on his right. There was no cutlery because we ate with our hands, and sometimes the contestants' answers got lost in Dad's loud post-cooking meal analysis shouted down from the kitchen: whether the dal was salted correctly, if the rice was timed right and cooked well, whether the mirch (red chilli) in his lamb curry was too much, even if the meal was served at the right temperature. (He liked it hot enough to blister his fingers when he took his first taste.)

Talk of the meal was as significant as the meal itself, which is why, when I teach people about masala face to face, I start on the living-room floor with a discussion about what taste means in making masala.

What it means to taste

Background information is everything. In my job in hospitality in cellar doors and restaurants in Margaret River, I spend my whole day talking about what it means to taste. A lot of folks who come to taste wine do so from a standing start, with no prior knowledge. They want to know if the name of each wine comes from the grape variety that's used to make it – like chardonnay is called chardonnay because it's made from the chardonnay grape. They're often surprised to learn that the juice of red wine grapes isn't red, and that the eventual colour of red wine comes from contact with grape skins. And to know that there isn't *one* cabernet sauvignon: every winery produces cabernet with a different character, depending on the clone of cabernet grown; the terroir; and the influence of winemaker philosophy, winemaking techniques and brand identity.

For people in wine or accustomed to drinking wine, those sorts of questions don't seem like questions at all – they're just things that you know. But when you're new to it, everything's an unknown. And it's not until some of those questions are out of the way that we can start to talk about what we're actually tasting in the glass: you can't ask someone to pay attention to what's in their mouth until they understand what they're paying attention *to*.

It's the same for masala. So just like a good masala, we're going to start off with the spices and aromatic categories that provide the connection between our palate and our deep gut. In this section, your first taste, you'll find a starting point for what masala means for you.

'Every time I introduce another aromatic into the mix of masala, we're going to taste the raw spice together. Think of this as an interactive book: if I could make it both scratch 'n' sniff and lick 'n' taste, I totally would.'

How to taste masala

Tasting masala involves these six steps:

1.

Taste enough of the raw spice to get an experience of its texture, aroma and sensory stimulation, but not *so* much that its volume creates an experience of bitterness. All powdered spices, no matter how beautiful in the right quantity, will default to bitterness when used in excess. I normally take a pinch.

2.

Taste the spice and focus. If it's a seed or leaf, chew. If it's a powdered spice then work with it, moving and pressing your tongue across the roof of your mouth.

3.

Note how the spice feels texturally. Dried leaf spices will rustle. Seeds might feel dry or sticky or hard to chew, depending on the aromatic. Powdered spices might be rough or dense or heavy, or very light and ephemeral. Take note of what you can.

4.

Try the spice again. This time, move your attention to where the spice hits your mouth. You might feel it in the back of your throat, on the roof of your mouth, on the tip of your tongue, in the upper palate space, or around the sides of your jaw. You don't need to put the spice in any particular part of your mouth to gather this information – an aromatic will stimulate the area of the palate that it stimulates no matter if you lick it off your finger, toss it to the back of your throat or nibble it with your front teeth. The mouth's clever like that. It knows what to do with what you give it. You don't need to make any connections as to why you feel it where you do. Just note the sensations.

5.

Try the spice again and now focus on aromas – the smells and tastes. Spices are complex, so these will occur in plural and will generally segue from prettier or stronger primary notes through to the less obvious or uglier tastes. If you repeat this process a few times – tasting the raw spice and then searching for flavours – your acuity will develop as the aromatic content builds in your mouth. Name aloud the tastes you detect.

6.

Try the raw spice one last time and now – with all of your other information about texture, mouthfeel and taste as a reference – assess how the spice affects your sensory body. It might have a settling or calming effect. It might stimulate you and heat your face. It might invoke strong sensations that feel difficult or inspire a sense of distaste. There could be that sensation of pleasure and the joy of experiencing a beautiful or delicious flavour. You may feel nothing at all, but even that is an emotion. Again, you don't need to rationalise what you do or don't feel. Just note the sensations.

It's best to work like this with every spice. Once you've got this down, you'll find it easier to take in the recipes.

How to cook

Each spice in the book is followed by recipes that work as explanation and exploration. Some recipes showcase very traditional Kashmiri Hindu fare. Some show a more contemporary approach to spice. And some borrow from other regions of India where that particular aromatic is used most commonly – spice usage across India is a hyper-regional affair. In each instance I've selected recipes that will help you attach what you've noted in tasting the raw spice to the flavour of the final dish.

We're working this way because the recipes themselves act like masala code breakers. There's lots of focus on progression. Take the Aloo jeera (page 126) that I've chosen to help illustrate cumin seeds. The three variations of the recipe use different oils to show how small changes to masala affect our sensory body.

Building this kind of beginning-to-end awareness of flavour means we can learn to feed ourselves the way our bodies desire to be fed (see page 35). We know the individual spice and what it does. We understand the techniques we can use to shape and form flavour. We understand what to pay attention to throughout the cooking process so we can create the nourishment that serves us.

Spice slammers

One of the easiest ways to make that connection between tasting raw spice and masala is to line up the aromatics asked for in any recipe and try them all raw, one after the other. I call them spice shots or spice slammers. Trying base aromatics like this helps us understand how flavour builds, and the ways spices influence each other. Pay attention to the flavour sequence. How a spice you thought you knew changes because of what comes before. And also to how you feel at the end after the experience as the spices coalesce – that idea of emotive flavour. This can take a few minutes as the raw spices jostle and shuffle on your palate. Certain elements that were strident might soften. Subtle spices initially overrun by stronger aromatics may return to the fore. Ultimately you'll feel *something*. High-tone flavours will leave you feeling stimulated. Darker, more pungent aromatics might be grounding or invoke shadowed tastes that thump you in the solar plexus.

It takes a long time to get inside masala, but a trick like this works as an accelerant. And once you decide you'd like to experiment by creating your own masala, it's a good way to test out your aromatic combo before going to all the trouble of cooking it: line up the spices you plan to use and run through a raw taste. A spice slammer should be delicious and give you the feels, even in that raw state.

Getting used to spice

One of the most difficult aspects of masala for those new to spice is its weight and texture. Masala *feels* like a lot to an untrained mouth. By gradually introducing softer spices with stable structures – turmeric, salt, a little cumin powder – the uninitiated can acclimatise to complex flavour. If you need help with recipe suggestions to start you or someone else on the journey, try the Simple yellow dal (page 39), Jeera chawal (page 123), or even the milder version of the Butter chicken (page 209).

THE THREE-BODY STATE

Masala has its roots in Ayurveda, which means health is implicit in the food we make and eat. In Ayurvedic terms, 'health' refers to our ability to understand and feed our three-body state. The three-body state is a concept we'll return to continually, so here I'll just give a quick summary.

The three-body state takes in our **physical**, **emotional** and **metaphysical** forms. Together these three parts make up the sum of us. The ultimate purpose of masala is to feed our three bodies, and what 'feeding' means is a little different for each body:

- Feeding the **physical body** relies on the concept of nutrition and how each of us is best nourished: this means understanding a little bit about our body constitution, which is traditionally where an appreciation of Ayurvedic doshas kicks in (see page 26).
- Our **emotional body** requires emotional nourishment, which is where we get into masala's emotive tastes. We tap into these by being engaged with our sensory body.
- The **metaphysical or spiritual body** is the home of our lineage, where we're from in a long-back family sense, and what our people have believed and attached meaning to in the non-physical world. Pragmatism as a philosophy is a relatively recent phenomenon in the course of human history – for more generations than not, humans have believed in some form of the divine. This is what the spiritual body connects us to. It influences how we've come to move through the world (see Taste as touchstone versus taste as blueprint, page 41).

Masala connects to all of these aspects of who we are.

BITTER SPICES

Function in masala: Providing a strong and stable base for flavour construction.
Emotive quality: Providing an underlying stability, persistence and strength.
Traditional medicinal quality: Deep-gut structural support.

The first action I take when I cook is to use fats and salts. But my first *thought* circles around bitter spices.

Bitter spices dictate a lot of decision-making with masala. If I choose a softer bitter aromatic then I know that I can drive my spice combination with a bit more aggression and emphasise pungent or darker characters. If the bitter spice I use in a dish is heavy, then I might choose to be lighter, sweeter and warmer in my masala. In both cases that bitter choice will influence how I think about salts and fats. Together these three elements drive the masala forward.

Traditional Indian regional recipes all find their origin in bitter tastes: bitterness is the foundation, and masala's complexity means you can't build your structure until you know the strength and shape of the base. That's not to say you'll find bitter spices in every traditional recipe. Ancient food cultures tend to find more than one way to achieve an end goal. Sometimes the foundational structure in masala derives entirely from use of a bitter spice like turmeric powder or fenugreek powder. But sometimes masala's base structure is created through combining a certain type of oil and a particular heat application (see, for example, Chokhta, page 91), or by combining spice and produce in a particular way to draw out recessed bitterness in other aromatics.

It took me years to work out how to teach others about the role of bitter in masala construction, because – like much of the wisdom of the Indian householder – the bones of it were fed to me but never explicitly explained. I think the only two things ever related to me directly about the role of turmeric powder were that it should be used with a little sugar, and that it should be present but not tasted. Ammi told me that.

I can understand why in the past the internal workings of masala weren't spoken of. We ate from tradition and that was it. But contemporary masala use is different. We're all coming at it from diverse places. Maybe you're part of the diaspora living in a Western environment with non-traditional food habits. Or maybe you have no relationship at all to India or to masala but you just want to get closer to the health and taste benefits of spice. In either case, learning from both traditional and contemporary quarters will give you the most flexibility and the largest internal reference library. Which is why I've deliberately sequenced the following bitter spices and accompanying recipes to provide an easy-to-follow arc of understanding. Read and cook sequentially if you can.

'Maybe you're part of the diaspora living in a Western environment with non-traditional food habits. Or maybe you have no relationship at all to India or to masala and you just want to get closer to the health and taste benefits of spice. In either case, learning from both traditional and contemporary quarters will give you the greatest flexibility and the largest internal reference library.'

TURMERIC POWDER
HALDI

Category: Bitter spices.
Form: Powder from ground dried turmeric rhizome.
Colour: Dusky orange to turmeric yellow.

Turmeric powder is an axis spice between East and West. Everyone knows it. When Scott and I lived in Paris, I used to walk up the street every morning to a boulangerie that made an incredible *petit pain* with *curcumin et noisettes* – turmeric and hazelnut loaf. I'd never buy a big loaf because I couldn't stop eating it. This was back in the early 2000s, so turmeric's worldwide spread is not a new thing. And now of course it's the first spice people ask me about. They want all the secrets.

But the actual reason we begin with turmeric powder – haldi – is its elemental importance in our understanding of masala. For an Indian householder haldi is the cradle-to-grave spice. It's the first aromatic introduced to us as babies. Haldi doodh (over the page) – turmeric milk – is the morning drink for building young bones and a healthy body. Soft yellow dal made by your mother is the flavour of maternal presence: my son Ash says the smell of dal's pressure-cooker steam will forever remind him of me.

The softness in turmeric's bitter taste is what I love. And what makes it accessible.

Tasting notes

Turmeric powder is heavy on the tongue but also complex and beautiful. Primary characters move through **warm ginger, clay** and **bitter orange rind**. There are secondary **floral** qualities and a faint tail of **fine white pepper**. Its tertiary characters relate to its dual textural appearance: turmeric powder has a **round powdered** quality through the central mouth space before settling as **heavy clay** on the tongue.

Use in masala

The dominant use of turmeric powder relates to creating a framework – bitter spices work like coat racks from which we can hang prettier aromatics so they show themselves more clearly. It's one of the reasons turmeric powder is a staple spice in the Indian pantry – masala is so complex that, without a frame, it ceases to make any aromatic sense.

'Taste is taught, and turmeric powder is the A in the alphabet of this lesson.'

Emotive content

Soft bitterness is a difficult emotion to feel because the pain is so exquisitely gentle. In many ways bombastic emotion often feels easier because it's very straightforward: hard anger, giddy joy, devastating grief. I wrote my first book, the memoir *Spirits in a Spice Jar*, in a long phase of gently bitter melancholy. Turmeric was a spice I kept close by my side, tasting the experience in dal and paneer ... soft dishes where the ground dried rhizome offers a gently bitter quality. The Indian householder's approach to Ayurveda folds our activities in the kitchen into lived experience.

Traditional medicinal impact

Ayurveda views turmeric powder as a support for the structure of the deep gut, and as an anti-inflammatory for the internal body and the skin itself, while its bitter taste works as a mild appetite regulator – eating less at every meal over a lifetime is one of the tenets of Ayurveda when it comes to longevity. Including bitter tastes in our meals helps to satiate the body so we don't eat too much (see Satiety is more than a full stomach, page 121).

Haldi doodh

Turmeric milk is the Desi* equivalent of Milo for Aussie kids, Ovaltine for Brits or Nesquik for Americans. There's no real recipe. But there is real meaning.

Haldi doodh is super simple, super nutritious, super comforting and super important to the architecture of a young child's building relationship to masala. Taste is taught, and turmeric powder is the A in the alphabet of this lesson. Stir a teaspoonful or so of turmeric into a cup of warmed milk. It will change from creamy-milk white to palest turmeric yellow – the only colour more identifiably 'Indian' would have to be rani pink. The upfront palate is dairy-sweet, but fast on its tail is just the softest bite of bitter. You might also find a little sediment in the bottom of the cup.

It's these last aspects of the drink that count. Bitter taste is the core of masala, and discovering it gently through subtle fat and sweet sets kids on the trajectory towards comfort with complex flavour. The bottom-of-the-cup sediment is about getting used to physical texture, surprising texture and contrasting texture. You might never learn to love it, but you will understand that it's part of the picture – that smooth is not the goal and perfect is not the answer.

****Desi is a loose term used when talking about people and cultures from the Indian regions in a casual, intimate and affectionate capacity. The word desi means country or land in Sanskrit.***

Simple yellow dal

Turmeric powder is a base recognition spice for every Indian, of any descent, anywhere. As a spice thought to be native to India, it has historical blueprint. Unlike chillies, say, which arrived from South America much later, turmeric's earthy and gingery base-note bitterness has always underwritten the message of masala. It's what I mean when I speak of its elemental importance. Most dals contain turmeric for this reason: it's the thread that ties us through our regional flavours to a collective experience (see Taste as touchstone versus taste as blueprint, page 41).

For those not of Indian descent or experience, the use of turmeric powder in dal provides a point of connection to the root experience of masala. It conveys, in a basic dish, the powerful simplicity of tradition.

Soaking your channa dal overnight in cold water is your best chance of success. Soak in a bowl large enough to hold more than twice as much water as lentils: dal swells significantly when soaked. And though harder lentils like channa need longer soaking times, they're a better beginner's choice: strong lentil structure results in a more articulate expression of masala. And that matters a lot when we're learning, because it makes it easier to taste our mistakes or successes.

>

Serves 4–6 as part of a shared meal

24 hours before cooking
2 cups (400 g) channa dal (split chickpeas)
plenty of cold water, for soaking

For pressure cooking
soaked channa dal (above)
3 cups (750 ml) water
2 teaspoons fine pink salt
½ teaspoon turmeric powder
scant ½ teaspoon fine white salt
1 × 2 cm (¾ inch) piece of jaggery

Tadka
2 tablespoons ghee
3 teaspoons cumin seeds
3 teaspoons finely grated fresh ginger
½ teaspoon Kashmiri chilli powder
scant ½ teaspoon ginger powder

To finish
1 heaped teaspoon Ammi's garam masala (page 156)

Put your channa dal in a large bowl and cover with plenty of cold water – more than twice as much water as lentils. Leave to soak overnight.

Drain and rinse the dal under cold running water, then transfer to your pressure cooker and add the water and spices.

Lock your pressure cooker (or see If you don't have a pressure cooker, right) and set to high until it releases two or three hard jets of steam, then turn to low. The cooking time will depend on the size and type of pressure cooker, so you'll need to get to know your equipment. Dal cooks in a pressure cooker in as little as 10 minutes (see note). Once the dal is cooked, let the pressure cooker depressurise on its own.

Once your dal is cooked, take a look at it and have a taste. The texture should be soft but the lentil shape should still be just visible (see note). It should be well seasoned, with a structured taste that's clear and communicative. When done right, you'll taste the sweet nuttiness of the cooked lentils, the drive of salt, the rounded subtlety of jaggery. An under-seasoned spoonful of dal is heavy and bland and not at all delicious – there's no impetus to take a second mouthful.

In a small frying pan, heat all of the tadka ingredients over medium–low heat until the ghee is bubbling and the spices are fragrant. Watch carefully to ensure it doesn't go too far – powdered spice in particular burns within the minute on a too-hot flame. Tip your tadka into the dal and stir.

Add the garam masala just before serving. It will both refresh the aromatics bedded into the foundation of the masala, and put an aromatic lid on the dal so that those aromas don't escape.

If you don't have a pressure cooker: Use a slow cooker or large heavy-based saucepan. Be sure to soak your channa dal for the full 24 hours. If using a slow cooker, cook the dal with 2 teaspoons of fine white sea salt, 1 teaspoon of turmeric powder and a scant ½ teaspoon of fine pink salt. If using a saucepan, cook the dal over medium heat in a high volume of boiling water with 2 teaspoons of fine white sea salt, a scant 1 teaspoon of turmeric powder and a scant ½ teaspoon of fine pink salt for 10–15 minutes, skimming off any scum. Reduce the heat to low and cook on a low simmer for a further 35–40 minutes or until tender. Now move on to preparing the tadka.

Note: Get to know the aroma of properly cooked dal – a sweet, slightly starchy and gassy smell is emitted via the steam once the dal is softened.

Rescuing burnt dal

At some point you will burn your dal. If you're using a saucepan this is something you can keep an eye on as you cook, but if you're using a pressure cooker, it can get away from you. If you can smell that you've let the pressure cooking go too far, let the pressure cooker depressurise on its own. This allows the dal to relax. If not *too* burnt, you can then just stir whatever is sticking to the bottom of the pressure cooker back into the body of dal – the slow reabsorption of steam 'unsticks' what's caught on the bottom. If you know, however, that it's properly burnt, scoop from the top and transfer the rescued dal to another pot before stirring through the tadka. It will be a little smoky for sure, but still passable.

Not umami (but close)

As a bitter spice, turmeric powder acts as a coatrack for the other aromatics. Imagine a pile of clothes on your bedroom floor – it's pretty hard to see what's what. Hang everything on the coatrack, however, and suddenly they'll take shape. You'll be able to distinguish your orange shirt from your red jacket and your striped tee.

Without the structural support of a spice like turmeric powder, the other spices will expend their aromatic energy in creating stability and shape. But with stability already present, we can experience all of that aromatic content as taste. In essence, turmeric powder allows everything to taste more of itself. I'm often asked if that makes turmeric powder umami. It's not umami, but it's close.

Over the page: Large saucepan: Masoor dal (page 276). Copper bowl: Simple yellow dal (page 39). Glass bowl: No-soak masoor dal (page 219), with tadka being poured on.

Taste as touchstone versus taste as blueprint

There are libraries of books on the power of food nostalgia – the way that touchstones of taste can recall people, periods and occasions in our lives. Taste touchstones are created in lots of ways. Sometimes it's via storytelling: recently I took Ash and Cailean to Melbourne to eat hokey pokey at Jock's Ice Cream & Sorbet. It was Dad's favourite treat for our boys. Dad, their Baba, died when Ash was nine, but the last real time they spent together was before we left Melbourne for Europe, when Ash was four. Eating that ice cream while telling Ash the story of Baba and his hokey pokey fixation is reinforcement of a memory Ash doesn't know he has, in order to maintain a connection to a pivotal figure in his life of whom he has limited recollection.

But taste as blueprint goes a little deeper.

Taste blueprints are genetic memories of tastes built in to us via ancestry and heritage. These are the tastes that link us to our mothers and grandmothers and great great grandmothers. They're the tastes our three bodies know, and that make sense to us; the tastes we pass on to our children or our friends or the people we come to love. In doing so we – sometimes consciously, sometimes unconsciously – propagate personal connections in order to reinforce our own understanding of ourselves.

The first time I made Gobi sabji (page 290) after years of rejecting masala, I stood at the stove and cried. Somehow I knew what to do. My hands moved like Dad's. I spiced like Ammi. I tasted Mum. Of course, I'd grown up at their stovetops and seen and eaten this dish many times, but it was more than that. I felt it *in* me. And the relief was intense. When we know what's inside us, we find a stability that doesn't need to rely on external supports.

luxe

The point of mentioning taste as blueprint is that we all have it. Those of us who tell the stories of ourselves through food find it easier to recognise. This book is your opportunity to seek, to develop curiosity about which tastes work as touchstones and which as blueprints for you as an individual.

A quick cheat: taste as touchstone invokes a strong memory of a person, experience or thing external to us; but taste as blueprint stimulates a powerful moment of self-recognition. Masala needs both.

TURMERIC POWDER AS ANTI-INFLAMMATORY

There's a strong tide of information flooding in through popular culture about turmeric as an anti-inflammatory and the theory that it can help control physical ailments, particularly issues associated with the natural course of ageing.

While Western medicine tends to focus on the physicality of ailments, Ayurveda considers inflammatory conditions across the three bodies – the idea of emotional, spiritual and physical inflammation and the links between them. This might take in lung inflammation caused by grief, skin inflammation caused by stress, or emotional inflammation – anger, stress, hyperactivity – caused by combinations of inferior nourishment of body and spirit.

Ayurveda uses turmeric powder in masala to help address these causes, because masala allows a single spice to express multiple facets in one mouthful. In any one masala we can learn to blend aromatics so that turmeric powder shows its weight, its inherent **oiliness** and its **bitter** tail. Ayurveda says that each of these three aspects soothes a specific type of inflammation:

- Turmeric powder's **weight** on the palate is said to connect the sensory body to the deep gut, triggering holistic support for the physical body. A strong and steady body is a counterpoint to inflammation.
- Turmeric powder's **oiliness** is said to soothe and stabilise a frayed and erratic nervous system.
- Turmeric powder's **bitterness** is said to give structure and form to formless worry, helping us to find steadiness and see ourselves in a clearer space.

A spice like turmeric powder is important not because it's special, but because it helps newcomers to masala understand that for the Indian householder medicinal approaches begin in the kitchen and connect to an understanding of healing that considers the whole person.

Masala as anti-inflammatory

Within Ayurveda, inflammation is seen as the leading cause of disease. As our primary means of maintaining health, masala is geared towards cooling bodily systems to prevent inflammation from occurring.

The concept of cooling itself is flexible, and what it looks like in masala depends on your dosha (see page 26), your age, your stress levels, your physical environment, your levels of exertion, how much external support you have – friends, family, finances – and your emotional and spiritual condition.

As you make your way through this book, you'll begin to see how to manipulate spices, fats, salts, cooking techniques and produce in an effort to keep inflammation at bay. The conversation here is a starting point, because knowing a concept exists is the first step towards understanding that we can apply it.

Turmeric chaaman

Serves 4 as part of a shared meal

- 2 cups (500 ml) vegetable oil
- pinch of turmeric powder
- pinch of salt (any kind)
- 400 g (14 oz) Paneer (page 110), diced or sliced
- 1 cup (250 ml) water, plus extra as needed

Masala

- 2 teaspoons aniseed powder
- 1–1½ teaspoons fine white salt
- 1 teaspoon turmeric powder
- 1 teaspoon ginger powder
- pinch of hing (asafoetida) powder

Finishing spices

- 2 tablespoons ghee
- 3–5 green cardamom pods, husks cracked
- 4 cloves, split with a mortar and pestle

Dad would use the words 'paneer' and 'chaaman' interchangeably. It was only as an adult that I realised chaaman was the Kashmiri word, paneer the word more commonly used in Hindi, from Urdu. I'm a language nerd, and so while both words hold love, chaaman also contains identity. And the first time I made this dish I tasted that.

Cooking turmeric and chaaman in water is a traditional Kashmiri Hindu cooking technique that alters the appearance of turmeric powder. Most of the time, turmeric powder comes through in masala as a soft and round bitter taste. But boiling water gives this spice a square edge. It's a reflection of the mountains and the people in the food on the table: Kashmiri Hindus are Pandits (see page 163) and there's a legacy within that of adherence to the strictures of faith.

When we were kids, all of us cousins conducted a seance in Ammi's living room in New Delhi one night after we thought the adults had gone to bed. Ammi came in to find us and was livid. It was the only time I ever saw her like that. She was spiritually steel-rod straight and strict. What we were doing was playing with the foundation of our faith practice.

These are the dishes that give the concept of masala its depth. Plunging in to feel the sternness and the steel helps us to discover masala's origins.

You'll need to make your paneer the day before you make this dish.

Heat the vegetable oil over medium heat in a kadai, stable cast-iron wok or heavy-based saucepan large enough that the oil comes up no more than halfway. Prepare a bowl of cold water while the oil is heating and keep it beside your stovetop. This is where you'll put the chaaman after frying – floating it in water straight from deep-frying removes excess oil. It also keeps the fried chaaman soft.

Once the oil is hot, add the turmeric powder and salt. (A pinch each of turmeric and salt when deep-frying *anything* will magically prevent it sticking to the pan.) Working in batches so the oil stays hot, gently fry the paneer until just browned, then transfer from the oil to the bowl of water using a slotted spoon.

Drain the fried chaaman and transfer to a large frying pan. Place on the stovetop with the heat off and add the water – the chaaman should be almost completely covered, with just the top visible above the waterline; I call it the iceberg effect. Add more water if needed to achieve this.

>

Turn the heat to medium–high and bring to a simmer. Keep simmering until the water level has reduced by half. You shouldn't need to stir the paneer at this point – just check it's not sticking to the pan.

Once the water is reduced by half, add the masala and stir through gently.

Reduce the heat to bring to a slow simmer. (The idea is that the heat is tempered to match the evaporation intensity of the water. When these two elements are in balance, you won't have to stir the pan, and so will avoid breaking up the delicate chunks of chaaman.) Keep simmering gently until the water has almost evaporated, about 20 minutes – don't panic if it's longer. There should be enough liquid just to produce a thin gravy and prevent the chaaman sticking. In a separate pan over medium heat, melt the ghee (see note) and add the cracked cardamom pods and cloves until the ghee is sizzling and the spices are fragrant. Add the ghee and cracked spices to the chaaman. Allow 2–3 more minutes of simmering before serving.

Note: Boiling the paneer is the start of building a particular type of structure, creating a certain tension that strings the paneer proteins 'tight' and prepares them for communicating a steelier view of masala. Using structural spices like cardamom and cloves to finish further reinforces the square and strong iteration of turmeric powder in this chaaman. The ghee is a nod to softness, and a connective point to the dairy base of the dish.

A little experiment

If you're finding it hard to envisage the idea of the same spice tasting square or round, try this: temper salt, ginger powder, fennel powder and turmeric powder in a small frying pan with ghee, and simultaneously temper the same spices in the same quantities in another small frying pan with water. Taste the two masalas side by side. Ghee makes it soft, water makes it angular.

'... turmeric's earthy and gingery base-note bitterness has always underwritten the message of masala.'

THE INDIAN HOUSEHOLDER

Just as masala began as medicine (see page 35), the concept of the householder's role has a religious origin. In the case of our Ganju family, the religion is Hinduism. The way Dad explained it to us, life as a Hindu is divided into segments. You have your childhood and your student years, two large bodies of time where moral and spiritual health are wrapped up in those of the family.

The householder role comes next and encompasses the productive middle years of our adult life. These are the decades when we work within the community, get married, have children and raise a family. Historically, for the regional Indian householder, the internal family structure mirrors the external cultural construct: in a traditional sense this means that it was the woman – the mother – who modelled, instructed and held the family accountable. The householder was female, and she ruled the home.

My aunt Bui recalls that growing up, Ammi put a framework in place that kept the family's 'Kashmiri-ness' at the forefront, making it the strongest aspect of who they were – the scaffolding of their selves that they could understand and rely on. And this was articulated through the kitchen. So breakfast was only served after 9.30 am, at the completion of Ammi and Papa's *puja* (household worship ritual). Mutton was the primary protein: Kashmiri Hindus traditionally viewed chicken as an unclean meat. Meat could only be cooked on certain days. Even though Ammi had the privilege of house help, in Bui's words, she 'held everything in her hands'.

'On food, religion has a definite impact, because of some foods being taboo. Mama would want to do the food, she would like to cook it herself, or have it cooked her way. In the day-to-day household running, the religious thing was paramount: if it's a Tuesday, meat won't be made, there is a *puja* today and this is what will be made.

'Mama was rigid in that. The Kashmiris were much more traditional, because when I went to school I saw the girls from other families were different. What they wore. How they were. I was aware of that difference. Rebellion was not encouraged.'

There's a picture from 1979 pinned to the board above my *puja* of Ammi and Papa with all of us grandkids clustered around them – there were seven of us back then. Ammi and Papa are on two cane chairs in the front garden of the old Ganju family home in Defence Colony, New Delhi, seated like smiling monarchs. I'm two years old, sitting naked on Ammi's knee. The photo was taken about three decades after Bui's own childhood, the time she framed in recollection.

Pivotal to the connection between Bui's memories and this photo is the work Ammi did as a householder for all those years so that she could find herself in this position – as the matriarch of a Kashmiri Hindu household filled with grandchildren who fleshed out the frames of meaning she had scaffolded into her own children, Bui included, all those years ago. She trusted that the strength of her householder framework would continue for generations to come.

When I took Scott to meet Ammi for the first time, she was living with Chachu in Bengaluru. When we walked into her bedroom, Scott sat next to her on her bed. Ammi grabbed his jawline in one hand and turned him to face her. She asked about his parents. Married? Divorced? Dad alive, Scott replied, Mum passed away from cancer six years earlier. Ammi murmured acknowledgement. Then, still silent, she used her hand to turn Scott's face, studying first one side and then the other. Bringing his face back to centre, she finally dropped her hand but kept his gaze. She paused before she spoke.

'You will have beautiful children.'

She meant your parents are honourable. You are honourable. You will run your home in the way we have instructed, and pass the meals we made for you into the mouths of your own children. And in all of that you'll carry our messages onward.

Like masala, the householder role isn't a single message. It's a body of information that can be structured in different ways to tell a different story, across multiple generations. It's communicated through patterns, our understandings of which change over time. And just like spice within masala, the humans within a household sometimes create relationships through distance and disputes, sometimes via friendship and intimacy. Sometimes we'll find who we are with family. Sometimes we'll see who we are without them.

Three-egg turmeric scramble

Turmeric powder does amazing things to eggs. They'll never taste as creamy as they do with the addition of a small amount of a really good-quality haldi.

This is a great way to work with turmeric powder. Make it quotidian. Make it easy. Make it friendly. Taken out of context, haldi has developed a mysticism that is at odds with its traditional place in masala. Understand its complexity, of course. But also understand that it isn't special in the way that your mother isn't special. She's just everything, and you know her, and she's yours.

Serves 1

- 3 eggs
- 1 tablespoon sour cream
- 2 tablespoons milk
- salt (any kind), to taste
- scant ½ teaspoon turmeric powder
- a little cracked black pepper and fine white pepper
- chilli powder or chilli flakes (optional), to taste
- 1 tablespoon olive oil
- 1 tablespoon butter and/or ghee

Lightly whisk your eggs in a small bowl with the sour cream, milk and spices until just combined.

Heat the olive oil with the butter and/or ghee in a small frying pan over medium–low heat until melted and foaming slightly. Reduce the heat to low and pour in the egg mixture. Wait until the edges are cooked, then use a wooden spoon to push the eggs into the centre of the pan from the outside, moving deliberately around the circumference. Continue to do this gently and methodically until all the egg is just cooked.

Serve immediately, as is or on buttered toast.

TRAINING THE WORLD AROUND US

One of the householder's hallmarks is the energy they extend towards ensuring their family construct makes sense outside the home. The most obvious way this occurs is through the cultivation of social circles – choosing people to be around who reflect our values. But more nuanced are the places we select to insert our family *into* every day. The grocer we choose. The butcher we frequent. The coffee shop or dosa stand we make our local.

I know in modern Western cultures, and even in modern Eastern ones, a lot of the places we choose to put our family are commercial behemoths. Big-ticket supermarkets. Multinational cafe chains. But even in those places there is an element of choosing what suits your householder ideal. Maybe it's speed or convenience, two pretty common modern householder messages.

But for householders aligning more closely with tradition, the nature of shopping lends itself to the butcher, baker, candlestick-maker format: shopping for traditional foods that require traditional preparations carried out by real people. Maybe it's the grocer handpicking the ripest tomatoes from the storeroom when I need them for the Kashmiri lamb dish that uses ripe tomato as part of the masala carrier. Or the butcher deboning a shoulder and cutting the bones to the size I need for Chokhta (page 91).

In Aya Nagar in New Delhi, just up the road from our Ganju family home – Mum and Dad's house when they were alive – there's a butcher in a clutch of three stores facing Mehrauli Road. My brother Shyam took me there after Mum died. Both Dad and Bui trained the butcher how to cut mutton for a Kashmiri Hindu house. Unlike kosher or halal, it's not about how the animal is killed. It's about how to cut the meat and the bone to suit our traditional dishes. It's about how much fat to trim off different cuts for different preparations. The shared experience of training between customer (in this case Bui and Dad) and butcher creates a relationship that lasts for generations.

These interactions go to the heart of the extended householder role, which is to effectively train the world around us to reflect our culture back upon us. Or to phrase it perhaps more generously, so that we can share some of the intimate aspects of how we live with others, extending our household beyond the home's physical borders to create strong and lasting connections.

FENUGREEK POWDER
METHI

Category: Bitter spices.
Form: Powder from ground dried fenugreek seeds.
Colour: Soft cream to papyrus yellow.

Fenugreek powder is a bitter spice with a strong Indian accent. I don't remember it as a spice from when we were kids because it doesn't play that role – it's not the aroma on which we hang childhood memories.

It tends to be a spice bought once to fulfil a recipe and then pushed to the back of the cupboard. Because its aroma isn't naturally delicious or even particularly recognisable, it's not an easy spice with which to experiment. It took me time to learn how and when to use it outside of traditional masala. Try a taste. At first it's just about the tasting notes – bitter celery leaf and apple seed. But the feel of it in your mouth explains more. Whereas turmeric powder is round and fills the palate with weight and warmth, fenugreek powder is square. It's cold and sticks to the roof of the mouth and the back of the front teeth like setting concrete. It's structure, but open structure, like a multistorey car park.

So that's how I use it – to give structure but also to make space.

Tasting notes

There are a few iterations of fenugreek – powder, seeds and leaves. Each is different. The seeds and powder belong here, in the bitter category. You'll find the leaves in the forest-floor spices (page 266). On its own, fenugreek powder has primary notes of **bitter celery leaf** and **apple seed** that are followed by a **cyanide** aftertaste – I always connect it to that slightly toxic taste that comes with biting down on apple seeds (which I love, by the way). Subtle secondary and tertiary notes of **licorice** and **lemon rind** create a palatable framework.

Use in masala

Fenugreek powder gives masala a strong frame, while also working as a preservative in generic 'curry' blends produced by spice companies: Madras curry powder, hot curry powder, mild curry powder and so on. Fenugreek powder provides structure and stabilises aroma at the same time. But the more familiar it becomes, the more you'll appreciate this spice for its subtleties.

Emotive content

Fenugreek powder's bitterness is cool and open-ended. For me it's the most difficult type of emotive exchange to handle. Which is possibly why when I use this spice, I tend to wrap it in masala or other ingredients.

Traditional medicinal impact

In Ayurveda, fenugreek powder stabilises and preserves the functional health of the gut. It's frequently used as a base-note ingredient in the quest for three-body health.

Chocolate fool

Some cooks know that a bit of salt will create texture and interest in a sweet dessert. But maybe less appreciated is how the cool and blunt structural quality of fenugreek powder can leaven the weight and heaviness of rich fat combinations such as milk chocolate and cream.

Serves 4–6

Stage 1

- 400 ml (14 fl oz) whipping cream
- ¼ cup (55 g) caster (superfine) sugar
- scant ½ teaspoon fine pink salt

Stage 2

- 100 g (3½ oz) milk chocolate buttons
- 70 g (2½ oz) ruby chocolate buttons (see note)
- ½ teaspoon fenugreek powder
- 1 tablespoon sour cream

Combine the cream and caster sugar in a medium bowl and whip using hand-held electric beaters until soft peaks form (or complete this step in a stand mixer). Whisk in the salt by hand.

Set up a double boiler by placing a heatproof bowl over a saucepan of simmering water over medium heat (ensuring the bottom of the bowl is not touching the water, now or at any point during the process). Add all the chocolate buttons with the fenugreek powder and melt while stirring frequently. Alternatively, melt in a microwave-proof bowl in the microwave.

Remove the chocolate from the heat and stir in the sour cream (for a little more fat, a bit of tartness, extra weight and creaminess).

Gently fold the chocolate and sour cream mixture into the whipped cream, then spoon into small serving glasses. Tasting at this point tells you everything you need to know – the fool is rich and creamy and delicious, but somehow incomparably light and digestible. That's thanks to the fenugreek powder.

Note: Adding the fenugreek powder to the melting chocolate won't mess up the melting process or make the chocolate grainy.
Using the ruby chocolate in addition to the milk chocolate creates a bit of added texture, an important consideration when working with unusual aromatic contrasts. If you're using all milk chocolate or all ruby chocolate, reduce the quantity of fenugreek powder by half.

Functional fenugreek powder
As baking powder is a rising agent and gelatine is a setting agent, consider fenugreek powder in baking as a 'lightening agent'. Adding ¼–½ teaspoon to heavier desserts – such as a rich caramel macadamia cheesecake – will increase palatability without diminishing any of the indulgent sweetness. For dessert fans, that feels like a win.

Osso buco

Serves 4

- ½ cup (60 g) cornflour (cornstarch)
- 2 generous pinches of fine white sea salt
- generous pinch of cracked black pepper
- 4 pieces of veal osso buco

For the flameproof casserole

- 2 tablespoons mustard oil
- 2 carrots, finely diced
- 1 white onion, finely diced
- 3 celery stalks, finely diced
- 8 garlic cloves, finely diced
- scant ½ teaspoon fine white sea salt
- ½ teaspoon cracked black pepper
- generous ¼ teaspoon fenugreek powder
- 2 dried bay leaves
- a good glug of olive oil

To finish

- 1 cup (250 ml) tomato passata (puréed tomatoes)
- 3 cups (750 ml) good-quality beef stock or bone broth
- 3 generous pinches of fleur de sel
- pinch of fenugreek powder
- ½ teaspoon caster (superfine) sugar
- ¼ teaspoon fine white pepper
- ¼ teaspoon fine black pepper

To serve

- ⅓ cup finely chopped fresh parsley
- 2 tablespoons finely grated lemon zest
- green salad
- basmati rice or polenta

Mum made this recipe pretty regularly from her *Australian Women's Weekly* cookbook when we were kids, but it was never frequent enough for me. I completely *love* osso buco. We'd go to the main street butcher in Torquay – a small beach town on Victoria's south-west coast – and Dad would only let us walk out with the cuts if it was proper veal. You can tell by the colour. Very white flesh means it's actually veal and not yearling beef. As Hindus it was the only beef we ever ate. Even Dad ate it, which says something about just how delicious this osso buco is.

I took Mum's *Women's Weekly* cookbook when I left home so I could make it for myself. Which I did, for years. But once Cailean came along, the way I cooked had to change a little. Ashy loves heavy, delicious, fatty, spice-packed food as much as I do. But Cailean is different – lighter, cooler. Too rich is too much.

I'm often asked how to cook for different body types in the same family. The answer is in not just knowing spice, but in understanding masala (see Domestic Ayurveda, masala & feeding a family, page 56).

I now know that I can add fenugreek powder to a deliciously heavy, umami-rich, tomato-ey slow cook like this to ensure it's not too much for that beautiful first son of ours. Yet for the rest of us, it still carries the weight that makes it so special.

Tip your cornflour, salt and pepper onto a large platter and mix the seasoning through the flour with your fingers. Dredge the osso buco pieces through this mix so they're well coated.

Heat the mustard oil in a heavy-based flameproof casserole over high heat. (I love my Le Creuset casserole for this.) When the mustard oil begins to smoke (see note), lay the osso buco pieces flat in the oil. They should sizzle straight away. You want them to brown, so don't move them around.

Once the osso buco pieces are browned on one side, flip them over and let them brown on the other side. The heat should be high enough that the browning on each side is complete within 2–3 minutes.

Remove the browned veal pieces from the casserole and set aside on a clean plate. Leave the casserole over medium–high heat with all the yummy flecks of meat and seasoned flour in the bottom and toss in the carrot, onion, celery, garlic, salt, pepper, fenugreek powder and bay leaves. Stir everything through and take a deep smell. You'll get mustard oil, garlic and just a hint of that celery-like, vegetal fenugreek powder. Pay attention to how subtle it is.

Add the olive oil and stir it through, then take another deep whiff. Instantly the aroma of fenugreek powder jumps right out of the pot. (The thin quality of olive oil loosens the aromatics around the fenugreek powder at the same time as its inherently grassy and bitter quality reaches into the vegetal bitter of fenugreek powder and, for want of a better word, explodes it.) Stir for 2–3 minutes over medium–high heat, then return the veal to the pot.

Add the passata, stock, fleur de sel, fenugreek powder, sugar, and white and black peppers. Taste the sauce now and it will feel quite light and aromatically sparse. Don't be alarmed. As the dish cooks down, the rich depth of bone and marrow will come in to bolster and deepen flavour around the space fenugreek powder and olive oil create.

Reduce the heat to medium–low, put on the lid and leave to bubble away at a low simmer for 2–3 hours. The longer you can leave it, the more tender the meat and the more complex the sauce. Remove the lid after the first two-thirds of the cooking time.

To serve, mix together the parsley and lemon zest to make a gremolata (see note). Use this to top the osso buco, then serve immediately with a green salad and basmati rice.

Note: Mustard oil is traditionally heated to smoking point before use so that it's not *kachcha* – 'raw'. I use mustard oil to brown meats for most dishes because it adds a layer of texture and complexity that results in a more delicious and richer finish (see Browning meat, page 97). You might like to add crushed garlic to your gremolata.

Using tomato passata

Whenever I add tomato passata to anything, I toss in fenugreek powder, one or two types of salt, fine white pepper, finely ground black pepper and a little caster (superfine) sugar. Add ¼–½ teaspoon of each. It's a way to introduce passata to any dish without smothering the existing aromatic profile.

DOMESTIC AYURVEDA, MASALA & FEEDING A FAMILY

Like ours, pretty much all families will have members with varying degrees of appetite for rich or complex foods. Strict Ayurvedic practice can make finding a middle ground difficult, because the three body types – and the myriad permutations of each of our constitutions – have such disparate needs.

But masala falls more into what I call domestic Ayurvedic practice, the practice of the Indian householder. These are the anecdotal snatches of information passed down via oral tradition through families. As the child of an Indian householder, you might learn about the heating and antiseptic quality of fresh ginger via consumption of Ginger honey tea (see page 258), thus getting to know the spice as one of benefit to the respiratory system. Just as you'll likely learn not to eat bananas when you have a chest cough because elders say they increase phlegm.

Combining information about domestic Ayurveda with an understanding of masala gives us the ability to modify dishes with spice, fats or even salts in order to soften any unwanted bodily impacts.

There's a generosity that results from cooking in this way. Together these two concepts create a loosening of restriction, one that removes much of the stress that comes with contemporary understandings of 'wellness'. Masala allows ways of eating foods that might be considered out of reach under stricter regimes.

***Jolie-laide:* fenugreek powder**

Of course the French have an elegant term for a dichotomous ideal. Translated literally, *jolie-laide* means 'pretty-ugly'. In conceptual terms it refers to the kind of beauty that's strong and striking, and more arresting for its blunt, disturbing or angular edge. It's an ideal description for fenugreek powder.

FENUGREEK SEEDS
METHI DANA

Category: Bitter spices.
Form: Stout, squarish pebble.
Colour: Tan yellow.

For an Indian householder, fenugreek seeds are like the hammer in the toolbox of masala. They're a spice for pickles and digestive teas. Functional.

The texture – teeth-breakingly hard – makes them difficult and unpleasant to chew when raw, and only marginally less unpleasant to chew when cooked. Aromatically they're actually pretty beautiful once you break through the form: they have a nutty, apple-y, maple-syrupy quality. If your reference is colonised North American culture, then I imagine they're a little Thanksgiving-esque. It's important to note, from a common usage perspective, that the whole seeds don't have the bitterness of fenugreek powder.

Tasting notes
Fenugreek seeds are the seed form of the fenugreek plant. It's a difficult spice to taste because its primary notes hide behind the seeds' pebble-like texture. Bite into it for a subtle reveal of **apple skin** that gives way to **almond shell** and a slightly sweet finish of **old apple flesh**. Secondary notes reference aromas of **yellow mustard seeds**. A recessed **maple syrup** quality comes forward when the seeds are heated.

Use in masala
It's likely a limited vision, but fenugreek seeds don't move beyond pickles and teas in my kitchen. At least, they didn't, until I bumped into the incredible Fenugreek chicken butter sauce recipe (page 59) from Dan Gedge, the head chef at Leeuwin Estate winery. While I find the form of fenugreek seeds a little prohibitive, I can imagine that after softening them by soaking overnight, they would make a strong and interesting addition to a sprouted salad.

Emotive content
I feel like fenugreek seeds are one of those aromatics that sneaks in sideways. They're a 'pillar' spice – a structural support but only subtly so, like a friend in the distance. Allow time and use to develop your own intimate relationship with this spice.

Traditional medicinal impact
There's a strong tradition of using fenugreek seeds as a digestive spice in hot water alongside other carminative (gas-reducing) spices – fennel seeds, perhaps, or cumin and coriander seeds. If you're not a fan of teas, you can soak the seeds overnight in water and then eat them in the morning – make them delicious by heating in ghee and then stirring through porridge. I'd add honey, too.

Fenugreek seed tea

Fenugreek seeds steeped in hot water are a digestive aid. The taste is mildly bitter with a tail of apple seed. It's strangely delicious.

Digestion matters in domestic Ayurveda, because good digestion is considered a baseline for good health. And it doesn't have to be complicated. We do little things all the time to improve our digestion, and just let them add up: fenugreek seed tea in the morning, dahi (yoghurt) with lunch, mukhwas or candy-coated fennel seeds – a small, heaped spoon sipped off the palm of our hands – after dinner.

One of the biggest causes of disease in the body is stress, and one of the biggest daily stressors is the idea that only big changes have any impact. The discipline and disappointment of diets. Hiding restrictive regimes behind a vocabulary of wellness.

Please don't. Or do. But know there is another way.

Masala isn't about immediacy. It's about building a long-term relationship with ourselves through taste. It's about cumulative wellness taken in small and permissive doses. For me, after a long day of restaurant service energised by the adrenaline of waiting tables and fuelled by meals gulped back of house among unpolished glassware, a cup of fenugreek seed tea is a small pause, a connection to heritage, and a gentle reminder to build my internal strength.

✱

Not-Madras curry powder

Make up this masala in small batches and use as a whole blend to cook your favourite 'curry'. It's well suited to lamb, and to orange vegies like pumpkin and sweet potato, and will be subtly beautiful with fish – as long as you use a little less than you would with lamb. When you taste the raw mix, you'll notice how elegant this masala is, and how easy that is to discern – that's the fenugreek powder. It muscles up the prettier spices – cinnamon, sumac and all that fennel – while still allowing them their natural flounce.

Makes 25 g (1 oz) or enough for one curry to serve 6–8

- 2 teaspoons fennel powder
- 1½ teaspoons fennel seeds
- 1½ teaspoons ginger powder
- 1½ teaspoons fine pink salt
- 1 teaspoon cinnamon powder
- 1 teaspoon Kashmiri chilli powder
- ½ teaspoon fenugreek powder
- ½ teaspoon sumac powder
- ½ teaspoon turmeric powder

Mix together and store in an airtight container for up to 3 months.

Ratios: extrapolating masala

One of the hardest things with masala is working out how to adjust ratios when increasing the overall quantity of a dish. Spice ratios don't operate on a clear-cut 2:1 basis – because of its complexity, the weight of masala becomes heavier than the weight of produce if both are doubled or tripled. The important notion to share here is that if you're doubling or tripling a masala quantity, give yourself room to move. If one of the spices feels like too much for you, reduce it. If another feels like not enough, increase it. The experience you accumulate with ratios is part of finding the you in masala.

A way to accelerate that experience is to read recipe books widely. The first thing I do when I look at cookbooks is flick through a few recipes and get a feel for how the aromatics are handled. Are there combinations or quantities that surprise me? Can I discern a pattern in how certain spices, fats or other ingredients are put together? Yotam Ottolenghi is fascinating. Fresh parsley, cumin powder, black pepper and sesame oil, say. Or sherry, fresh tarragon and celery. Angular tastes that build fresh and communicative food. Nigella Lawson is at the other end of the scale – opulent with the weight of her food but simple with its structure. It has a different voice.

Noticing patterns in the ways others handle spice allows us to see more clearly our own habitual patterns, limitations and uniqueness. It gives us insights into how to work with ratios in a more freehand way. The more perspective we gain on how we work in the kitchen, the more opportunity we're giving ourselves to grow as cooks.

Chef Dan's fenugreek chicken butter sauce

When Dan Gedge, head chef at Leeuwin Estate in Margaret River, asked me about using fenugreek in his chicken butter sauce, I thought he was talking about the leaves, not the seeds. I'd never thought about using fenugreek seeds as an ingredient in a dish that wasn't pickled, fermented or medicinal. The sauce was the flourish on the fish dish paired with the vineyard's Art Series Chardonnay. The result was unexpected. I'm used to fenugreek seeds being structure, but in this sauce they're also texture and body.

Use this sauce on fish, chicken or shellfish for a rich finish. You could deep-fry a few fresh curry leaves as a garnish for a little extra sweetness and flourish.

Makes 1 cup (250 ml)
or serves 6–8 people

Sauce base

400 ml (14 fl oz) good-quality chicken stock
200 ml (7 fl oz) whey
2 teaspoons fenugreek seeds

Tadka

150 g (5½ oz) butter
6 garlic cloves, thinly sliced
12 fresh curry leaves
pinch of fine white sea salt
¼ teaspoon nigella seeds
¼ teaspoon yellow mustard seeds
juice of 1 lime

Combine the sauce ingredients in a medium saucepan over medium–high heat. Bring to the boil then keep boiling for 10–15 minutes, until reduced by half, watching to ensure it doesn't boil over.

As the liquid boils down, taste. Then remove from the heat and taste again. Gradually the bitter apartness of fenugreek seeds wraps itself in the cushion of cooked-down stock, while the whey creates opulence (see Working with whey, page 168). At this point the sauce is more texture than taste.

To make the tadka, heat the butter with the garlic in a separate medium saucepan over medium–low heat. Keep cooking until the butter foams and turns nut-brown. You'll smell the caramelisation as well as see it. Add the curry leaves, salt, nigella seeds and mustard seeds. Give the tadka just a minute to temper, then add the lime juice.

Strain the tadka, discarding the garlic and spices, then add to the cooking chicken stock, whey and fenugreek seed reduction. Emulsify with a hand-held blender until the sauce thickens and stabilises.

As long as the sauce isn't refrigerated or boiled it will remain intact. You can leave it in an airtight container at room temperature for 2–3 hours then reheat gently to serve.

Note: Working with a tadka allows us to build masala in components. The tadka spices of nigella seeds, yellow mustard seeds and fresh curry leaves add flesh to the bones of the sauce.

SALTS

Function in masala: Communicating and driving flavour.
Emotive quality: Creating clarity in masala, which makes emotive messages more easily understood. The result is clearly communicated flavour, a fundamental pre-requisite for deliciousness.

Coming out of bitterness into salts is like exiting a warren of tunnels into the openness of endless prairies and fresh air – it's so *expansive*. Salts are the drive in masala. The volume. They allow every other aromatic in the pan to speak clearly. Masala's relationship with salt has the quality of epiphany.

When I teach people about masala, salts are my first port of call because of this revelatory aspect. As an aromatic in Western kitchens, it gets paid the least attention after black pepper. You might think that choice when it comes to salt is just how much to use, or whether to use it at all. But salts are like any spice. Every type is different. When I need a strong masala I turn to white sea salts. Softness and subtlety have me reaching for pink salts. The stimulation of surprise or unexpected encounters is about kala namak, Indian black salt.

As a kid I remember how much more present salt was at Ammi's New Delhi table. The nightly salad of cucumber, fresh onion and lime was kissed by it, her dal popping with it. Even in her Salan walah chawal (page 286) there was just this muscle behind the spice that was detectably driven by salt. It was the one criticism Dad had of Mum's food, and often even of his own. To be clear, it's about not just taste, but the communication of what masala means: inadequately salted masala is akin to taking a call from a missed loved one on a phone connection so distant you can't make out their words.

Understanding salt's ability to clearly communicate taste is the revelation. Trying salts one by one, side by side, and viscerally experiencing the at times radical differences in their aromatic profiles feels so *surprising*. And then working out how to integrate this new kitchen knowledge into making the kind of food that reaches into the soft spots of your own heart and those of your loved ones? Well, that's masala.

The easiest way to understand this category is to use different types of salt in recipes or dishes you already know well. Next Tuesday taco night, when you make your bean or chilli con carne mix, instead of using whatever table salt you have stashed in the cupboard, use a fine pink salt. Or a white lake salt. If you always use a pink salt, then try one night with an industrial table salt just so you can taste the lack. With known ingredients, this kind of experimentation is the easiest way to break down any apathy or habit so that you can work that aromatic into your own building experience of masala.

Lastly, like fats, salts are one of the primary filters that work to establish, reframe or direct masala's overall tone. In the following pages, I provide an explanation of how each particular salt shapes the spices around it.

Tiering salts

'Tiering' is a technique in masala that involves using more than one aromatic in the same category to create a textured effect. I also refer to it as 'scaffolding'. Tiering or scaffolding salts means that, instead of using one salt in a dish, I might use two or three. In this section, you'll see that each salt has its own unique personality, function, expression and relationship to masala. By tiering salts we exponentially increase masala's complexity.

FINE WHITE SEA SALT

Category: Salts.
Form: Fine grains that together have a slightly fluffy appearance.
Colour: Soft white.

The differences between salts are determined by their origin – the landscape from which a salt is harvested underlies its taste profile. A fine white sea salt is oceanic, a little seaweedy but often only subtly so – in the way seawater has that soft element of iodine when you swallow it accidentally at the beach.

I emphasise the 'fine' sea salt here because the texture of the salt influences its taste, mostly due to the way the salt dissolves on the palate: the finer the granule, the more upfront the initial salty and mineral hit. The nature of soft and fluffy fine sea salt means that absorption is quite soft. Try it next to standard white table salt to see what I mean.

And yes, every sea salt will taste a little different. As will different batches of salt from the same source. That's why it's always good to try your ingredients before cooking them, even if it's something as simple as salt. It will help you to work out your ratios, and to appreciate that there's never a time with masala when assumed knowledge is wholly reliable. The subtly shifting qualities of all spice and produce are what keeps us on our toes.

Rather than write out long-form recipes, here are a few classic dishes in which you might use a fine white sea salt and note its effects. Other than standard table salt, fine white sea salt is the default salt choice for many kitchens. You'll get to know it better through simple usage and comparison with the salt you normally use. To do this, try:

- **Tomato or avocado on toast:** Make two pieces of either. Season one with a good-quality fine white sea salt. Cut the second piece in half: season one half with table salt and the other with a white lake or flaked salt. Toast seasoned with sea salt will feel more textured and the produce will be more 'present'. Toast seasoned with lake salt will feel heavier on the saltiness. Toast seasoned with table salt will feel 'empty' or industrial in comparison to the other two.
- **Oat cookies or Anzac biscuits:** Make two batches of your favourite oat cookies or Anzac biscuits. You'll be adding a little salt, just to season – for a recipe that makes twelve cookies, a generous ¼ teaspoon should suffice. In one batch use a fine pink salt. In the other use a fine white sea salt. The pink salt batch will have a sweet salt taste. The sea salt batch, in contrast, will have a savoury salt taste.

Tasting notes

A fine white sea salt has a saltiness that's **direct** and **strong**. It also has that **seaside taste** that so many of us know from summers at the beach, in Australia at least. I use fine white salt when working with produce that tends to flatten spice, such as beef or skinless, boneless chicken. When used with these protein foods, white sea salt makes sure that the other aromatics are 'heard'.

Use in masala

All salts are used to create drive and clarity, but each will perform this function in a unique way. A fine white sea salt draws forward an 'anvil' quality in masala. Try this experiment: taste turmeric powder on its own. Notice its earthiness, warmth, slightly oily texture, ginger–orange rind bitterness, and weight dispersal – it's felt evenly across the front to mid-palate. Now lick a good quality fine white sea salt off your finger and follow that with another taste of turmeric powder. Feel how the turmeric powder changes. The spread of its aromas pulls together tighter and the weight sits heavy on the mid-palate alone. Sea salt consolidates turmeric powder so that it becomes strongly beautiful: from Disney princess to tribal queen. Sea salt has the same effect on aromatics across the breadth of masala. It makes the spice around it bolder, stronger, more angular and aromatically tighter. A fine white sea salt will create direct and – if you desire – quite muscular masala.

That said, one of my favourite ways to use fine white sea salt is in combination with a fine pink salt. The white salt is the fabric and the pink salt is the flounce; the result is an aromatic bed with a clear structure but greater detail and nuance.

Emotive content

You need to think quite deeply about salts in order to connect to an emotive quality. For me, they seem to work more like mirrors of expression. For example, I reach for turmeric powder when I want to feel its bittersweet strength, but I use fine white sea salt to reflect my own strong certainty. The difference is a little *Alice through the Looking Glass*: emotionally speaking, I draw myself *out* of spices and I put myself *in*to salts. Understanding the nuance in that distinction will help you become more creative in your salt usage.

FINE PINK SALT

Category: Salts.
Form: Fine grains with a sandy texture.
Colour: Soft rose pink to pinkish white.

I love fine pink salt for the gentle underbelly it brings to masala. Its saltiness is soft and has what I can only describe as a spiral quality. It swirls and fizzes on the palate. To get a feel for this, try a white lake salt and then segue to pink salt – the linear drive of the former makes the circular movement of pink salt easier to discern.

I also love it because it gave me a personal access point into a tradition that I'd been looking for a way to make my own. Old cultures can be a lot to find yourself in, even when you claim ancestry, but the softness of pink salt made room for me. I find that many people respond to it like that – in a line-up tasting of salts, they instantly fall in love with what pink salt does to spice, how classically beautiful masala becomes, and how approachable it feels.

Fine pink salt isn't only harvested in the Himalayas, though it's this that most think of. Australia has some beautiful pink salts harvested from mineral lakes. The salt owes its colour to its mineral composition, which in turn determines its aromatic content. And while pink salts from different regions will taste a little different, any fine pink salt will offer masala that same soft filter. Perhaps with subtly different accents that will be indiscernible to all but the most acute observers of taste.

Tasting notes

Fine pink salt is an effervescent experience. It hits the palate with a direct intensity because of the way it dissolves – all at once and fast. The secondary bloom of its mineral qualities smooths and sweetens its initial salty hit. This is where the gentleness comes in: pink salt's finish is soft and long. Aromatically, the primary taste is intense **saltiness** that segues to secondary **mineral** characters and a lively **popping fizz.** It has a **round** and **slightly sweet** finish.

Use in masala

Whereas fine white sea salt consolidates the strength in masala, fine pink salt offers a classically beautiful interpretation of the spices with which it's surrounded. Fine pink salt makes turmeric powder appear warm and gingery. It highlights Kashmiri chilli powder's floral and sweet qualities. And cumin seeds under the influence of fine pink salt are warm cedar. When I want a simply beautiful masala, fine pink salt is my first port of call.

Emotive content

Fine pink salt is a chance to impart a gentle touch to food. With such a soft foundation as the masala filter, creating a taste of kindness becomes effortless. A little cinnamon powder. A subtle microplaning of fresh ginger. Kashmiri chilli powder for floral heat. And fennel seeds – sweet, wet and green. I like to give love without any hidden barbs or sinkholes. I feel like – in a food on a plate sense – fine pink salt allows me to do that.

Pink salt's patterning

One clear benefit of pink salt is its even 'patterning'. Patterning with aromatics refers to the way taste is experienced throughout the course of a mouthful. With pink salt, this means that if you use too much, the too-muchness will be dispersed evenly across the dish. The saltiness might still be a little striking, but it likely won't be offensive (unless you've *really* gone overboard). A white sea salt, white lake salt or table salt won't offer the same degree of forgiveness.

Simple aloo gosht

Serves 4–6 as part of a shared meal

Aloo gosht is the North Indian version of lamb casserole. Every family has their own recipe and it's that one universally loved dish because it's comforting, easy, delicious and familiar all at once. I'm a fan of tiering salts (see page 62), but this dish works better when fine pink salt alone provides the drive. Everything from the cut of the lamb to the minimal browning process and the method of cooking is about cushioning an already soft masala. A harder salt would be discordant, and not in a good way.

As an exercise, you could try making this dish using the same quantity of a fine white sea salt and notice the difference in overall emotive tonality. It will no doubt still be beautiful, but some of that gorgeous gentleness will be lost to the more aggressive salt.

Preparation

- 3 tomatoes

Browning phase

- 100 ml (3½ fl oz) mustard oil
- 2 pinches of hing (asafoetida) powder
- 2 dried bay leaves
- 1.2 kg (2 lb 10 oz) lamb shoulder, chopped into 5 cm (2 inch) pieces

First masala

- 1 teaspoon Kashmiri chilli powder
- ⅓ cup (80 ml) cold water, plus extra as needed
- 2½ teaspoons fine pink salt

Tomato tadka

- 3 teaspoons coriander powder
- 2 teaspoons cumin seeds
- 1 teaspoon ginger powder
- ½ teaspoon turmeric powder
- ½ teaspoon cumin powder
- ½ teaspoon cinnamon powder

To finish

- 400 g (14 oz) potatoes, unpeeled, cut into 3 cm (1¼ inch) cubes

Pop the tomatoes in a pressure cooker and add enough cold water to half-cover them. Pressure-cook until the steam releases once. Turn off the heat and leave to depressurise. If you don't have a pressure cooker, completely cover the tomatoes in boiling water and leave until the skin starts to soften and wrinkle away from the flesh.

Drain, skin and core the tomatoes, then blitz them using a hand-held blender until smooth. Set aside.

Heat the mustard oil over high heat in a flameproof pressure cooker or a large heavy-based saucepan until smoking. Set aside to cool off. This step reduces the pungency of the mustard oil.

>

Reheat the oil over high heat, then add the hing powder and bay leaves. Stir briefly, then add the lamb and brown it for about 15 minutes. You want it to look like the protein is a little tensioned but the meat itself isn't too caramelised. It should have a soft colour.

Stir the Kashmiri chilli powder into the cold water, then add to the lamb. This will deglaze the pot and disperse the chilli water evenly. Taste now – there will be heat, and you'll get a sense that the meatiness and richness of the lamb is a little out of reach.

Immediately add the fine pink salt. Taste now to get a feel for what the salt adds – it draws the lamb forward again, and creates a sweet, meaty mouthful.

Mix the tadka spices in a small bowl and set by the stovetop.

In a small frying pan over medium–low heat, warm the puréed tomatoes, taking care that they don't boil. Add the tadka spices and stir through until aromatic.

Add the tomato tadka to the lamb, using 2–3 tablespoons of extra water to swirl the last of the mixture out of the frying pan (this will also help prevent the curry sticking).

Add the potato. Adding it raw rather than cooked creates additional subtlety in the masala.

At this point all that's left to do is add the lid and turn to high heat. Once the pressure cooker emits three or four jets of steam, reduce the heat to medium and leave to putter for 25–45 minutes, depending on the strength and size of your pressure cooker. Let the pressure cooker depressurise on its own (see page 27). This can take up to 25 minutes. If using a saucepan for the whole cooking process, you will need to simmer everything for 90 minutes or until tender.

Serve with Simple yellow dal (page 39) and Jeera chawal (page 123).

The size of the dice

The way we prepare produce has an important influence on the final character of a dish. This is true for all cuisines, and masala is no exception. In aloo gosht, gently pressure cooking or parboiling the tomatoes, then skinning them and breaking them down with a hand-held blender, results in a softer bed for masala than simply dicing fresh tomatoes and throwing them in the pan.

FINE WHITE LAKE SALT

Category: Salts.
Form: Crystalline grains that are smaller and squarer than sea salt.
Colour: Hard white.

I didn't use lake salts for a long time because it was enough just to learn the different impacts of pink salt and sea salt on masala. If you're still there, then feel free to head straight to kala namak – Indian black salt (page 72).

Fine white lake salt isn't an imperative but an addition. I only got into its use after discovering salt from Lake Deborah in the Western Australian outback. The landscape is big and expansive, and the salt from this part of the world is so beautiful I found it impossible *not* to engage.

White lake salt has an exposed saltiness: you can taste the dried-up bed of the inland waterway. Texturally, it's not a 'melty' salt, if I can use that technical term – it's granular. This granular texture and exposed saltiness combine to create a salt that's both blunt and spacious, with an uneven salty drive. We'll get into what this means for masala in the Khichdi (page 70). For now it's enough to know that the best use for fine white lake salt is as a second-addition tiering salt (see page 62).

Tasting notes
Fine white lake salt is a little **crunchy**, with a **bright** and **clear** salty quality and a recessed **garlic tang**. Focus hard on the initial primary notes for an **earthy** hit reminiscent of a dried lake bed, and a subtle tailing aroma of **clay**.

Use in masala
I use fine lake salt as a secondary salt to make masala pop. It adds additional complexity to the base structure that a single salt can't achieve on its own.

Emotive content
Dry and drawn back, fine white lake salt has a quality of constriction – it's ideal in the Khichdi recipe (page 70), where we're keeping the impact on the sensory body light.

Khichdi

Serves 2–3

1 cup (200 g) basmati rice
½ cup (110 g) toor dal (split yellow pigeon peas)

Simple masala

1 teaspoon fine white lake salt
1 teaspoon cumin seeds
pinch of hing (asafoetida; optional)

Khichdi is rice and dal cooked in a pressure cooker with water and barely there masala. We eat it medicinally – for an Indian householder, coming back to health in the wake of an upset stomach or long-term and serious illness starts with bolstering deep gut health.

A lot of the khichdi recipes online include tomato or asafoetida or perhaps even onion or green chilli. But omission is the key with this dish: in the world of Ayurveda, for every aromatic element included in masala, the sensory body must undergo a process of both recognition and allocation of that taste. When someone is weighed down by stress, inflammation or illness, this additional effort demanded of their bodily systems can quickly veer into the territory of too much. Think of it like having to answer a list of questions when you've walked in the door from a long day at work. You just want the conversation kept simple.

If you have time, soak the basmati and the dal in plenty of water in separate bowls for 2–3 hours. This helps them soften, release starch and be more receptive to soft masala. Rinse the basmati and dal in clean running water then drain and transfer both to your pressure cooker, slow cooker or large heavy-based saucepan.

Add the masala and enough water to just cover the rice and dal. Pressure-cook or slow-cook the dal and rice on high heat. If using a pressure cooker, cook on high heat until one or two jets of steam emerge, then reduce to low–medium heat for 7–10 minutes, depending on the power and size of your cooker. If cooking in a saucepan or slow cooker, cook over low heat with the lid on until the water has been absorbed and the khichdi is tender. (If the water runs out before the khichdi is cooked, add a little more.)

Serve with plain yoghurt, or instead of plain rice with all your favourite dishes.

KALA NAMAK
INDIAN BLACK SALT

Category: Salts.
Form: Very fine powder with no obvious grains.
Colour: Pale pink or lavender. The 'black' in the name refers to the unrefined salt crystals, which are deep purple, almost black. It's a volcanic salt harvested in the Himalayas then kiln-fired to enhance its sulphurous quality.

Kala namak is like mustard oil and ajwain (carom seeds) in that it's one of only a few aromatics that aren't commonly used or known outside of regional Indian cooking. The vegan community's love affair with kala namak as an egg-taste replacement has done something to raise its profile, but only in niche quarters.

Unique subcontinental ingredients like kala namak are great to get to know when learning about masala because they contain strong cultural codes. Tasting it raw tells you a lot about the Indian palate. It tells you that we see ourselves clearly in strong, pungent aromas, such as pickles, salty drinks, and food heavy with aromatic texture. Kala namak tastes like streetside pani puri, or Fresh nimbu soda (page 75) drunk in the high peak of Delhi summer heat.

A final practical note: kala namak has a low sodium content so it can't carry complex masala on its own. In most cases, I combine it with a sea salt or lake salt – white or pink, depending on the message I want to convey.

Tasting notes

Kala namak is complex, distinctive and divisive – a strong upfront taste of **boiled egg** elicits an immediate love, loathe or 'What the hell just happened?' reaction that this spice owns completely. The boiled-egg aroma comes courtesy of its heavy **sulphur** component. There's a secondary taste of **seaweed**. There are accents of **movie butter popcorn**, **chicken skin** and **shellfish**.

Use in masala

Kala namak isn't a spice used in daily masala in any regional Indian kitchen. It won't be in the essential masala dabba by the stovetop. To be honest, it might not even be in the house. In a traditional domestic sense, kala namak is an ingredient for nimbu pani (nimbu soda) and not much else. Where it really shines is as a component in the aromatic arsenal of the street food vendor's chaat masala. Of course, I love kala namak because of its ability in a raw tasting to bring a whole group of people to immediate attention. It's that deep dive into tradition I spoke of earlier. And if you adore flavour experimentation, kala namak has an easy ability to redirect masala in unusual ways.

Emotive content

Kala namak is a doorway into collective cultural memory. When I was less than eight years old, I saw my Badi Ammi – my Kashmiri great grandmother – on what would become her deathbed. I remember the experience for how terrified I was. I was very young and soft, a quiet girl with her hair in braids, in love with Dad's stories of Hindu myth and Mum's very

beautiful material interpretation of her Kashmiri husband's world: rich colours, gold braid trims sewn onto couch cushions, not a spare inch between floor rugs or tapestries hanging on walls. Mum was from the south-eastern suburbs of Melbourne and had a penchant for princess fantasies that became her life: marrying a Kashmiri Brahman in New Delhi in 1975, taking on a new name – Amba – and remaking herself as a henna-haired, blue-eyed Devi. Our home traditions lined up with the quotidian beliefs of Kashmiri Hindus everywhere, albeit softer, not so strident. The influence of Mum.

Coming face to face with Badi Ammi was an energy I hadn't encountered before. She was the power of a proud Kashmiri Hindu woman at full force. She spoke Farsi, Kashmiri and Hindi, the linguistic expression of her direct connection to old tradition – Kashmir and Persia share roots seen through masala. I remember her enormous dogs and the energy that shouldn't have been emanating from a woman so ill. Even flat on her back with pillows plumped and a blanket pulled up to her neck, Badi Ammi ruled the room.

That's kala namak. That's what it contains – an unadulterated taste of an India unsoftened by either Western influence or Eastern modernity.

Traditional medicinal impact

Although salts are generally considered in Ayurveda to have a heating effect on the body, that's not the case for kala namak. Through the summer months, householders across India employ the lauded cooling qualities of kala namak in simple drinks and snacks designed to help lower internal body heat with subtlety (see page 75).

Cooling, not cold

An Indian householder doesn't look to temperature when it comes to cooling the body, but to sensory body chemistry. While the modern approach for eating in the heat is focused on food temperature – with ice-cold drinks, salads for dinner or, maybe for the adventurous, a Spanish-style cold soup – in regional Indian tradition cooling the body is seen as something we regulate through clever use of masala. This might be drinking Fresh nimbu soda (page 75) on a hot day (its masala content is considered to be hydrating and non-inflammatory) or eating a little raw onion with lunch (though inflammatory in high quantities, raw onion in low doses is said to draw heat from the body).

A cooling salt

The idea that a spice can be 'heating' or 'cooling' is Ayurvedic shorthand created by the Indian householder to convey a broad set of information within a single word. A heating spice is one we eat less of when the weather is very hot, when suffering from stress, when dealing with inflammatory conditions, as we age, for an upset stomach, when grief is big, or when the general pace of life is just too weird and too much. On the upside, a heating spice is said to help drive metabolism, shift heavy energy, provide lift for a flat-lining mental state, and increase general alertness and vibrancy.

A cooling spice, on the other hand, is one we eat less of when the weather is very damp, if struggling with heavy physical energies, or for a sluggish metabolism. On the plus side, a cooling spice such as kala namak is an aromatic we turn to for combatting excessive internal (inflammatory) or external (seasonal) heat. For this reason it's included in the natural Powerade of India – nimbu pani.

A breakfast seasoning

In the summer, mangoes are everywhere in India, in all forms, and everyone has a personal favourite. Fresh mango breakfasts are squeezed with lime and finished with kala namak – a cooling element to reduce the inflammatory effect of a fruit that ripens at the hottest time of the year.

In the winter it's guava season, and the softer and pimplier the skin, and the more flecked it is with black, the sweeter and more jelly-like its savoury interior. Kala namak sprinkled on cut guava at this time of year – when Delhi's December cold clutches your ankles on concrete kitchen floors – is a pungent morning wake-up call. It's a moment of delicious intensity during a season when intensity can be flattened by morning fog and dim light that barely penetrates heavy skies.

In Australia, I sprinkle my kala namak on avocado toast with pink salt, cracked black pepper and fine white pepper. It tastes at once like the egg I can't be bothered to fry, and opens a side-door connection to home.

✱

Fresh nimbu soda

The simplest nimbu pani recipe is more a list of ingredients with no official measurements or method. Squeeze a few limes into a jug of soda water (club soda) or just plain water. Add sugar syrup or sugar to taste – a little less than a teaspoon per glass – and then about ½ teaspoon kala namak per glass. The black salt will react with the nimbu (lime) and the drink will fizz. Drink it fresh, over ice, with a sprig of mint and a sprinkle of toasted cumin powder. For a more intense nimbu soda experience, you could replace the kala namak with a teaspoon of chaat masala.

Over the page, left to right: Clay cup: Jeera pani (page 125). Bottles: Haldi doodh (page 38). Fizzy glass: Fresh nimbu soda. Stainless-steel cup: Shivani's namkeen lassi (page 278). Still glass: Fenugreek seed tea (page 57).

Mess and fuss: an Indian tradition

There were a lot of reasons I didn't take to picking up the tradition of thali and kadai in my kitchen once I left home. Many of those reasons were emotional – my book *Spirits in a Spice Jar* explains them if you want to find out more. But one strong reason for resistance was the practical reality that cooking traditional regional Indian food is incredibly time-consuming. And messy. Pots and preparation and fats and spitting oil and spice jars. Dad used to try to convince me it wasn't the case, but when I finally did set up my Kashmiri kitchen and start cooking Indian food proper, he owned up to what any householder knows … there are few shortcuts, many ingredients, and much time and space required to pull together a meal with all the traditional components.

Eventually I reached the tipping point in my early 30s where it mattered more to me to cook than it did to worry about the clean-up or the time. I always find time to do the things I really want to do, and cooking has become one of them. But part of the benefit of learning about the internal workings of masala is that it's possible to produce similar outcomes with less hassle. By similar outcomes I mean food that will approach the sensory body in the same way, if perhaps not with the same depth or intensity. Dishes like the Haloumi-baked eggplant opposite. They can be good stand-ins for nights when you want flavour but you just don't have the fortitude to go the full monty.

Two ways with eggplant

Segueing from a traditional dish to a contemporary dish, both of which use the same produce and the same star spice, is a good way to introduce traditional Indian regional cooking techniques into a non-Desi kitchen. The masalas for these two dishes use the same base with a few variations. Traditional regional Indian dishes often take time. Looking at two dishes side by side in this way shows how knowing about masala means we can cook dishes with similar aromatic sensibilities to regional classics but with less mess and fuss (see left).

Baingan bharta

Serves 4 as part of a shared meal

2 medium eggplants (aubergines)

Masala

2 tablespoons mustard oil
1 tablespoon crushed garlic
1 teaspoon tamarind paste
1 teaspoon fine white sea salt
1 teaspoon fennel seeds
½ teaspoon kala namak
½ teaspoon hot chilli powder
½ teaspoon amchur
½ teaspoon cumin powder
½ teaspoon chilli flakes
scant ½ teaspoon sumac

To finish

½ cup (125 ml) water
1 teaspoon Ammi's garam masala (page 156)

To serve

fresh coriander (cilantro)
plain yoghurt or raita (page 130)

Start by charring the eggplant. A barbecue or tandoor is ideal, I char mine over my gas stovetop by holding them in metal tongs. Alternatively, roast them in a 200°C (400°F) oven or under the grill until the skin is charred and the interior very soft. When cool to handle, remove the skin and dice finely. Set aside.

Heat the mustard oil in a cast-iron casserole (I use my Le Creuset pot) or large saucepan over medium–high heat. Add the garlic and spices to temper, stirring constantly so they don't burn. Quickly add the eggplant and stir it through. Cook down for 2–3 minutes, stirring constantly.

Stir in the water, then bring to a simmer and cook for 2–3 minutes. Add the garam masala and simmer for 2–3 minutes more. Top with coriander and serve with yoghurt or raita.

Haloumi-baked eggplant

I love this recipe because it's one pot and no prep. My first test run making it was a few years ago as a vehicle for my Spirit of Spice Chilli Masala. The masala used here is a simplified version of my retail blend, but it has the same qualities – sweet heat and sulphur. And while the Baingan bharta uses garlic for extra tang, this dish finds it in the haloumi.

Serves 2

3 ripe tomatoes, chopped
1 small eggplant (aubergine), thinly sliced
1–2 tablespoons mustard oil
250 g (9½ oz) haloumi, thinly sliced

Masala

1 teaspoon fine white sea salt
1 teaspoon fennel seeds
½ teaspoon kala namak
½ teaspoon hot chilli powder
½ teaspoon amchur
½ teaspoon cumin powder
½ teaspoon chilli flakes
scant ½ teaspoon sumac

Preheat the oven to 180°C (350°F) fan-forced (200°C/400°F conventional).

The eggplant isn't pre-cooked here – it doesn't need it. Any small heavy-based ovenproof dish with a lid will do (I use my small Le Creuset). Put the tomatoes on the bottom, lay the eggplant on top, then drizzle with the mustard oil. Sprinkle all of the masala on top, and then finish with a layer of haloumi.

Bake for 35–45 minutes, until it's an oozy, spicy mess of deliciousness. Serve hot with a green salad.

FLEUR DE SEL
FLAKED WHITE SALT

Category: Salts.
Form: Snowflake crystals.
Colour: Bright white.

Fleur de sel is classically thought of as a finishing salt: those flakes that fall like snow across a charred steak. It's not a salt that finds traditional use in masala – the most famous fleur de sel is harvested on the Ile de Ré on the west coast of France, a long way from the salt mines of Himachal Pradesh and Rajasthan. I include fleur de sel when teaching people about masala because it's such a useful comparative tool. Try lining up white sea salt, a white lake salt and a white flaked salt and tasting all three. It will take you straight to the truth that within the frame of masala even salts have an interplay and a story to tell.

I chose Dal makhani (page 83) to showcase fleur de sel because it's the kind of traditional dish where it can have impact. The salt is a subtle aromatic addition but it nonetheless does a lot to lighten the weight of the dal, increasing its creaminess and its complexity.

Playing on the edges of masala with aromatics such as fleur de sel – aromatics, in other words, that won't impact the structure of the dish or ruin the integrity of its flavour – is a safe and simple way to begin to find your own masala voice.

Tasting notes
Fleur de sel initially presents as texture more than taste, from **angular** to **polished concrete**. Its **salty** quality is **subtle** and exhibits a slow decline into **recessed sweetness**.

Use in masala
I use flaked white salt in a few ways with masala. The easiest is as a third salt – when I want masala to be vibrant but using any more pink or white salt feels too heavy-handed. At this point, I'll add a generous ¼ teaspoon of a flaked salt with the rest of the starting spices as a turbo boost. It works well because the surface area of a flaked salt detonates little landmines of flavour. It's not another *layer* of salt. It's confetti.

The other way I like to use fleur de sel is to build it into dishes at the midpoint. Spice behaves in masala and in a dish just like it does on the palate. So just as fleur de sel fizzes like salty popping candy when tasted raw, so it works in food (see Palate to dish translation, opposite).

Applied in the middle of the cooking time – after the base masala has been tempered – the popping-candy salty quality of fleur de sel 'aerates' the mid-dish (see Not just which, but when, opposite). It's a useful technique with winter soups or slow cooks that carry heavy weight. Or with dals, as the Dal makhani recipe (page 83) shows.

The trick is to make sure you only add fleur de sel at the midpoint: the remaining cooking time and any later addition of aromatics will ensure its aerated quality is sealed inside the dish.

'Fleur de sel energises masala.'

Emotive content
Fleur de sel energises masala. It's frivolous when frivolity is needed.

Palate to dish translation
Tasting a spice raw will tell you directly how it will behave in a dish. If a salt is heavy around the front of the mouth upon tasting, it will hold and drive flavour heavily around the front of the mouth in a dish. If an earth spice like nigella seeds has a windy and hard-to-grasp quality in raw tasting, it will also have that effect in a dish, creating elusive movement in the accompanying aromatics. This 'aromatic logic' is a straightforward way to strengthen our understanding of how an unknown spice might behave in a dish.

Not just which, but when
Salt relies on masala to be able to express a particular portion of its drive. When added at the beginning, a salt will be present in the dish from root to tip. When added through the mid-dish, it will show itself from the third floor up. And when applied at the finish, the relationship of salt to masala is bright and surface-level, in the way of an untested friendship or a fresh herb garnish.

Salt for beginners
One of the biggest challenges when coming fresh to masala is to have the confidence to colour outside the lines and still rely on those mistakes being edible: cooking with beautiful ingredients is both expensive and time-consuming. Produce and time are precious. You don't want to sacrifice either. One of the ways to work with this conundrum is to create relationships with forgiving spices. It's your starting point. Aromatics like cumin seeds, fresh ginger, ginger powder, softer chilli powders, coriander powder, fresh curry leaves. Spices, in other words, that aren't punishing if you use either a little too much or not quite enough. For salts this means fine pink salt.

Dal makhani

Serves 8 as part of a meal

This isn't a dish on our regular family roster, and I can safely say that this is pretty much true of any family across India's regions. The weight and richness of dal makhani makes it a 'sometimes' dish, one that's ordered when eating out, probably alongside tandoor-cooked naan. I've included it here to demonstrate the impact of fleur de sel, showing how a single change in masala introduces a new library of sensory information.

24 hours before cooking

¾ cup (150 g) urad dal (black lentils)
¼ cup (50 g) rajma (red kidney beans)
plenty of cold water

For pressure cooking

3 cups (750 ml) water
2 teaspoons fine white sea salt

For the main cooking phase

40 g (1½ oz) salted butter
40 g (1½ oz) ghee
1 onion, finely chopped
1 tablespoon crushed garlic
1 tablespoon finely grated fresh ginger
½ cup tomato paste (concentrated purée)

Masala

2 teaspoons fleur de sel
1 teaspoon Kashmiri chilli powder
1 teaspoon Ammi's garam masala (page 156)

For simmering

1½ cups (375 ml) water

To finish

20 g (¾ oz) salted butter
¼ cup (125 ml) pouring cream
½ teaspoon red chilli powder (optional)

Soak the urad dal and rajma in plenty of cold water in separate bowls for 24 hours or at least overnight. Drain the soaked dal and beans and put them in a pressure cooker with the water and salt. Set on high heat and cook until the pressure cooker emits three or four jets of steam. Turn to medium, then cook for a further 15–20 minutes. Let the pressure cooker depressurise on its own, then check the dal. When cooked, the lentils and beans should hold their shape but be soft enough to mash. If not, pressure-cook for a little longer, then mash.

>

Alternatively, cook the dal and rajma in a slow cooker or large heavy-based saucepan. Ensure the lentils and beans are soaked for the full 24 hours then cook in plenty of boiling water for about 90 minutes, until tender. Mash when cooked.

For the main cooking phase, place a large heavy-based saucepan (I use my large Le Creuset casserole) over medium heat, then add the butter and ghee and cook until melted. Add the onion and cook for 5–7 minutes, until translucent but not caramelised. Add the garlic and ginger and stir for 2–3 minutes, until the raw aroma dissipates. Add the tomato paste and cook for 2–3 minutes until it no longer smells raw.

Add the masala and stir. Add the mashed urad dal and rajma mix and stir again. Lower the heat and add one-third of the water. Stir frequently, to prevent it sticking and burning, and to ensure a creamier result. When the water has worked into the dal, add another one-third and cook as before until worked into the dal. Repeat with the remaining water until the dal is rich and creamy.

To finish, stir in the butter and cream – and the chilli, if using. Serve with basmati rice and a light sabji.

Over the page, right: Top tray, clockwise from top: yoghurt, olive oil, water, milk. Lid and spoon: vegetable oil. Bottom tray, clockwise from top: Ghee, macadammia oil, peanut oil, sesame oil, coconut oil, mustard oil.

FATS

& other masala carriers

Function in masala: Providing activation. When fats aren't used at some point in the cooking process, the expression of masala is curtailed.
Emotive quality: Fleshing out the message of masala, and creating a general underlying emotive tone.
Traditional medicinal quality: Bolstering natural resilience, protecting organs, lubricating joints, providing dense energy, and helping reduce consumption through increased satiety.

When I introduce people to masala, we do fat tastings. I line up olive oil, ghee, mustard oil, coconut oil, sesame oil, peanut oil – you name it, we taste it. Most people find it novel, but for some the idea of swallowing a few teaspoons of oil is just too confronting. I always try to sway them – fats are too important to skip.

In the same way that the choice of bitter aromatic underpins a dish's structure, and the choice of salt influences the expression of masala's emotive content, the choice of fat/s affects overall tone. Ghee is like the Sydney Opera House – with it, masala takes on classically beautiful song. Coconut oil is the outdoor amphitheatre – it makes masala feel joyous and open. Mustard oil is a basement club – it gives masala a grungy, low solar-plexus voice. Each of these tones has a particular resonance for different Indian regions. And when fats are used in conjunction, the overall tonal complexity of masala increases.

Functionally, fats are important because they hold masala in the mouth. Technically, as soon as a mouthful is swallowed, the flavour information dissipates. That is unless we use fats and oils well: any fat and oil residues that hang on the palate will hold the aromatic content of a dish. With time, the sensory body will decode tastes, emotive content and cultural or metaphysical messaging. Only once those messages are decoded can the sensory body act upon them. Fats that hold or lengthen flavour buy the body that processing time.

With masala it's never as simple as flavour, but it's not removed from it either. Sometimes I think masala is just about teasing out the reasons why we do what we do when we're cooking, so that we can understand the implications and then make decisions.

Tradition, the original harbinger of health

I'm liberal with fats as a rule – chiefly because they make food delicious, but also because they communicate the messaging of masala beautifully. Some people have a general fear of fat consumption. But in Indian cooking we use a lot of fat because it's a harbinger of health. Fats diminish our need for quantity when it comes to consumption, and Ayurvedic tradition views minimal consumption as one of the keys to wellness and a key indicator of longevity.

The only functional way to minimise how much we eat each day is to focus on beautiful food that satisfies our three bodies with each mouthful. That way eating less isn't a stress or something we have to focus on. It's a natural occurrence. Achieving that level of satiety relies on being able to hear the messaging in masala, and fats provide the kind of rich and meaningful mouthful that naturally minimises hunger. Tradition encourages us to be full in our approach to food and thoughtful in our means and method of consumption.

GHEE

Category: Fats and other masala carriers.
Form: Changes depending on the temperature. In the heat it has an oily melted-butter consistency. In cold weather it solidifies to a firm dulce de leche consistency.
Colour: Bright butter yellow.

Ghee is the mother fat of India. There's not a Desi kitchen anywhere in the world that doesn't have a tub of ghee by the stovetop or in the cupboard. On a subcontinent with swathes of desert and tropical jungle in its geographical mix, and a culinary tradition that can be heavily reliant on dairy, a dairy-based fat that doesn't go rancid is the perfect solution.

Ghee is made by churning, separating and then clarifying butter, from either cream or milk. This results in most of the lactose being removed along with the milk solids, which is chiefly why it won't go rancid, and also why it can be okay for people with lactose intolerance. Its cooking point is higher than that of butter but lower than that of most oils.

Emotively, ghee is about nurture. In Ayurveda it's considered a *sattvic* food – one that's neither heating nor cooling but rather sits in balance with the body (see page 200). There's an evenness to the experience of ghee, whether that's in its texture, carriage of masala or relationship to the sensory body. Stir a little ghee through hot rice and it is instantly a cradle.

No specific ghee recipes follow directly here, but to see differing uses and expressions of ghee within the frame of masala, turn to:

- **Jeera chawal** recipe (page 123), where ghee provides a soft cradle for the produce and masala, and allows the body a subtle digestive experience.
- **Kabargah** (page 135), which uses ghee to deep-fry heavily cooked and spiced lamb ribs. Ghee as a frying fat is opulent and rich.
- **Rogan josh** (page 302), where ghee ensures rich Kashmiri-style caramelisation of the meat.
- **Three-egg turmeric scramble** (page 49), where ghee blended with olive oil softens the aromatics.
- **Matar paneer** (page 230), which uses ghee in a classic way. Complex masala that speaks clearly of a region and a family is tempered with ghee and only ghee. In any of my recipes where ghee is the only fat used, don't substitute. The ghee is telling a special story.

Tasting notes

The tasting profile of ghee can change radically depending on where and how it's made. It can be floury in the way of shortbread, very rich and buttery, or possessed of a strong element of 'cow'. Generally, ghee is **buttery**, **dense**, **sweet** and **floury**.

Companion fats
Mustard oil will sharpen ghee's sweetness. Sesame oil will lift its weight. Coconut oil will excite and sharpen its softer quality.

Emotive content
Ghee sweetens and softens masala. Dad always said it was a healthy fat, but I think that's because there's almost no Indian alive who can imagine eating ghee in moderate quantities. How can we possibly restrict our access to the maternal message of ghee? Even for non-Indians, ghee with masala is soothing.

Traditional medicinal impact
Ayurveda encourages daily consumption of ghee because it is believed to have important nutritional qualities and a long list of benefits, including enhancing brain function, pacifying the doshas, and reducing anxiety.

Vegan masala
The inherent beauty of spice makes it easy to use in vegan dishes, but authentic Kashmiri Hindu cuisine uses a lot of yoghurt, ghee and milk. Dairy-based fats have a transformative effect on masala that's impossible to replicate: not just soft and sweet, ghee creates richness and fullness.

If you can't or don't want to use ghee, macadamia oil (page 114), though expensive, does replicate its very broad quality, the way it flat-coats the bottom of the palate. Macadamia oil has buttery tones, and mixed with coconut oil can mimic ghee's thicker texture and sweetness. The cuddly quality of ghee is, however, missing.

VEGETABLE OIL

Category: Fats and other masala carriers.
Form: Relatively slick. A little less viscous than most extra virgin olive oils, though with a more insistent oiliness.
Colour: Straw to bright yellow.

The stripped-back nature of vegetable oil creates a hard stop at the base of the dish. This hard stop provides a strong upward force for masala – tastes stand out in relief. In the kitchen this means a few things. Firstly, cooking in vegetable oil suits emphatic spice that isn't too complex and that tells a clear story. Secondly, vegetable oil has a broad storytelling capability – even those who don't know India or Indian regional cuisine at all understand what they're eating.

That said, vegetable oil is definitely not for all the time. Unless specifically stated in a recipe, don't use it as a replacement for ghee or mustard oil.

Tasting notes
Vegetable oil is **brutish**. The solid taste hits you in the face and settles into the mouth like the feel of a **sodden coat** – it has as much flavour as a wet coat, too. Its taste is predominantly the experience of weight.

Companion fats
Adding some mustard oil to your vegetable oil will create a more viscous and pungent quality. Yoghurt gives vegetable oil density, but without the natural cohesion of yoghurt and ghee or yoghurt and mustard oil. A little sesame oil will add body and fragrance.

Emotive content
Vegetable oil offers an opportunity to construct flavour from a neutral emotive space, which means a simpler experience of the dish.

7411737004

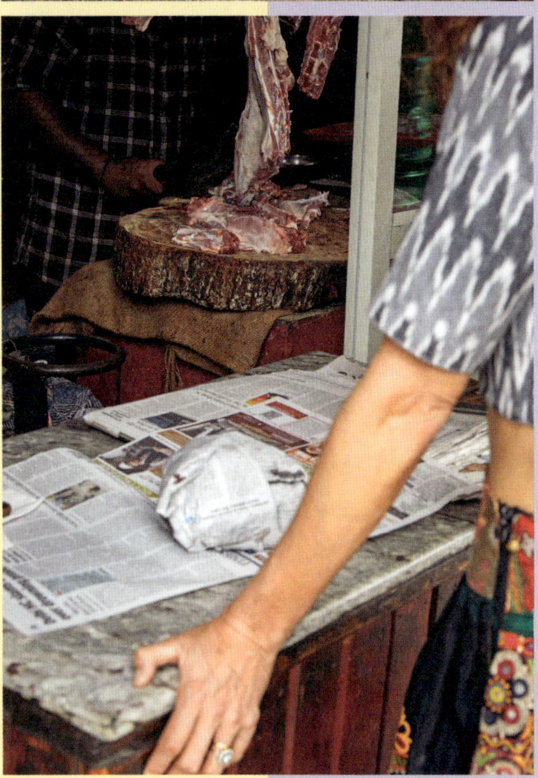

Chokhta

This is the most beautiful lamb. Roasty, like the roastiest roast lamb you'll ever eat, but Kashmiri-style. One of the Kashmiri Hindu blueprints is the use of hing (asafoetida) and ginger powder, and this recipe follows that model. This is a family recipe published by a once-removed aunt in a little recipe book. I've kept true to her version – I never ad lib, because it's already perfect. Pay attention to the choice of cut. I use lamb leg – the meat needs a tensile muscle structure in order to hold up when cooked in vegetable oil over high heat. Roasting the bones separately and returning them later creates another tier of flavour.

I was nervous the first time I made this dish – actually, to be honest, I'm nervous every time I make it – because at different moments during cooking the meat will look hard and boiled. To find success, stick with the recipe and be confident with the changes from very high to low heat.

Serves 4–6 as part of a shared meal

6–8 lamb bones about 5 cm (2 inches) long
900 g (2 lb) lamb leg

Base masala

1½ cups (375 ml) cold water
½ cup (125 ml) vegetable oil
1½ teaspoons fine white sea salt
2 teaspoons Kashmiri chilli powder
1 teaspoon ginger powder
2 pinches of hing (asafoetida) powder

Chilli water

1 teaspoon red chilli powder
2 tablespoons cold water

To finish

scant ½ teaspoon ginger powder

Preheat the oven to 180°C (350°F) fan-forced (200°C/400°F conventional). Pop your lamb bones on a baking tray and roast without oil or seasoning for 20–25 minutes. (You want to keep this step simple – adding the lamb bones to the dish later is not so much about aroma but texture.)

Meanwhile, trim the lamb leg of fat and chop it into large chunks of at least 5 cm (2 inches). (Use discretion when trimming: you'll need to retain a little extraneous fat for added sweetness and mouth-hold for the masala. Leave more than your heart surgeon would condone.)

In a large kadai, stable cast-iron wok or heavy-based saucepan, combine the water and oil and place over high heat. When bubbles begin to form on the base of the pan, add the base masala spices. Bring to a rolling spicy boil then add the lamb chunks.

Cook over very high heat for 2–3 minutes, turning the lamb through the boiling oil and water. Reduce the heat to high and cover with the lid. Boil until the water reduces by half, about 15 minutes.

You'll need to keep an eye on the pot, stirring occasionally. The tension created by the high heat and oil will leave the meat looking tight, chewy and boiled.

After the water has evaporated by half, remove the lid. If the meat feels very hard, then you're there.

Reduce the heat to medium–low and cook, uncovered, for about 10 minutes. This step is about creating a softer-heat tension that allows the lamb to imbibe the spiced oil. The lamb should soften while the oil and water mixture becomes a little creamier. Cook over low heat until the liquid has mostly evaporated and mainly oil remains.

Prepare your chilli water by stirring the chilli into the water. Set aside near the stovetop.

Return the heat under the boiled lamb to high and add your roasted lamb bones. Stir them through for 2–3 minutes at this high heat, then reduce the heat to medium–low and cook for another 5–7 minutes. As the bones settle in, and the low temperature reduces the tension in the lamb pieces, you'll notice the appearance of the dish change. Taste the dish now. If it's starting to feel intense, creamy and umami-rich, you're almost there.

Turn the heat back up to high. Add the chilli water and use its sizzle to deglaze both the meat and the cooking vessel.

To finish, add the ginger powder and reduce the heat to low. This will allow components from the bones to render into the lamb glaze and provide that missing fatty sweetness that the spice of this dish won't provide. Taste again. If the oil is masking the spices, keep cooking for a few more minutes, until the last of the 'oiliness' cooks off – when you no longer feel a residue of vegetable oil after a taste. If that oily sensation dominates the mouthful, it's not quite there. Cooking off the last of the oil unearths chokhta's story.

Serve straight from the kadai with flaky paratha (such as Methi fried flatbreads, page 271) and a tangy raita (pages 130, 229).

Heat, tension and taste

One way to build flavour structure in meats is to hit them with multiple heat applications through the cooking process. In this recipe, you'll see striking changes in the meat as you turn the temperature from very high to a slow medium and then back up to high, before finishing low. High heat creates a hard tension. This is infrastructure. As the heat slows, the tight scaffolding of the internal protein is set, but the flesh around it relaxes to let the masala penetrate. We repeat this sequence throughout the cooking process. Tension, relax. Tension, relax. The masala will find expression through the differing tensions that have been scaffolded into the lamb, increasing complexity. It's how we can use minimal spice, vegetable oil and water to achieve a rich result.

MUSTARD OIL

Category: Fats and other masala carriers.
Form: Very viscous, with an almost syrup-like oily consistency.
Colour: Honeyish brown.

Mustard oil is the workhorse fat of the Indian householder's larder, particularly in the north. In a culinary sense, it's used to deep-fry, to make pickles and to brown meats. In the medicine cabinet it's used as a hair and skin oil in the dry winter.

From a faith perspective, we used it as kids when we had to perform a *Shani daan* – an offering made on a Saturday (Saturn's day) to offset the malefic aspect of Lord Shani, son of Surya (the Sun) and embodiment of the planet Saturn. We performed the ritual during times of personal trial or threat as designated by our *varshphal* readings (yearly interpretation of our personal astrological chart; see page 94).

The mustard-oil-filled katori was put by our beds by Dad on a Friday night; the first thing we had to do the next day, even before we opened our eyes, was drop an iron nail or copper coin into the mustard oil. I used to stress out about that *sooo* much. What if I forgot? And how could I drop in the coin or nail without looking? Vexing! I normally resorted to a half-squinting peek, hoping no one was there to see that my eyes weren't shut.

In these three roles, mustard oil defines masala's purpose: food as emotive carriage, medicinal support and spiritual conduit.

Tasting notes
Viscous and **sharp**, mustard oil creates a long-lasting seal for the palate, ideal for supporting complex spice. This fat draws forward the pungent, hot, floral and shadowed character of all spice. Mustard oil makes chilli sizzle and earth spices glitter. It strengthens and blunts warm and sweet aromatics. On its own, mustard oil is **hot** and **pungent**, with a taste that recalls **wasabi**, **fresh horseradish** or **hot English mustard** – depending on your food reference map. The hidden **floral body** of mustard oil steps forward when it's tasted raw.

Companion fats
Ghee will soften with mustard oil's intensity. Coconut oil will raise its pitch. Sesame oil will increase its heat and pungency. Peanut oil will reduce its viscosity.

Emotive content
Mustard oil has a strident voice. Its emphatic nature heralds a quality of strength: of purpose; of directive. Its floral and shadowed profile represents light and shade.

Traditional medicinal impact
Mustard oil's heating and pungent quality makes it a traditional remedy for joint pain and respiratory issues (via topical massage). Internal consumption is said to benefit skin tension and improve blood flow.

Mustard oil and our use of language
Pungent taste is the doorway to some of the deepest understanding of masala (see page 183), but it's not always an easy door to walk through. Masala loves to use aromatics that are sulphurous or bitter, and fats like mustard oil that are strident and pervasive. It rejoices in dishes that are oily and fermented, spices that are gritty. When you don't grow up with it, it becomes a lot to digest from a standing start.

Language is important when it comes to taste. If we describe a dish as 'pretty' or 'fragrant' it means we like it. When we find a dish too much we might say it's 'bitter' or 'pungent'. Fairly soon, 'pretty' and 'fragrant' become good, and 'bitter' and 'pungent' become bad. But in masala we rely on those brutish tastes to construct nuanced, complete and communicative flavour.

The easy answer is not to change our language but to drop the emotional implication. Think of words as descriptors and not judgements. Bitter is bitter, that's it. A spice with a soil-like and cranky character is just a spice with a soil-like and cranky character.

Once we drop any linguistic implication, we achieve clarity with taste. And we understand that every contribution is equally prized. That process goes to the heart of connecting with masala.

ASTROLOGY, HINDUISM AND MASALA: OPENING A PORTAL

A *varshphal* is a yearly interpretation of a Hindu devotee's *janampatra*, the Vedic astrological chart used to map an individual's lifetime. At birth, the time, place and date of birth are sent away for the *janampatra* chart to be drawn up. Traditionally this was done manually by a Vedic astrologer, but nowadays the calculations are done by computer program. In either case, the *varshphal* is like an annual chapter of the *janampatra*, and its astrology is read by a guru – a Hindu family priest. It's read every year on our birthday to give a feel for what the immediate future holds. It's not a magic prediction but a method to prescribe specific mantras and specific *daans*. Mantras are added to the daily recitation of the practising Hindu; the *daans* are offerings to be performed at certain points in the year to offset perceived malefic planetary aspects.

Indian householders use masala to teach our children the language of our culture and of our family because masala is bound into the root systems of their particular ancient faith tradition – Hindus, Muslim Sindhis, Sikhs, Jains, Christians, Buddhists, Parsis, Jews. The nature of masala as a storytelling tool means each faith tradition has its own spoken language through spice. Dad introducing my brothers and me to the *Shani daan* practice was one of a series of pillars that tied masala to our faith and identity. It didn't matter that we didn't understand all the whys. Creating awareness of that pillar's existence was enough to make the connection between masala and myth.

You don't need to believe in or to understand the specifics of the Hindu faith in order to understand this book. But you need to know that those connections and practices exist and relate to the traditional meaning of masala. As a discipline, masala is expansive. It's all about letting go of the edge. Masala requires surrender. Sometimes that act of surrender is easier to make when we know we're attempting to cross not a swimming pool, but an ocean.

Rova
ನೇತ್ರಾ | NETRA
BENGALURU CITY POLICE

Browning meat

One of the ways to get inside masala is to give an exotic ingredient a regular job in your kitchen. Make it a utility. Like using ghee to scramble eggs (page 49). Sprinkling kala namak on avocado toast (page 75). Or using mustard oil to brown meats, even if they're not destined for a traditional Indian recipe.

When I make Chicken cacciatore (page 294), I brown off my cornflour-coated chicken Maryland (leg quarter) pieces in mustard oil and reserve what's left in the heavy-based pot to start off the recipe. I do the same with lamb shanks destined for winter slow-cooking. Mustard oil's pungent and blunt qualities establish a strong base profile in the meat. And that's what we need to support textured aroma and complex structure – which is where deliciousness lives.

1.
Make sure the mustard oil is very hot but not quite smoking before adding the meat. I use a deep vessel and a significant amount of oil, as the browning process is protracted and a volume of oil is required so that it's not eaten up in the first instance. The meat added at this point will hit with a sizzle and instantly crust and brown, which is perfect.

2.
With large cuts, don't constantly turn the meat. With smaller pieces, refrain from constantly stirring. Browning is different from stir-frying. The meat is moved by folding it back *into* the oil, rather than constantly stirring it *around* the oil. This allows a complex tension to be built into the meat. We keep at this stage of the browning process until the oil begins to look 'harder' and the meat is well browned. To get a feel for the flavour that's developing, you can taste the oil at this time – especially given many of the recipes will have added whole spices and salt, and maybe even chilli alongside the meat.

3.
Now we begin to add liquid or yoghurt to 'elongate' the browning process. We add this liquid or yoghurt a little at a time, watching the oil become creamy and the tension in the meat soften. We keep resting the meat then folding it into the oil (see point 2), waiting until the oil hardens and the meat protein tenses again before adding more liquid or yoghurt. We can carry on with this process for anywhere from 15 to 90 minutes, depending on the dish and the complexity of taste and structure we're building into the meat.

4.
The last stage of the browning process is different for every dish, but in general, the oil and any added yoghurt or liquids should be cooked down, and the browning arrested at the desired tension. For a dish like Chokhta (page 91), this is a hard tension. For a dish like Simple aloo gosht (page 67), it's a softer tension. Hard-tensioned meat looks tighter. If we then go on to pressure-cook (or cook further on the stovetop), whatever is left of the oil and liquid should be transferred along with the meat into the next pot. That oil will be imbued with much of the foundational taste of the dish.

Bhavna's mum's winter carrot pickles

Bhavna Kalra Shivalkar is both @moderndesi.co and @justagirlfrommumbai on Instagram. The former page circles around her work as a teacher of regional Indian cuisine and a teller of culinary stories. The latter offers a more personal account of her writing and unique point of view that's beautifully melancholic and enchanting in the sense of fragility it evokes. I chose her mum's winter carrot pickles recipe to tell a story of mustard oil because of the way Bhavna recounts the Desi love affair with pungent tastes, and the emotion we embed there.

Because this is a winter pickle made without brine or vinegar, it needs to be kept refrigerated and must be consumed within two to three weeks.

Note: You can use cauliflower florets instead of carrot sticks, but boil them for 2–3 minutes longer. To sterilise the jar, either put it through a hot cycle in the dishwasher or wash in hot soapy water then dry thoroughly in a 110°C (225°F) oven.

Previous pages, left to right: Dried mint, Mum's raita (page 229), coriander (cilantro), Coriander and mint chutney (page 278), green chillies, Toasted cumin powder raita (page 130), Bhavna's mum's winter carrot pickles, Imli chutney (page 190).

Makes 1 × 700 ml (24 fl oz) jar

- 25 g (1 oz) mustard seeds
- 500 g (1 lb 2 oz) carrots (see note), cut into 4 cm (1½ inch) sticks
- ¾ cup (185 ml) mustard oil

Masala

- 25 g (1 oz) finely grated fresh ginger
- 15 g (½ oz) chopped red chilli
- 15 g (½ oz) crushed garlic
- 1 tablespoon fine white sea salt
- 1 tablespoon caster (superfine) sugar, or to taste
- 2 teaspoons red chilli powder, or to taste
- 2 teaspoons turmeric powder

Using a spice grinder or mortar and pestle, grind the mustard seeds to a coarse powder and set aside.

Bring a medium saucepan of water to a rolling boil over high heat. Add the carrots and cook for exactly 2 minutes. Drain immediately, then spread the carrot sticks on a clean tea towel (dish towel) and leave them to dry completely – moisture can decrease the shelf life of the pickles. You could even leave the carrots out in the sun for 2–3 hours.

Meanwhile, heat the mustard oil in a large kadai, stable cast-iron wok or heavy-based saucepan over high heat until it smokes. Leave it to cool completely. (The heating and cooling step softens its sharp pungent smell.)

When ready to make the pickles, reheat the oil over medium heat and add the masala. Temper for about 30 seconds, then add the dried carrots and stir well. Cook for 2–3 minutes only, then remove from the heat.

Once the pickles are cool, spoon them into a sterilised jar (see note). Leave to mature in the sun for 2 days before refrigerating. Always use a clean spoon to scoop out the pickles. Use within 2–3 weeks.

COCONUT OIL

Category: Fats and other masala carriers.
Form: The texture of coconut oil changes depending on the temperature. In the heat it melts to an oily melted butter consistency. In cold weather it solidifies to a firm dulce de leche consistency.
Colour: White.

The mix of coconut oil and jasmine flower woven into the long plaits of the women around our home in what was then called Bangalore is pretty much the signature aromatic memory of my early teens. We moved to Bengaluru in the early 1990s before the tech boom, when it was still a small town. Mum and Dad bought a textile factory there and we lived in Koramangala in a fourth-floor apartment with a big balcony and a rooftop terrace. Across the way was an empty marshland. Giant monkeys sometimes occupied our terrace. Banyan trees lined our walk home from the bus stop, and water buffalo were as populous as people. As kids we'd spent a lot of time in Delhi and even Hyderabad – both fairly hard climates. But Bangalore was pretty and soft, a much gentler environment than the north. And that's how coconut oil translates as a fat.

Coconut oil is a cooling fat. In the south, householders rub it into their hair and onto their skin. Ayurveda prizes it as an aromatic to soothe the nervous system. Perhaps you avoid using coconut oil because you don't like the coconut taste. But the taste of coconut oil itself is not really the point.

Coconut oil is about building in brightness. As a fat it reveals hidden recesses of acidity, sweetness and light within individual aromatics. Tempered in coconut oil, fresh ginger becomes sharper and less earthy. The floral heat of Kashmiri chilli powder speaks louder than its brick smoke. Even cumin seeds lose that intensity of cedar in favour of menthol. The overall effect is masala that trills with a high and clear tone.

As a fix, adding coconut oil at the end of a dish will lift a dark, flat masala by raising the volume on the masala's recessed sweetness and acidity. Add a tablespoon when you've been heavy-handed with earth spices, or when you want to carry more heat and acidity through leaner and cheaper beef cuts with heavier fibrous tissue and less fat.

Tasting notes

Coconut oil is **cool** and **slick**. It lingers on the palate and **soothes** bodily systems. For me, coconut oil is about wrapping the mouth in brightness. Masala responds to coconut oil with openness and generosity. As a fat, it draws forward **sweetness**, **light** and **acidity** in a spice, and these are all points of pleasure for the palate. Coconut oil is a natural inclusion in Southern Indian street-food-style salads and vibrant seafood dishes, just as it is across South-East Asia. When I want to make a festive, high-toned dish, coconut oil is my go-to fat.

Companion fats

Coconut oil will heighten the 'hot' quality of mustard oil, lighten ghee's rich mouthfeel, and shift sesame oil into a heavier and warmer gear.

Emotive content

Coconut oil is uplifting. It has the effect on the sensory body of a day of sun at the end of a dark winter – joy just kind of unfurls.

Masala is symphony, not solo
Individual aromatic tastes don't have the same significance in masala as they tend to in other types of cooking. Using coconut oil is about providing a certain type of filter for masala. I don't like nutmeg powder or whole cloves or clove powder on their own, but I use them in masala. On the other hand, loving a spice is no reason to include it all the time. Masala is a *symphony*, not a solo. I don't understand orchestral music enough to make a good metaphor, other than to say you might dislike the tone of an oboe, but in accord with the instruments around it, that sound is required to tell the music's story.

Coconut oil is a powerful conduit of high-tone emotion. And it's a blueprint taste for many regional southern Indian, Sri Lankan and South-East Asian dishes. Masala requires us to drop the idea of like and dislike with individual spices and fats in order to embrace the whole picture.

Sapna's breakfast channa sabji

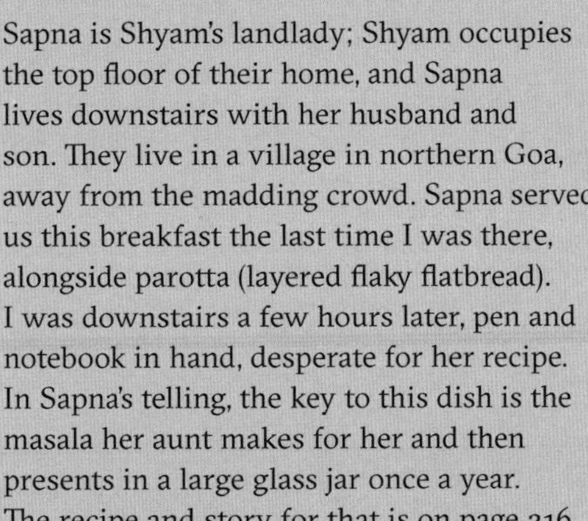

Sapna is Shyam's landlady; Shyam occupies the top floor of their home, and Sapna lives downstairs with her husband and son. They live in a village in northern Goa, away from the madding crowd. Sapna served us this breakfast the last time I was there, alongside parotta (layered flaky flatbread). I was downstairs a few hours later, pen and notebook in hand, desperate for her recipe. In Sapna's telling, the key to this dish is the masala her aunt makes for her and then presents in a large glass jar once a year. The recipe and story for that is on page 216.

While this dish is rich, it speaks more of the masala than it does of the coconut (see Masala is symphony, not solo, left). The coconut brings weight. The coconut oil ensures a base lightness. The masala connects the two fat elements with texture. All three elements combine to project a picture, not just of Goa, but of Sapna's Goa. It's joyous, sustaining and delicious.

Coconut oil and fresh coconut are key to this recipe. If you can't get fresh coconut, you can buy frozen coconut in some supermarkets and from most Asian grocers. Fresh is of course best.

Serves 4

- 1 cup (200 g) dried safad channa (chickpeas/ garbanzo beans), soaked in cold water overnight, or 400 g (14 oz) tinned chickpeas
- 1½ cups (375 ml) water, plus extra as needed
- ¾ cup (55 g) grated fresh coconut
- white salt, to taste

Initial masala

- 2 tablespoons coconut oil
- 4 French shallots, finely chopped
- 2–3 fresh curry leaf sprigs
- 2 tomatoes, finely chopped
- 1 large handful of fresh coriander (cilantro), finely chopped
- ½ garlic bulb, cloves peeled and finely chopped

Second masala

- 1 tablespoon Sapna's auntie's ready-made masala (page 216)

Drain the soaked chickpeas and rinse under cold running water, then transfer to your pressure cooker and add the water, ensuring the channa is well covered. Pressure-cook on high until the pressure cooker releases two or three hard jets of steam, then turn to low. The cooking time will depend on the size and type of pressure cooker, so you'll need to get to know your equipment. Dal cooks in a powerful pressure cooker in as little as 10 minutes. Once the dal is cooked, turn off the heat and let the pressure cooker depressurise on its own.

If you don't have a pressure cooker, use a slow cooker or large heavy-based saucepan. Be sure to soak your chickpeas or dal for 24 hours. If using a saucepan, cook over medium heat in a high volume of boiling water for 10–15 minutes, skimming off any scum. Reduce the heat to low and cook on a low simmer for a further 25–30 minutes or until tender.

For the initial masala, heat the coconut oil in a large frying pan over medium heat and add all the remaining ingredients. Stir until the masala forms a thick paste and the oil splits the paste. Transfer to a food processor and grind to a smooth paste.

Combine the ground masala paste, drained cooked channa and fresh coconut in the frying pan. Season to taste with white salt, add Sapna's auntie's masala and cook over low heat for 2–3 minutes more, until the sabji comes together.

If eating for breakfast, it's usually served with parotta. It can also be served with rice, and a cucumber and onion salad dressed with lime juice and seasoned with salt.

'The coconut brings weight. The coconut oil ensures a base lightness. The masala connects the two fat elements with texture.'

YOGHURT
DAHI

Category: Fats and other masala carriers.
Form: You'd struggle to find someone who didn't know what yoghurt looks like – the dairy version of a drift of snow.
Colour: White.

Categorising yoghurt as a cooking fat is a little odd even in the context of masala, but it's here as a masala carrier because so much of how masala is expressed through Kashmiri Hindu cooking relies on yoghurt in the cooking process.

Yoghurt is mostly a subcategory fat, typically used as an adjunct to a higher-heat oil to create a modified interpretation of masala – using yoghurt will soften the browning process, make nightshade-based sabjis more gentle, and curtail the impact of pungent masala. The exception to this rule is the canon of dishes listed under the yakhni banner. Yakhni is a traditional style of cooking prevalent in Kashmiri Hindu kitchens that uses yoghurt as the primary fat and signature filter for masala. Yakhni is typified by gentle cooking and soft spicing. These dishes are considered to be cooling, more easily digestible and ideal for the summer heat. A mutton yakhni follows opposite, but there's also a recipe for Bottle gourd yakhni on page 133.

Tasting notes
Heavy and cooling, full-fat yoghurts have a **tang** that gives shape to their dominant **broad quality**. They are **cool**, with a recessed **fermented** quality.

Companion fats
Yoghurt works well across the entire fat spectrum. It preserves the heat of mustard oil while simultaneously clarifying its recessed floral qualities. Kashmiri cooking pairs yoghurt with ghee for added richness.

Traditional medicinal quality
Traditionally made fresh in the home, yoghurt has strong probiotic qualities. In a domestic Ayurvedic sense, yoghurt-based dishes are fed to help unsettled stomachs.

The impact of yoghurt on browning
Achieving that browned crust normally involves a hard oil, but a harder oil drives harder flavour, which isn't always desirable. And that's when we can use yoghurt.

Yoghurt in hot oil splits to form a curdled milk crust on the exterior of browned meat. Just that small amount of dairy protein and subtle yoghurt acidity helps to soften both the impact of the hot oil and the response of the meat proteins. See page 97 for more on this technique. The message here is that yoghurt permits a less aggressive means of browning meat, allowing us to create softness under the pressure of high heat.

MILK
DOODH

We don't typically think of milk as a cooking fat. But just as within the framework of masala the definition of spice is broad – including, for example, salts – the idea of fats is similarly expansive. Essentially, the term 'fat' refers to any body of liquid or liquidised solid that we use to carry masala into produce.

In Kashmiri Hindu kitchens, milk has a significant place. It serves as one of the few primary fats used in Kabargah or milk-cooked lamb ribs (page 135). But as in other cultures, it's also a utility ingredient: we use milk to make paneer, khoya (thickened milk solids) and dahi or yoghurt (pages 110–11). These are simple processes, but they rely a lot on learning visual cues, so you might want to take a look at my YouTube channel, The Spirit of Spice, for some pointers.

When we were kids in Delhi and teens in Bangalore, milk often meant buffalo milk. In Australia, of course, I use cow's milk.

WATER
PANI

We use water as a masala carrier in regional Indian kitchens not to reduce calories but because it allows a different style of masala. See, for example, Turmeric chaaman (page 45), Chokhta (page 91), Shivani's mutton yakhni (right) and Kalia (page 292).

Water as a rule will carry masala in a broader capacity. Heavier fats and oils create concentric tension in masala, squeezing things into a tighter spiral, but water disperses, making masala more river delta than river rapid.

Dishes that use water as a vehicle for masala will all – at least in this book – also include a conventional fat. Think of these fats as elements of regional personality introduced to give masala a point of specificity. Water is general. It applies to anyone and anywhere. But the way we use traditional fats reflects regional character. In other words, when using water as a masala carrier, introducing a little bit of a familiar fat will strengthen the identity of the dish.

Shivani's mutton yakhni

Shivani made this recipe for and with me during a stint of filming in her Bengaluru kitchen. She was having friends over for dinner and they'd requested – in their words – a Kashmiri Pandit meal. This yakhni was the star of the table.

Yakhni carries emotive messages of maternal nurture and comfort. Shiv says it's the dish she made for her daughter, Kaira, every time she came home from boarding school: being away from family is tough, and the re-entry to the home can be a time of grief as much as happiness – grief in the knowledge that home is not where you spend your time, and in the joy of arrival being overshadowed by awareness of imminent departure. A dish like mutton yakhni in a family culture like ours is subtle enough to acknowledge that difficulty and support it with love.

For those with a more distant relationship to Kashmiri culture, mutton yakhni is an intimate experience of masala. It's not the 'spice' expected of regional Indian cuisine, and so it introduces an alternative insight – masala as subtlety.

Yakhni is a dish that doesn't like a lot of excess fat. It interferes with the yoghurt and the expression of masala. If you can't get mutton and you have to work with lamb, trim off the fat. If using lamb leg or shoulder, the end result may not be as tender.

>

This recipe uses fine white lake salt because lake salts are cleaner, sharper and brighter than sea salt. For this dish, we need a driving agent that will be strong but not too complex. As there's not a lot of textural variation in this dish, the salt needs to be quite 'clean' and linear.

Serves 6 as part of a shared meal

For the first stage

- 1.5 kg (3 lb 5 oz) mutton chest and shoulder, cut into 5 cm (2 inch) pieces
- 2 cups (500 ml) water
- 5 black cardamom pods, husks cracked
- 4 dried bay leaves
- 3 teaspoons fine white lake salt

For the second stage

- 500 g (1 lb 2 oz) plain yoghurt
- 3 teaspoons fennel powder
- 2 teaspoons fine white lake salt
- 1½ teaspoons ginger powder

Tadka

- 2 tablespoons ghee
- 9 green cardamom pods, husks cracked
- 5 cloves
- pinch of hing (asafoetida) powder

Combine all the first-stage ingredients in a large pressure cooker and turn to high heat. Wait for the ejection of steam, then turn to medium–high heat and cook for a further 12 minutes or so. Allow the pot to depressurise on its own. The mutton should be tender. If not, pressure-cook for 2–3 minutes more, until you're confident the mutton is subtly delicious. (Using water as the spice carrier softens the input of the whole spices and creates a less driven and broader structure.) Alternatively, cook in a large heavy-based saucepan over medium–high heat until the mutton is tender, about 60 minutes (or 90 minutes for lamb).

Leave the mutton for about 40 minutes to cool almost completely. Pick out the whole spices as well as you can – we want the yakhni to look as smooth as it tastes (see The contribution of visual texture, page 134).

Whisk the yoghurt in a small bowl until smooth and a little thinner – whisking yoghurt naturally draws out its acidity. If your pressure cooker is flameproof, add the whisked yoghurt to the cooled meat and stir through. Otherwise, transfer both to a large heavy-based saucepan. (If the meat is cool, the yoghurt doesn't split.)

Add the remaining second-stage ingredients and stir through. These spices will bring body and warmth to the masala. The extra salt is included to drive the softer aromatics through the broad bed of yoghurt.

Place over medium heat and bring to just below the boil. This might take up to 10 minutes, courtesy of the volume of food.

Now prepare the tadka. Heat the ghee in a small frying pan over medium–low heat. Once the ghee is hot, add the aromatics and stir through for 2–3 minutes until fragrant. Tip into the yakhni and stir through.

The tadka builds in a strong frame of aroma that holds the mutton in a firm grip. It's a way of using spice to push the central aromatic profile – the soft mutton – forward without having to rely on heavy oil or heavy spicing.

It's now ready to serve. Typically, yakhni is served with basmati rice. Haakh (see page 252) makes a delicious and colourful addition to this dish.

Khoya

Makes 200 g (7 oz)

5 cups (1.25 litres) milk

The most important things about making khoya are having the right cooking vessel – a deep cast-iron or stainless-steel kadai or wok – the right temperature (very low) and the patience and time to stir and scrape as required. It can take 2–3 hours – smaller quantities of milk are a little quicker. You don't need a lot of khoya – it's very rich and only lasts for 2–3 days in the fridge. The heat should be low–medium for the entire process.

Bring the milk to the boil over medium heat, then reduce the heat to medium–low and cook, stirring constantly with a spatula as the milk simmers, scraping the milk solids off the pot and gently stirring them through.

As the moisture starts to reduce, bubbles will appear on the surface of the condensing and solidifying milk. This is an important time to keep stirring so that the milk doesn't caramelise and stick to the bottom of the kadai and burn. You're aiming to simmer until no more bubbles appear in the milk solids. The milk solids should also become more granular. When you get to this point, remove from the heat. The khoya is ready.

I use khoya as a rich vehicle for savoury masala, such as Matar khoya (page 180), but it's also a foundation ingredient for many Indian desserts. If you want to make your own barfi or laddu, think about setting aside the time to make your own khoya first.

Paneer / Chaaman

Makes 600 g (1 lb 5 oz)

12 cups (3 litres) milk

1 tablespoon plain yoghurt

juice of 2 lemons

Bring the milk to the boil in a large saucepan over high heat, stirring occasionally so it doesn't stick and burn. Keep the yoghurt and lemon juice handy. When the milk starts to bubble up, remove from the heat, add the yoghurt and stir through, then add the lemon juice 2–3 tablespoons at a time, stirring after each addition to see how much more acidity is needed to properly split the milk and create the curds and whey (2). (Curds are the white lumpy bits, whey the yellow liquid that remains.) Too much lemon juice added at once can split the actual curd, making it less plump and rich.

Once the curds and whey have split, strain through a piece of muslin or cheesecloth, a clean thin old tea towel (dish towel) or a clean Chux (3). I lay the cloth over a colander, and then balance the colander over a pot to ensure I catch the whey.

Tie up the muslin or cheesecloth and hang it over the sink or a container (4, 5). When the paneer has been hung for 24 hours, unwrap it from the muslin and cut into 1.5 cm (⅝ inch) cubes (6), ready to make Turmeric chaaman (page 45), Matar paneer (page 230) or Lal paneer (page 212). See the QR code on page 107 for a video with directions for making paneer.

1
2
3
4
5
6

Yoghurt

'Traditionally made fresh in the home, yoghurt has strong probiotic qualities.'

2 tablespoons yoghurt starter culture (see note)
2 cups (500 ml) milk
1 chilli, fresh or dried (optional)

Choose a bowl or container with an airtight lid and spread the yoghurt starter on the bottom of the bowl. Bring the milk to the boil in a small saucepan over medium heat, then remove immediately from the heat and leave to cool to the temperature of drinkable tea or coffee. Pour the milk into the bowl and whisk well. Cover with the lid and leave at room temperature to set. In a warm climate, this can take as little as 4 hours.

Bui says if it's cooler and you're having trouble getting the yoghurt to set, place a single dried red chilli on top of the bowl once it's left out on the bench to settle – in some sort of alchemy, the chilli assists in the setting process.

Once the yoghurt is set, refrigerate and use within 1 week.

Note: A yoghurt starter culture is akin to a sourdough starter. In India, *jamun* or starter can be bought from mithai or sweet shops. A scoop of store-bought or home-made pot-set yoghurt can also be used as a starter.

SECOND-TIER FATS

Second-tier fats don't make the front row in my pantry, but I always keep them in stock. Obviously, my second-tier fats will be someone else's first-tier fats and vice versa. My second-tier fats don't carry a dish or a full thought in my kitchen, but I use them to deepen and create further texture within the message of masala.

SESAME OIL

When used as a finishing touch, sesame oil is perceived by the mouth as warm and thick, lending a unique nutty lift. Its viscosity and distinct aromatic profile make it an interesting oil to use with broader oils such as coconut, macadamia and ghee that can carry its flavour. Within the framework of masala, sesame oil draws out astringent notes in warm spices, heats acidic spices and emphasises the grounded quality of earth spices while bringing them to the fore and making them more pungent. It also stimulates hot spices. Sesame oil can be used at high heat if paired with a high-heat oil, which protects the sesame oil from burning.

A little bit of sesame oil has a big impact. Use it when cooking with mustard oil to accentuate nutty and hot characters in a dish. Liven up earthy dishes by using it as a finishing oil. A touch of sesame oil adds an elegant end polish to a Mexican mole, for example.

Companion fats

When frying at higher temperatures, combine sesame oil with peanut oil, mustard oil or vegetable oil for an aromatic combination.

PEANUT OIL

Peanut oil is nutty yet neutral and sits in the centre of the mouth. It has a mild taste and a light feel on the palate. It's thinner than mustard oil, but more viscous and textured than olive oil. This oil is used in central and South-East Asian cuisines because it's ideal for high-heat cooking. It can also carry vibrant, fresh aromatics, and makes an excellent base for the salty, umami-laden liquid condiments common to recipes from these regions. Within the framework of masala, peanut oil flattens the flavours of dried spice tempered at low heat. Counteract this by using it in combination with a brighter fat, such as coconut oil or even ghee.

When frying pakoras or samosas, try peanut oil in combination with mustard oil to increase the crispiness of the pastry.

Companion fats

Combine peanut oil with mustard oil for an aromatic combination when frying at higher temperatures.

MACADAMIA OIL

Broad and sweet, slightly bitter and mild, macadamia oil has an unctuous mouthfeel akin to that of ghee. It's slippery and without edge. Much of its aroma is recessed by the oily quality of the fat, but this can be drawn forth by intelligent use of spice and companion fats. Within the framework of masala, macadamia oil is a valuable vegan replacement for ghee: its broad, slightly sweet and relatively neutral profile – along with its round mouthfeel – makes it similar. It smooths the gritty texture of earth spices, rounds out the edges of acidic spices, and thins warm and bitter spices.

In general use, macadamia oil tends to flatten flavour, so I rarely recommend using it on its own. If cooking vegan, pair it with a companion fat such as coconut oil to lift the dish. This is a low-heat cooking oil, so when cooking at higher temperatures, it's essential to buffer it with a high-heat oil such as peanut oil to protect it from burning.

Companion fats

Sesame oil draws out macadamia's nutty quality, while mustard oil lifts and brightens its dense, buttery weight.

OLIVE OIL

Olive oil has multiple flavour profiles, since it's produced from different types of olives. It can be peppery and biting, grassy and herbaceous, green and mild, or any combination of these. Regardless of flavour, olive oil has a uniform consistency: slightly more viscous than other vegetable oils but thinner than mustard and nut oils. In masala, olive oil thins out complex spice structures and draws out peppery, pungent and grassy characters. Dried spices in particular all have at their core a bitter and pungent quality that olive oil emphasises. Within the symphony of masala, this aromatic emphasis becomes hard noise, like too much percussion and not enough harp. Olive oil is not part of India's taste blueprint (see page 41), so one of my only edicts is not to make olive oil a default primary fat with masala.

Companion fats

Pair olive oil with butter to approximate ghee. Mustard oil will increase the peppered heat of olive oil, peanut oil will increase its aromatic complexity, and coconut oil will make it appear creamier.

OTHER FATS

Butter

Butter browns and caramelises at low heat, changing the profile of tempered spice and proving itself too light to support complex aromatic blends. Butter is most useful for mellowing strong oils and pungent fats, or for adding texture and weight to thin or 'slippery' oils.

Lard

Fat reserved from roasted meats can be used to temper masala when using very light produce, such as leftover greens like wilted lettuce or sad broccoli, for a delicious no-waste side dish.

Grapeseed oil

In the regional Indian traditions, grapeseed oil doesn't work as a base fat in sabjis or in meat-based dishes. It is slippery and thin, creating a film between masala and the palate. If I do use it, it's to deep-fry ingredients where the dish is better served by not taking on any additional texture from fats.

2

TEXTURE

THE KITCHEN BENCH

Part 2 is about the triumvirate responsible for creating texture: earth, warm and acidic spices. Then, before we move on to Part 3, we'll take an interlude to look at two other equally important but very different categories: sweet spices and hot spices. We treat them separately because their job is to transmute texture.

What texture means in masala

Anyone who's ever sat down to a thali (see page 28) will know what I mean when I say that texture in masala is only notionally about crunch versus cold versus silken. In Western culinary traditions chefs combine different elements to create texture: a bite of rich protein, a slice of sweetly pickled vegetable, a swipe of astringent purée, and a balance of crunch from a beautifully seasoned crumb – five elements to create a single textural mouthful.

But for an Indian householder, texture means creating a very complex aromatic structure within a single element. A mouthful that is aromatically sophisticated, with structure and an eloquently executed story will offer up an experience of taste that we can metaphorically chew on. An obvious way to observe this is to try a raw spice slammer (see page 34). Experience firsthand the way a mouthful of spice can segue from salty, hot and sharp, through earthy, bitter and square to a starburst of acidity, and then be folded in a blanket of warm-sweet before the whole experience coalesces and settles into a sort of full-body hum. I think of it as like the three-course chewing gum from Roald Dahl's *Charlie and the Chocolate Factory* – the texture inherent in masala becomes the taste that not only keeps on giving, but also changes shape as it's doing so. This is why texture in masala is really the creation of shape and form.

The meaning of shape and form

When I look at a flat-lay of masala in a cold pan (opposite), I don't see a bunch of seeds, dried powders and whole spices but a clear shape and form.

Earth, warm and acidic spices play a primary role in establishing the body of shape and form because, to the palate, these spices have the most identifiably solid expressions. The mouth can *feel* their shapes. Just as a fairground clown blows into balloons and twists them to make an animal, masala takes shape when earth, warm and acidic aromatics are added. You won't get a poodle, but you will introduce a very distinct shape and form.

Shape and form are how masala expresses texture, and texture tells us we're eating. *Knowing* that we're eating is elemental not only to the experience of masala, but also to our ability to cook with masala in a deliberate way.

Texture: the other seasoner

Salt and acid are generally the go-to additions when it comes to seasoning. Here I mean seasoning in the sense of giving a dish that extra bit of oomph. But with masala, you also have to think about the role of texture in seasoning. Texture has impact on masala because we use aromatic contrast to construct and express specific shapes. Think of *shape* here as the way a spice appears aromatically. And think of *texture* as a tool we can use to alter that shape.

For example, using ghee with ginger powder makes the ginger rounder, softening its bite and drawing out a friendly ginger flavour. If we then add cumin seeds, the addition of texture makes the angles in ginger powder reappear, laying an angular heat on top of its rounder expression. Texture splits a spice into its different bodies, and adding texture to a flat dish can create shape and interest in a way that salt and acid can only envy.

TEXTURE: AN INDIAN HOUSEHOLDER'S VIEW

In a Western kitchen, texture means physical sensation: the crunch of the crust of freshly baked bread, the silkiness of panna cotta or custard. But when we talk about texture in a regional Indian kitchen, we mean texture of thought.

Texture of thought

This is the way we think about the connections we have to food. For the Indian householder, connection to food is a central pillar of identity and so our thoughts around it are complex. It's less a question of whether the broccoli is soggy, and more whether the texture of soggy broccoli can carry the message we wish to feed to our loved ones today. Just as masala is about more than food, and spice is about more than flavour, texture is about more than deliciousness. For the Indian householder, tastiness is a perspective, the result of a message thoughtfully conveyed.

The texture of thought encompasses three main strands:

1. **The texture of tradition**
   The techniques we use to ensure that the dishes we make today retain connection to those that our family has made for generations.
2. **The texture of aroma**
   The way we construct masala to establish certain experiences of taste. Aromatic texture is influenced by the fats we use, our choice of spice, how we treat produce and heat ingredients, our choice of cooking vessel, and the sum of all these parts.
3. **The texture of time**
   The way we use time to create recognisable structure in traditional dishes. Time has a taste, and it can be approximated, but not replicated, through the clever use of aromatics.

EARTH SPICES

Function in masala: Bringing texture to the mid-palate to build central flavour.
Emotive quality: Stimulating the mid-palate, which has a grounding effect that feels at once quieting and familiar.
Traditional medicinal quality: Considered in Ayurveda to have a strong digestive effect.

Once, when teaching a group of men and women about masala, I opened my six dabbas and was met with an exclamation of horror. I was so used to people responding with excitement that it took me a second to realise that one of the men had thrown his hands up as if he'd already given up. It was just too *much*. As soon as I looked at the benchtop through his eyes, I totally got it. It *was* too much. So I gave him a taste of cumin seeds.

In the most unglamorous way, earth spices are recognisable because the tastes and textures of the better-known aromatics in this category – cumin seeds, ground cumin, ground coriander – evoke grit and soil. As kids, we all put dirt and soil in our mouths. It's a taste we know. And knowing those tastes in that innocent and basic way gives them a stronghold in our foundational experiences. They are literally grounding.

In a culinary sense, these same spices are used across many traditional cultures and tend to be on fairly high rotation in modern Western homes. In a world of exotica they're 'safe haven' spices. Even in terms of ratio, earth aromatics are way friendlier than others. A little too much fennel or nigella seed, or not quite enough coriander or cumin powder. It isn't going to kill anything.

In Masala, we primarily use earth spices to create texture, to link us to the experience of being connected to our earliest environments, and to facilitate feelings of satiety across all three body states (see page 35). There are no sharp edges in any of that.

And so that's how I offered cumin seeds to that overwhelmed man – like a strong familiar hand to hold as we waded into masala's waters. He was appreciative of that. It's the strength of this category in a simile.

Another important function of earth spices is to act as conduits for flavour. As a general rule, the texture and weight of earth spices occupy the mid-palate – it's the space in the mouth that aroma passes through on its way from one part of the mouth to the other. Including earth spices in masala allows for the complex exchange of aromas.

Satiety is more than a full stomach

Masala is more than food, and hunger is not just physical.

Every aspect of any part of our three bodies – the emotional, the physical and the metaphysical – affects the others. We eat poorly, we feel down on ourselves, we sink into low spirits. On another day things feel right and our appetite for life returns.

This seesawing happens to us all. Think of it like adjusting a tripod – the legs will always tilt before levelling. Imbalance precedes balance, and balance precedes imbalance again. If we're only focused on one aspect of ourselves we're more likely to topple during those in between times. But remaining aware of our physical health, our relationships, and our mental and spiritual health means we're coming from a stronger base. The practice of masala encourages us to be more like that, more often.

CUMIN SEEDS
JEERA

Category: Earth spices.
Form: Elongated seeds with a fine tail and close-textured ribbing.
Colour: Silvered khaki.

Cumin seeds exemplify the concept of texture. Tasted raw, jeera feels stick-like, desiccated. With the spices, salts and fats we've encountered in this book so far, it's largely been about visualising different sensitivities on the palate – conjuring an idea of rounded bitter as it relates to turmeric powder, for example. But there's no need to imagine with a spice like cumin seed. You're literally chewing it. The sharp points of the seeds might catch in your gums or between your teeth. There are actual bits you have to swallow. All earth spices are like this – their textures speak as loudly as their tastes.

1
2
3
4
5
6

Jeera chawal

We don't really need a recipe for jeera chawal. The process of preparing and cooking basmati rice is really the key here – texture in jeera chawal isn't about just cumin seeds, but the contrast between their woody, pointed husks and the aromatic lightness of a beautifully cooked basmati.

Rice in India is like tea in Japan – a culture is built around it. Different regions will have different endemic varietals best eaten with the masala of that area. My younger brother Shyam lives in Goa and is mad for Keralan red rice. It's fluffy and dense and nutty, beautifully suited to indigenous spices like *kadi patta* (curry leaves), and coconut milks and fats.

Basmati is my jam. When we lived in Barcelona with the boys, I found an Indian grocer who sold the most incredible basmati rice, the likes of which I've never been able to buy in Australia: a grain three times as long as a standard supermarket basmati, with all the delicate fragrance you'd expect from such an elegant rice. Basmati at its best is a little nutty and sweet, with an alluring complexity. The boys used to walk in the door from school and ask if I was cooking popcorn. In India you'll find all sorts of aged varieties – the most aged will take on a deep yellow hue, the same shade as the long-cured fat of prosciutto.

Such dedication and delicacy is why basmati is bloomed by soaking it in water before cooking. Without soaking, the aroma gets trapped inside the hard grain. Think of it like throwing a beautiful scotch fillet on the barbecue straight from the fridge – the protein will seize around the flavour instead of releasing it. Basmati rice is the same.

Rinse the rice in a bowl with cold water. Dad always said to rinse it three or four times (1). Sometimes it needs more. Essentially we're looking to rid the rice of grit and small stones while also washing off some of the starch. You've rinsed enough when the rice no longer turns the water cloudy. Drain one last time, refill with cold water and set the now-soaking rice aside. I soak my rice the night before or the morning of the day I plan to cook it.

When you're ready to cook the rice, fill a large pot with water and set to boil with the lid on. While you wait, compare the soaked rice and unsoaked rice (2). The unsoaked rice is hard, white and will crumble when bitten into. The soaked rice is soft, a little opaque and has the consistency of partially cooked pasta – the grain will have external bite that gives way to a gluey texture. In essence, soaking the rice has hydrated it to the point where it feels partially cooked.

When the water is boiling, remove the lid, drain the soaked rice and pour it into the pot (3). You don't need to put the lid back on. Don't venture too far from the stovetop. Once the water comes back to the boil, the rice will only need 2–3 minutes to cook. It's ready when the grains are still slightly opaque: translucent rice is overcooked rice. Taste a grain if you're not sure. It should be al dente.

Strain the rice using a large colander with small enough holes not to lose the rice grains. Place the rice-filled colander over the empty pot, off the heat, and put the lid on the pot. We're now steaming the cooked rice (4). This second process dries off excess water, ensures the rice is in individual grains, and sets the aroma. As kitchen techniques go, it's akin to resting cooked meat. Rice can be steamed this way and kept warm for up

>

to 30 minutes while the rest of the meal is prepared. Serve now if making plain rice.

If making jeera chawal, temper the quantity of cumin seeds you desire in the amount of ghee you see fit to use (5). Once the rice is cooked and steamed to sweet perfection, tip the tadka over the top and use two forks to toss it through (6).

I love to finish with a sprinkle of fleur de sel.

Curing illness with kindness

Ash hardly ever gets sick, but when he does, towards the end his illnesses tend to cease being physical and instead fall into the category of emotional melancholy. It's that last ten per cent of fatigue: not really sick enough to stay home, but also not back to full resilience. This is the bit that I cure with jeera chawal.

Whereas Khichdi (page 70) is about bolstering the foundation of a body still under attack, jeera chawal is brighter. The way the rice is cooked is lighter. And the textural component – the tadka of ghee and cumin seeds – rouses without dismissal: there's nothing worse than a motivational push based on the opening sentence, 'Come on, it's not *that* bad.' Yeah, well maybe not to you ...

Jeera chawal acknowledges for Ash that I know he feels a little emotionally tender, but also lets him know that there's a family in place to walk with him back out into the world again. The cocoon can feel so good, but we can always keep it inside us somewhere. We don't have to unwind our bedcovers and replace them with battle armour.

Culturally, if there were to be a reigning monarch of masala across all regions of India, then I feel like cumin seeds would be it. Cumin seeds are in every kitchen and possibly even every masala dabba. It's difficult not to dwell on their meaning, because they mean so much. There is a feeling from those new to masala that it's the 'special spices' that make masala unique, when really it's the way we handle the ordinary that tells the truest tale (see page 125).

Tasting notes

Cumin seeds have **warm** and **woody** primary aromas that segue to **mint**, **eucalyptus** and a residual **pungent cedar** quality, with a soft **bitter** finish. It's a complex spice, given structure by its firm dried seed husk, and it's one spice where buying organic makes an enormous difference. Low-quality cumin seeds don't have the subtlety and tend to feel dry, hard and wooden on the palate.

Use in masala

Cumin seeds increase the feeling of volume in masala because they're so textural – they give physical form to taste, which helps us feel fuller sooner: if the mouth *feels* like it's eaten, so will the body. They also work as a central exchange in the movement of masala – they fill the mouth and enable other spices to track from one section of the palate to the other without falling into a mid-palate sinkhole.

Emotive content

The element of cumin seeds that speaks most to the sensory body is their familiarity. You'll read this a lot in the recipes that follow. But iteration has its uses, not the least of which is allowing us to pay attention to our own subtle day-to-day changes. External environments are noisy places and things move fast – there's often not enough time for or sanctity given to noticing the small stuff. Paying attention to the shifts of a spice like cumin seeds gives us the chance we need to notice movement in familiar patterns.

Traditional medicinal impact

There's a gentle bias around the idea that medicinal taste, practice and energy are intrinsically unpleasant in some way: the bitter for the better. Cumin seeds are the first spice in this book whose medicinal impact is rooted in the grounded and familiar. It's like learning that physical affection lowers our risk of heart disease.

Jeera pani

Like Fenugreek seed tea (page 57), jeera pani works as a digestive. But unlike fenugreek seed tea it's sharp, like a grass seed in your sock. Domestic Ayurveda sees this organic sharpness as a pointed nudge that turns us back towards self-reflection – a sip of jeera pani is the stimulant that can tell us how close or how far we are from ourselves emotionally. Because just as texture in masala helps us know that we're eating, it also helps us to know that we're feeling.

It seems obvious to say there's no recipe for this. Just a teaspoon or so of cumin seeds in a cup of hot water. Cumin seeds are so strong they barely need time to steep.

✱

The spice next door

While the end result of masala gives the impression that expertise is found in understanding the exotic, the actual magic is found in understanding how to reconfigure the familiar.

I sometimes feel I should get tired of using the same spices, but the approach required by masala doesn't allow for that. Instead, every time I use them, I see them with a fresh eye, a phenomenon that results from the time and attention it takes to cook traditional regional dishes: the techniques are so hands-on that it's not possible to be distracted by other tasks. Because of this we notice things, like when a masala we make all the time suddenly tastes sweeter or darker ... and we ask ourselves, how did that come about? Was it the spices themselves? Or the tone of the produce? Or the impact of our need and our mood?

These subtle differences are noticeable because we use spices we know, on high rotation. For Kashmiri Hindus that means turmeric powder, cumin seeds, fennel powder, ginger powder, Kashmiri chilli powder and hing. For other regions it will mean a different set of aromatics. But in the same way we experience the repetition of our spices, they will experience the repetition of theirs. The process of tasting and compiling and structuring familiar spices to create new masala ensures an enduring relationship to our spice-next-door aromatics.

Aloo jeera, three ways

On its own, aloo jeera just means potato and cumin seeds. The word 'just' isn't really justified though, because there's nothing small about this dish – it graces millions of tables every day and has as many iterations as there are Indian kitchens.

This recipe is about seeing how oil influences texture with a familiar spice, and how the combination of different cooking techniques with different oil bases gives masala a different shape and form. In all three we're looking at the textural shifts against the backbone of cumin seeds.

The three versions of aloo jeera here each say something different. Two of them involve a two-step cooking process, the last is quicker. While the masala ratios and potato weights are the same for each recipe, the fats, the process and the timing change. I prefer to use kipfler (fingerling) or royal blue potatoes.

Serves 4 as part of a shared meal

- 500 g (1 lb 2 oz) potatoes, peeled and cut into 2 cm (¾ inch) cubes
- 2 teaspoons cumin seeds
- 1 teaspoon fine white sea salt
- 1 teaspoon ginger powder
- 1 teaspoon Kashmiri chilli powder
- ½ teaspoon hot red chilli powder (optional)
- pinch of hing (asafoetida) powder

Mustard oil aloo jeera

- 1 cup (250 ml) mustard oil
- 1 tablespoon ghee

Pour the mustard oil into a kadai, stable cast-iron wok or heavy-based saucepan large enough that the oil comes up no more than halfway. Heat over high heat until very hot but not smoking. Fry the potato in batches until crisp but not completely browned. Drain on paper towel.

In a large frying pan, heat the ghee over medium heat and stir through all the spices until aromatic and gently bubbling. Toss in the fried potatoes and cook for 20–45 minutes, until the potato is cooked through and any moisture it releases has cooked away. The masala and the potato should look rich – the longer you intend to cook, the lower the heat should be (it should range from medium–low for a longer cooking time to medium for a shorter cooking time).

Potatoes fried in mustard oil before the masala is added have a weight and depth. The mustard oil draws out their shadows and subterranean vibe. I use the ghee to create an extra body of texture – this masala is earthy, and simple enough that the cumin seeds shine.

Right: Middle: Potatoes after first fry in vegetable oil. Right top: Mustard oil aloo jeera. Bottle: Mustard oil, with cumin seeds to its right. Tin: Ghee. Bottom right: Vegetable oil.

TIMES CITY

Ghee aloo jeera

1 cup (250 ml) vegetable oil

2 tablespoons ghee

Heat the vegetable oil over high heat in a kadai, stable cast-iron wok or heavy-based saucepan large enough that the oil comes up no more than halfway. When the oil is hot but not smoking, fry the potatoes in batches until crisp but not completely browned. Drain on paper towel.

In a separate frying pan, heat the ghee over medium heat and stir through all the spices until aromatic and gently bubbling. Toss in the fried potatoes, reduce the heat to medium–low and cook down for 30 minutes. Raise the temperature to a higher medium for the last 5 minutes to crisp off the aloo before serving. The end result is soft and light, with a less obvious or rousing body of flavour.

Potatoes fried in vegetable oil before the masala is added have a lighter weight and less complex taste than those cooked in mustard oil. This is reflected in the masala. The cumin seed is less angular and more homely. The chilli shows its floral side. Even the ginger is rounded out, its heating nature subtly neutralised by the slick of the vegetable oil and the softness of the ghee to a comfortable warmth.

Vegetable oil aloo jeera

This is a one-pan process, so a little faster than the previous two variations.

¼ cup (125 ml) vegetable oil

Heat the vegetable oil over high heat in a kadai, stable cast-iron wok or heavy-based saucepan. When the oil is hot but not smoking, add the potato all at once. It doesn't matter if the oil cools slightly here – we actually want this to be a little less frying and a little more cooking than the other two variations. Let the potatoes cook for about 5 minutes, stirring frequently. They should be a little cooked through, but not to the point of browning.

Add all of the spices and keep frying over a relatively high heat – you don't want the oil to get too cold. Because of the high heat and the reduced quantity of oil, you will need to keep stirring pretty constantly so the potatoes don't stick. Cook for a further 15 minutes, until the oil cooks down into the masala and potatoes to create a rich base.

This is a very basic method that you'll see used at roadside stands, and even in home kitchens across India's regions, when the aim is to put together a relatively fast masala that will satiate the appetite. The vegetable oil has a high energy content, but it also works to create blunt and head-on masala – the kind that speaks directly to hunger.

Toasted cumin powder raita

When whole cumin seeds are toasted in a dry frying pan over medium heat until lightly golden and then ground, they have a solid presence. In raita, this taste feels like stepping on a patch of dry clod in a melting snowdrift – reassuringly stable. The dried mint can dominate, so add it in pinches to ensure you don't use too much.

Because cumin seeds are the star, they should be toasted and ground fresh.

Makes about 1 cup

1 cup (260 g) plain yoghurt

2–3 tablespoons milk

Masala

2 teaspoons freshly toasted and ground cumin powder (see left)

1–1½ teaspoons fine white sea salt

1 teaspoon caster (superfine) sugar

2–3 pinches of dried mint

Combine the yoghurt and milk in a small bowl and whisk together. (Kashmiri Hindu cooking uses a lot of yoghurt or curd, and it is always whipped and quite often thinned with water or milk before use. It's a technique that both draws the acidity forward and ensures a silken consistency.)

Going a little easier with the salt and the mint in the first instance, add the masala and stir through. Add more salt and mint only if the taste feels flat – the freshness of your toasted cumin powder will dictate how much salty drive is required, and how much of the strong dried mint the raita can balance. (When paired this way, the dried mint ceases to demonstrate sweet herbaceous notes and becomes earthier – more 'decomposed leaf' than sweet herb.)

Serve immediately. Unlike Mum's raita (page 229), there's no driving acidic component here that requires time to settle and harmonise.

Toasting spice

Don't automatically toast your spice every time you begin a process with masala. It seems that somehow, through popular culture or the grapevine, the message has got out that toasting spice is always the way to go. Sometimes it is. Maybe. In our family we almost never toast spice except for this raita recipe. I didn't even know that people did toast spice until I left the family kitchen to head out into the world.

Toasting spice fundamentally alters its texture and aroma. When a spice comes into contact with dry heat, two things happen – its texture is flattened and its aroma is sealed. We'll get to how this affects taste in a minute, but first let's talk about why this happens. When spices and fat hit the pan together, they're in a relationship. Because of that, they naturally communicate. So instead of sealing, the aromatics tell their story through the fat and through each other. In the same way, the fat speaks through the spice. It's this process that creates nuance in the aromatic bed of a dish, and it's key to the beauty of masala.

But when spices hit a dry pan – dry meaning no fats – and are then subjected to heat, the toasting creates an aromatic shutdown. Without a relationship with fat, a spice will instantly seal. There will be no communication. This is true even if multiple spices are toasted together in that same pan: there'll be no intermingling of aromas. On top of that, the spices will more closely resemble each other texturally, so there'll be less interest in terms of overall spice shape.

As an explanation of how this affects actual flavour, dry-toasted spice is generally blunt, a little woody and more pungent than raw spice (though even here there is variation – the pungency of toasted spice is brittle in comparison to pungent raw spice tempered through fat).

This technique of toasting works when we want to figuratively vacuum-lock a particular aromatic quality – to create a taste that's unchanged and stable. We use it only when the expression of a dish calls for masala that's inherently darker, deeper, broodier or just flatter. Toasted spice does also have a slightly longer shelf life.

As you'll see in the recipe opposite, what does change the toasted spice is grinding. Grinding toasted spice re-releases aroma and re-creates complexity. What's interesting about this process is that toasted and ground spice has its own unique character, and offers a third aromatic alternative; the whole spice, the powdered form of the whole spice, and the toasted whole spice ground into powder.

DIGESTION AND EMOTIVE TONE

Gut instinct. Gutted. Stomach flip. It's not a new thing to connect emotion to the gut, but Ayurveda and masala join hands to deepen the notion.

Emotional states impact digestion. You'll know that if you've ever suffered any kind of extreme stress. For some in those circumstances, the digestive engine becomes like a relentless furnace, driving, driving, driving appetite and consumption like a summer fire. For others (including me) the engine of digestion seizes, the fire goes cold, and consumption becomes difficult. Most of the time, most of us sit somewhere in the middle of those two extremes.

If we can develop a feel for where we sit on that scale at any given time, then we can begin to weave this understanding of ourselves into our masala construction. It's a valuable skill to develop, and not just for reasons of health. Food that's digested well is perceived by the sensory body as being more satisfying and more delicious.

A final observation from Ayurveda is that our dosha (see page 26) influences our resting digestive state – where your 'neutral' is on the scale from overactive/hot to underactive/cold.

Bottle gourd yakhni

Yakhni is the name for a style of cooking that goes to the heart of the Kashmiri Hindu tradition, and is a shortcut term for any dish cooked in a bed of yoghurt. Yakhni is soft and shows masala in that same light. As a style of cooking it's used to cool an overheated body in summer, to provide nourishment for a digestive system under stress, or to soothe an overstimulated nervous system with gentle messaging.

Yakhni also handily subverts the natural inclination to think about texture as only crispness or crunch, and of earth spices as dry. Almost as a rule, the shape and form of yakhni is broad and gentle. I often swim of an evening where the Margaret River – Wooditjup Bilya – meets the Indian Ocean: here, the textural experience of water transmutes a brackish ecosystem into something soft and dispersed. Yoghurt and low heat do the same thing to cumin seeds in this dish.

If you don't have access to bottle gourds (calabashes), replace them with kohlrabi or zucchini (courgettes).

Serves 4 as part of a shared meal

1½ bottle gourds (calabashes), 4–5 kohlrabi or 3–4 zucchini (courgettes) peeled and cut into 2–3 cm (¾–1¼ inch) pieces

First phase

1½ tablespoons vegetable oil
1–2 pinches of hing (asafoetida) powder
½ teaspoon cumin seeds
2 teaspoons coriander powder
⅓ cup (80 ml) water

Second phase

2 small fresh green chillies
2 teaspoons fine white sea salt

Last phase

3 teaspoons fennel powder
½ teaspoon ginger powder
2 tablespoons plain yoghurt, whipped
1 handful of fresh coriander (cilantro), finely chopped

Heat the vegetable oil in a large heavy-based saucepan over medium heat. Add enough of the hing, one pinch at a time, that the oil becomes fragrant. Stir in the cumin seeds and coriander powder, then stir in the bottle gourd and water. Cook over medium heat for about 15 minutes, stirring frequently, until the bottle gourd is slightly soft (see note).

Continue building the masala with the second phase. Using your hands, break the chillies into two or three pieces and add them along with the salt, then cook for a further 5–7 minutes, stirring frequently, over medium heat. (These spices create drive – chilli gives a little punchiness, and the salt shape and strength, to the subtle masala.)

Now add the last-phase spices and yoghurt. Cook for 5 minutes, then add the fresh coriander.

Transfer everything to a pressure cooker – if you have one – and cook on high heat until it emits one jet of steam. Turn off and

>

leave to depressurise. If you don't have a pressure cooker, check there is enough liquid to prevent the bottle gourd sticking, put the lid on the saucepan, reduce the heat to low and cook for a further 20 minutes.

Serve with boiled rice or chapati.

Note: It's important to peel the bottle gourd so as to retain the character of the dish. In the same way that Bui doesn't add turmeric powder or chilli powder so as not to change the colour, we remove the skin so as not to interfere with the soft texture of the masala.

The contribution of visual texture

We tend to think of food texture as an oral term – the way a bite does or doesn't crunch, crack or make us chew. But when I cook with Bui and Shivani, they talk about the *colour* of a dish as texture. When I noticed Bui wasn't adding chilli or turmeric powder to her bottle gourd yakhni, I suggested that it was in order to keep the dish broad and subtle. Yes, she agreed, but also so that those two aromatics didn't interfere with the *look* of the yakhni: it should be pale. White.

A note on digestion

Masala embraces digestion as part of its DNA. For an Indian householder, the digestive system is responsible for maintenance of the deep gut, which serves as the soul and engine of our three bodies (see page 35). And we cater to the health of the deep gut through the sum of masala.

Practically, this means that when a householder thinks about digestion they focus not just on including a known digestive spice in cooking, but also on the cooking techniques, produce used, fats chosen and even the effects of the external environment. On a hot day when we're tired, we'll choose to cook bottle gourd yakhni – the yoghurt makes it easier to digest, bottle gourd is light, and cumin seeds have strong digestive properties.

FENNEL SEEDS SAUNF

Category: Earth spices.
Form: Plump and elongated dried seeds with distinct ribbing and a fine tail.
Colour: Soft green.

Fennel seeds after cumin seeds feel like diving into Wooditjup Bilya (Margaret River) in late November at my not-so-secret secret spot. It's fresh green everywhere. Even the river reflection. Texturally, the water feels like swimming through silk, warmed by the sun on top and cooled by the current where the eddies tickle my feet. Like the river, fennel seeds have a fluid, wet expression that's peculiar for dried seeds and unique among earth spices. Tasted raw, their texture – sticky to the chew – is soothing. Not even their close cousin aniseed replicates their aromatic spill – that little moat-like draw of saliva that pools in the bottom jaw, cool first, then sweet and warm.

Yes, I love them.

Not everyone feels the same. There's a clear dividing line between licorice lovers and haters that dictates their response to fennel seeds. In some ways it *is* a discretionary spice in masala: regional Indian cooking will typically never lead with fennel seeds. It's the weft to cumin seeds' warp – the contrast woven in and around sturdier structure to craft a more delicate aromatic fabric.

Texturally, fennel seeds are an important chameleon of shape and form: sweet and savoury, warm and cool, dry and sticky. These contrasting facets offer clear points of connection between earth and warm spices, and between dried and fresh aromatics.

Tasting notes

Fennel seeds are strong and distinct, but not at all hard or brackish. Their aromatic profile always has me thinking of that queenly archetype: soft steel. The seeds have a primary character of **sweet** and **wet licorice** followed by **salt** and a **cool, white mint** finish. They're **sticky** to the chew, a textural component that lays down velvet over strength. The higher the quality of fennel seeds, the greater the expression of their unique texture.

Use in masala

Generally fennel seeds are used to add warm texture. Used intelligently, they can lift an earthy masala into a higher key that feels gentle and approachable. Fennel seeds do something similar in masalas that have a surfeit of hot and/or acidic spices – they moderate the excitement and make the heat look pretty.

Emotive content

In a word, 'gentling'. The kind of spice that will take a dish from strident to communicative without ridding the message of nuance.

Traditional medicinal impact

A rare spice, fennel seeds are said to stoke *agni*, the digestive fire, without aggravating bodies susceptible to excess heat. They are seen as an appetiser and appetite regulator.

Kabargah

Kabargah is opulent. We take untrimmed lamb ribs, slow-cook them in milk, dip them in yoghurt, and then deep-fry them in ghee. The weight of fat and cooking time provide a sturdy dish structure that supports and carries elegant spice. And yet none of that beauty would come through effectively without the finishing application of fennel seeds.

Fennel seeds bedded into the outer cloak of besan flour embroider kabargah. They single-handedly lighten the dish by threading brightness into the rich fabric of masala.

Serves 4–6 as part of a shared meal

1 kg (2 lb 4 oz) lamb ribs
2 cups (500 ml) milk
2 teaspoons fennel seeds
2 cups (240 g) chickpea flour (besan)
1–2 cups (200–400 g) ghee

Masala

1 teaspoon red chilli powder
2 tablespoons water
2 teaspoons fine white sea salt
2 teaspoons fennel powder
1 teaspoon aniseed powder
1 teaspoon ginger powder
pinch of hing (asafoetida) powder
6 cloves
4 black cardamom pods, husks cracked
2 large dried bay leaves

>

Spiced yoghurt

1 cup (260 g) plain yoghurt

1 teaspoon fine white sea salt

1 teaspoon Kashmiri chilli powder

To finish

edible gold leaf (optional)

Combine the lamb ribs and milk in a large kadai or a large, heavy-based saucepan over high heat and bring to the boil, about 10 minutes. Reduce the heat to medium–low to achieve a gentle simmer. Continue simmering until half the milk has evaporated, about 1 hour. Don't stir the ribs too much – physical agitation in this initial stage impacts the build of texture. If you've chosen your pan well, this shouldn't be an issue. (This stage is about creating base structure, marrying dairy protein with meat protein to soften the lamb ribs and increase the overall fat density in the dish.)

Now we add the masala. First, stir the chilli powder into the water. (You'll notice we do this all the time before adding chilli powder to masala in Kashmiri Hindu cooking – it helps the chilli powder disperse evenly.) Add the chilli water to the milk and lamb, along with the rest of the masala spices. Continue cooking over medium–low heat, gently stirring occasionally using a folding motion, until the milk and lamb fats split, the liquid has evaporated, and the ribs are well coated in milk-solid masala and beginning to brown slightly, about 45 minutes. Continue stirring, using a scrape and lift motion. The aim is to prevent the lamb sticking and burning while ensuring we don't break up the density we've created using time, fats and spices.

Once the ribs have cooked down, remove the pan from the heat and set aside to cool.

Meanwhile, in a small bowl, make the spiced yoghurt by combining the yoghurt, salt and chilli powder. Whisk them together with cold water, 1–2 tablespoons at a time, until the yoghurt has the consistency of a thin pancake batter. Set aside.

On a thali (see page 28) or large plate, use clean fingers to mix the fennel seeds with the chickpea flour. Sift the fennel seeds through with your fingers until they are evenly distributed through the flour.

While the lamb ribs are cooling, heat the ghee in a kadai, stable cast-iron wok or heavy-based saucepan large enough that the ghee comes up no more than halfway but will still submerge the lamb ribs.

Once the lamb ribs are cool enough to handle, dip one rib at a time in the spiced yoghurt, then coat it in the besan and fennel seed mix. Set aside on a plate until all the ribs are coated. Once the ghee is very hot, fry the ribs in small batches for 15–20 seconds each, until golden brown.

Drain on paper towel. Apply gold leaf as an optional touch. Serve as part of a festive meal with pulao, raita and a pickle.

Regal spice, a definition

If I talk about street spices you'll probably instantly know what I mean – masala that's jazzy, bright and pungent, cooked high and fast. Regal spice is the opposite, and most of the time it's what Kashmiri Hindu cooking is all about: aromatics that combine deep and pervasive spice (black cardamom and cloves) with densely warm spice (fennel, ginger and aniseed powders), dry or fragrant heat (red chilli powder and/or Kashmiri chilli powder) and the tradition of earthy bitterness and elegant texture (turmeric powder and the likes of cumin, fennel and nigella seeds). Regal masala needs time and temperature to knit together. A lack of either is likely to tear the fabric of the taste experience.

Nadia's fennel seed shortbread

Makes 19

- 1 tablespoon fennel seeds
- 1 tablespoon finely grated orange zest
- 125 g (4½ oz) plain (all-purpose) flour
- 70 g (2½ oz) cornflour (cornstarch)
- ¼ teaspoon sea salt
- 70 g (2½ oz) caster (superfine) sugar
- 125 g (4½ oz) butter, softened and diced
- 1 egg yolk

I'm not a natural or particularly enthusiastic baker – Ash takes on that mantle in our family. Wanting to touch on this classic presentation of fennel seeds meant calling in one of the big baking guns of Margaret River, Nadia Haskell. She works a lot with gluten-free and vegan desserts, but I asked her for a straightforward salty/savoury version of those delicious Italian-style fennel seed biscuits that work as a bite with espresso.

I've include this recipe as an illustration of texture in all its facets. We saw earlier that fenugreek powder works in baking as a lightening agent (see page 53). Fennel seeds' texture means they can work as a binding agent in both baking and savoury cooking. In everything from this slightly crumbly biscuit to a fennel seed and pork sausage, they act as physical and aromatic glue. Blitzed in a food processor with the flours, sugars, fat and salt, fennel seeds are the savoury sticking point, while orange is for sweetness.

In Nadia's words: 'I wanted the fennel to be predominant but thought it needed a little fruity brightness and sweetness so it didn't seem too savoury. Orange and fennel are such good friends.'

The shortbread will keep in an airtight container for up to 4–5 days.

Grind the fennel seeds to a fine powder in a food processor or spice grinder. To ensure a fine consistency, you can grind them with the plain flour in a food processor on high speed. Process the ground fennel seeds, orange zest, flours, salt and sugar for 10 seconds.

Add the butter and pulse until the mixture resembles clumpy breadcrumbs. Add the egg yolk and pulse again briefly. You don't want to overwork the gluten.

Place a 40 cm (16 inch) square of baking paper on a clean benchtop and turn the dough out onto it. Gently bring the dough together with clean fingers, then wrap it in the baking paper and refrigerate for 1 hour for the dough to chill, or overnight for the flavours to develop further.

Preheat the oven to 160°C (315°F).

Unwrap the pastry and leave it on the baking paper. Place another 40 cm square of baking paper on top and use a rolling pin to roll out the dough to about 5 mm (¼ inch) thick. Peel off the top sheet of paper then flip the dough over and peel off the other sheet. Line a baking tray with one of those sheets.

Cut the dough into rounds using a 5.5 cm (2¼ inch) cookie cutter and transfer to the tray by lifting with a butter knife or angled palette knife. Leave 1–2 cm (½–¾ inch) between them. Gather together the offcuts of dough, then reroll and cut into more rounds. Add a little cold water if the dough is too dry, or refrigerate for 15 minutes if it's too sticky.

Bake for 10–15 minutes, until the edges brown slightly.

AJWAIN SEEDS
CAROM

Category: Earth spices.
Form: Ridged and elongated seeds, smaller than cumin seeds but larger than aniseed.
Colour: Bronze-khaki.

The taste of ajwain is dark. Though cumin powder is of the earth, ajwain goes deeper: its tonality is herbaceous, mechanical and stubborn – it throws us in the direction of thyme and caraway seeds combined. In masala it works as the roots beneath the soil, drawing flavour down and anchoring it there. Its intensity can be off-putting, and makes it tricky to use outside of recipes: I only remember having it as a kid in namkeen – deep-fried besan flour batons that Ammi would put out with chai in the early evening before dinner. It is one of those snacks that adults love and kids leave.

Ajwain seeds are best handled as an accent spice or as a depth creator. The former might be adding ajwain to Poori (page 140), the latter a small inclusion in a complex dish like Chicken thigh coconut curry (page 143).

Tasting notes

Ajwain seeds are a pungent spice with a distinctive triplet of primary aromas that segue from **eucalyptus** through **soap** and into **kerosene**. They leave a residual taste of '**garage floor**' that receives mixed reactions from many people who try them for the first time. Secondary aromatic notes include **bitter celery** and **thyme**.

Use in masala

This is a spice that speaks largely of distortion and difficulty. The fact of their aromatic strength strips ajwain seeds of any pretext of amenability, which seems unusual for this category – earth spices generally are about the grounded and the familiar. But once you consider the dynamics of Indian families you can see how it fits in. Loving pushiness. Argumentative affection. Intrusion as connection. In masala, ajwain seeds tell a very clear tale of what it is to be at home. They bring the texture of tradition (see below) to our thali.

Emotive content

The nature of ajwain is disruption, so it can be a hard spice to feel affection for: after all, who of us actively seeks out disruption in our day-to-day life? It exists though. And ajwain gives us a way to speak to it.

Traditional medicinal impact

Ajwain is considered a powerful cleanser and to have antimicrobial properties. It's used to make gripe water for relieving colic, and is seen as a headline digestive spice.

The texture of tradition

Like those distinctive aromatics kala namak (page 72) and mustard oil (page 93), ajwain seeds are Indian. They remind me of Dad and Ammi, and big family gatherings that for modern Australian culture would feel celebratory but for traditional Indian culture just spoke of how we lived.

My family name is Ganju and – just like the word 'ajwain' – its sound in my mouth tastes like tradition. Ajwain seeds mightn't be my favourite, but they are familiar: when we eat them, we definitely know who we are.

Poori

I look forward to the bite of ajwain seeds in poori: it's the ideal contrast of ingredient and cooking technique – a heavy fry with the bite of digestive spice.

Makes 6

2 cups (500 ml) vegetable oil, for deep-frying

Poori dough

2 cups (300 g) atta flour (Indian stoneground wheat flour), plus extra for dusting

1 teaspoon fine pink salt

½ teaspoon fine white sea salt

1 teaspoon ajwain seeds

1 teaspoon ghee

hot water, for binding

Place a kadai, stable cast-iron wok or heavy-based saucepan on the stovetop and pour in the vegetable oil – the pot should be large enough that the oil comes up no more than halfway but will still submerge a single poori. Don't turn on the heat until after you have rolled out the poori.

In a large bowl, combine the atta flour, salts, ajwain seeds and ghee. Run a thin stream of hot water from the sink.
Add a little at a time to the dough, mixing continuously by hand. The water must be hot – cold water will make the dough tense and stiffen, while hot water allows the atta flour to keep its natural stretch. Stop adding water once the dough is smooth and has the texture of a soft putty – malleable but not sticky.

Lightly dust a clean benchtop with extra flour. Tip the dough out onto the benchtop and knead it for 2–3 minutes to activate the gluten. Leave to rest under plastic wrap or wrapped in a clean tea towel (dish towel) for about 10 minutes.

Divide the dough into six small balls. Lightly dust the benchtop and rolling pin with extra flour, then roll each ball into a round 2–3 mm (1⁄16–⅛ inches) thick.

Now heat the vegetable oil over high heat until very hot. Fry the poori one at a time – turning just once – until puffed and delicious. Eat immediately with Channa sabji (page 102), Aloo jeera (page 126) or with mango pickles and Methi fried flatbreads (page 271).

Regional Indian flours: a key

- **Atta**: A stoneground wheat flour with a nutty taste that's used to make chapati, roti, poori and paratha. It has some stretch and creates a soft unleavened flatbread.
- **Besan**: Flour from ground chickpeas, with a squeaky texture similar to cornflour (cornstarch). A heavy flour, it's high in protein and suitable for coeliacs. Being naturally gluten-free, it has no stretch. A skilled householder can make beautiful flatbreads from besan flour that are nonetheless richer and heavier than those made with atta. More commonly, it's used as a binding agent in snacks like pakora/pakoda, or to make a batter.
- **Maida**: A refined, finely ground wheat flour used to make naan, bhatura and parotta.
- **Rice**: Finely ground rice flour used in the south and mixed with skinned urad dal to make idli or dosa.

Right: Bottom tray: Poori and yoghurt.
Top tray: Methi fried flatbreads (page 271).
Jars: Mango pickles.

Chicken thigh coconut curry

The masala in this dish uses pungent and earthy spices. But more importantly, it's focused on the cohesion created by individual aromatics that are strongly associated with traditional regional Indian tastes: kala namak, mace, fenugreek powder, ginger powder, cumin powder and, of course, ajwain. Reinforcing classicism is a way of building a texture of tradition into the dish (see pages 120, 139).

Serves 3–4

- 2 tablespoons mustard oil
- 1 tablespoon ghee
- 1 tablespoon yoghurt
- 1 teaspoon fine white sea salt
- 5 cloves
- 2 dried bay leaves
- 5 chicken thigh cutlets
- 5 small tomatoes
- ½ teaspoon fenugreek powder

Masala

- 2 teaspoons fennel powder
- 1 teaspoon fine pink salt
- 1 teaspoon Kashmiri chilli powder
- 1 teaspoon ajwain seeds
- 1 teaspoon cumin powder
- 1 teaspoon ginger powder
- ½ teaspoon kala namak
- ½ teaspoon turmeric powder
- scant ½ teaspoon mace powder

To finish

- 1 cup (250 ml) coconut milk
- 8–10 fresh curry leaves

Heat the mustard oil, ghee and yoghurt with the white sea salt, cloves and bay leaves in a large cast-iron kadai or heavy-based saucepan over high heat, stirring constantly. You'll notice how rich and thick the fat base is, even before the fat from the chicken skin can add to it. This very dense bed will provide some of the camouflage for the ajwain seeds.

Once the yoghurt starts to spatter and split, add the chicken thigh cutlets and begin browning. Keep over high heat and use the Kashmiri Hindu method of cooking (see page 97). Cook until the chicken is very well browned, about 20 minutes. As the yoghurt evaporates, the base fats will become oil-like. At this point you need to pay attention, stirring almost constantly to prevent the chicken sticking too much.

Meanwhile, combine all the masala ingredients in a katori or small bowl and keep by the stovetop.

While the chicken is browning, place the tomatoes in a pressure cooker and cover with water. Bring to pressure and cook for 1–2 minutes before turning the pressure cooker off and force-releasing the steam. Drain, skin and core the tomatoes, then purée them using a hand-held blender. Stir in the fenugreek powder.

When the chicken is browned, remove the pan from the heat briefly to prevent spatters and add the tomato purée. Add a little water to the purée vessel and swish it around to get as much of the tomato out as possible. Stir through, return to the heat and deglaze the cooking vessel, then immediately add the masala. The chicken will become rich and the oils will split the tomato. Cook together for 2–3 minutes.

>

Transfer the chicken and tomato to the pressure cooker, making sure you scrape out every last bit of sauce. Set the pressure cooker to high and cook until it emits one or two jets of steam. Lower to a medium putter, then continue to cook for 8–10 minutes. Turn off the heat and let the pressure cooker depressurise on its own. If you don't have a pressure cooker, continue cooking in the saucepan. Reduce the heat to low and cook for 45–60 minutes, adding more water if necessary to stop the chicken cooking dry.

Open the pressure cooker. If yours is flameproof, place it over low heat. If not, transfer the chicken and sauce to a large heavy-based saucepan over low heat. Stir in the coconut milk and cook for 10 minutes for the masala to thicken.

Just before serving, stir the fresh curry leaves through. The final sauce will be rich and creamy but also deep and strong, with a tail pungency courtesy of the ajwain seeds leading a marching band of charismatically pungent spices.

'... the idea of constructing a dish around a single taste can be applied to any spice. For newcomers, a spice like cumin seed can be a better place to start.'

Building around a single spice

It can feel arbitrary to say that a recipe like this is a recipe about ajwain seeds. It's one of twenty ingredients, most of them spices and fats. But of all the ideas around masala, intention is perhaps one of the most significant. When I think about masala, I think about the key theme and build from that point. With the focus on ajwain in this recipe, the theme is about showing a strong and distinct aromatic in a softer light: for me this masala eats like a pulled punch – you can taste the way the aromatic strength has been withheld.

Ajwain seeds are a complicated spice to build around, but the idea of constructing a dish around a single taste can be applied to any spice. For newcomers, a spice like cumin seeds can be a better place to start.

NIGELLA SEEDS KALONJI

Category: Earth spices.
Form: Teardrop-shaped seeds with no ridges.
Colour: Matte charcoal-black.

If fennel seeds are the earth spice that brings in a feel of water, and ajwain seeds the subterranean root, then nigella seeds – kalonji – are that touch of earth and wind. This is a spice of movement. Its aroma is veiled when raw: chew a clutch of seeds and the experience feels brittle, empty and a little sulphurous. But heat it through fat and weave it through masala, and you'll learn that the 'taste' of nigella seeds is not so much about what it *is* as what it *does* – kalonji blows in, tosses everything else up in the air, and reveals the hidden facets inside masala. I always refer to it as the worst kind of gossip ... kalonji knows all the secrets and tells them without revealing too much of itself.

Tasting notes

Nigella seeds are a spice that, like mustard seeds, release their aroma through heat. They are subtle as a raw spice. Obvious primary aromas include **charcoal** and **soot** with a **sesame seed** finish. Secondary characters invoke a **rancid garlic high note**. As a tertiary experience, nigella seeds offer the sensation of **emptiness** or **windiness**.

Use in masala

Kalonji is beautiful with seafood – I always think of its use in terms of the deliciousness it delivers with crustaceans. Traditionally in Kashmiri Hindu cooking we use it in lamb dishes alongside fennel and cumin seeds (like a panch phoron 'lite'). Its quality of movement means it disturbs dense and warm masala because it shifts aroma around. This propensity makes it useful as a linking spice to slip the body between states (see page 146).

Emotive content

I've always resonated with nigella seeds' windy element. It's a mirror for vata types (see page 26) and reflects the kind of hummingbird movements that can be perceived and experienced either as light and free or as erratic and unsettled.

SLIPPING BETWEEN STATES

In all my years of teaching people about spice, possibly their largest focus has been a desire for a better relationship with food. For some that means losing weight. For others it means finding or refinding pleasure in cooking. And for still others it means not feeling confused about what and how to eat so they can enjoy life more.

Beneath all of these desires focused on food, are basic desires focused on ourselves. Losing weight means wanting to feel okay in our skin. Finding joy in cooking means wanting to be okay in our everyday life. Feeling relaxed about knowing how to eat means feeling at peace with the bigger trajectory of our lives.

What we think we want in all of these cases is certainty. But for the Indian householder that idea of certainty is undercut from the youngest age. Dad always used to talk about planting and watering the fruit tree without looking to the fruit. It's one of the central tenets of Hinduism. Of most faith traditions, really. Doing the work without hanging on to the outcome. Because you never know how things are going to change, so how could it be helpful to focus on a set idea of what you want the outcome to be? It was a lot to chew for a small girl in plaits. It's still a lot to chew for the big girl me.

When I teach people about masala I offer information that allows them to develop a fluid relationship with the concept. Rules don't cut it because rules are about certainty. And domestic Ayurveda, lived experience, faith teachings, logic – they all teach us that there's not a lot of point hanging our hats on certainty. Instead, what we can learn to do is be flexible. Find ways to shift between states so we can better meet ourselves wherever we are in what we hope will be a long and stimulating life. When we create relationship to masala, we create that opportunity in our own kitchens every day.

Masala and domestic Ayurveda are never about negation. Physically, emotionally or spiritually, they're about recognising what's going on. When we know what's going on, we can more easily ascertain how our situation, illness or state of being is affecting us. Once we better understand how we're being affected, we can find the ways we need to move through and – hopefully – transition beyond that state. Which only takes us into the next one, by the way. So you can see how figuring out a gentler way to deal with change, uncertainty and distress is useful.

Have a look at the recipes and explanations in the following pages to gain insights into this way of using taste. It's a practice I worked with in earnest in my earliest days of learning the roots of masala for myself, and I still tap into it every day.

Masalas for slipping between states

We now move from concept to practice. This way with masala works by focusing on a singular spice that connects to the state in which we find ourselves. We then use other aromatics in sequence to transition into a quieter sensory body space where we can hear what's going on within us. While the process is the same for each of the three examples that follow, the aromatics we use to get there are different.

These masalas are intended to be used as presented, not toasted or ground. Heat the fat and then add the masala to temper. There are sabji suggestions beneath each. These masalas could also be used to marinate or slow-cook meats in line with Western cooking traditions.

Masala 1: Flightiness, nervousness, generalised anxiety

For vata imbalance

nigella seeds	1 teaspoon
Kashmiri chilli powder	generous ¼ teaspoon
fine pink salt	1 teaspoon
turmeric powder	generous ¼ teaspoon
fennel seeds	½ teaspoon
fennel powder	1 teaspoon
coriander powder	2 teaspoons
cassia powder	generous ¼ teaspoon
ghee	1 tablespoon

Here we're using the windy nature of nigella seeds to mirror the feeling of anxiety. Using the pleasure of taste, we connect to the masala and then step ourselves through a process of settling. Moving from nigella seeds into Kashmiri chilli powder escalates height, pointing our awareness towards where we are: that sensation of being high and outside of ourselves. Fine pink salt accentuates this sensation.

Once we're aware of where we are, our body is okay to settle down gently. And so that's what we do. We tamp down the movement with turmeric powder. Create a fluid feeling of grounding with fennel seeds. Ground ourselves further with the weight of fennel powder. Alleviate any heaviness but play into earthiness with the lightly floral quality of coriander powder. Embrace ourselves with cassia powder's warmth. And finally, soften, sweeten and temper our experience through ghee.

Use as a masala to make paneer with peas, cabbage or eggplant (aubergine). **See Matar paneer (page 230) for a guide to the method to use.**

Masala 2: Stuckness, stagnation and generalised low mood

For kapha imbalance

kala namak	generous ¼ teaspoon
fine pink salt	1 teaspoon
fine white sea salt	generous ¼ teaspoon
cumin powder	½ teaspoon
cumin seeds	2 teaspoons
fenugreek powder	generous ¼ teaspoon
red chilli powder	½ teaspoon
Kashmiri chilli powder	generous ¼ teaspoon
fine white pepper	¼ teaspoon
cloves	3
jaggery powder	2 pinches
cinnamon powder	generous ¼ teaspoon
cinnamon stick	1
ghee	1 tablespoon

Kapha is a little trickier than vata energy to rebalance because although the medicine is movement, it still needs a depth of strength and sureness. You can see that here with the sheer number of spices involved. First we begin with a 'flat' salt, kala namak. It's earthy and sulphurous, and so we get that feeling of acknowledging weight. We then start to move things on. Gently at first – fine pink salt. And then with more force – fine white sea salt. It will always take some push of energy to shift kapha after the initial connection phase. Not to scare ourselves off, we switch gears to cumin powder (heavily grounding and a little cranky) then cumin seeds (calming and familiar).

Now we are stabilised, fenugreek powder opens the door for more movement, with dried red chilli powder and an instant rise of heat. Kashmiri chilli powder chases this with a slight softening, like turning the flue down on the slow-combustion stove after the flame is lit. Fine white pepper disperses the heat further – kapha does better with dispersed heat. Cloves are warmth but also deep and pungent strength. Jaggery, deep sweetness. Cinnamon powder

and a cinnamon stick together provide structural and wooded warmth. It feels like integrity. Ghee again softens the experience.

Use as a masala to make aloo or gobi sabji. See Simple gobi sabji (page 290) for a guide to the method to use.

Masala 3: Anger, frustration and generalised dissatisfaction

For pitta imbalance

red chilli powder	½ teaspoon
fine white sea salt	1 teaspoon
fine white lake salt	generous ¼ teaspoon
sumac	½ teaspoon
amchur	generous ¼ teaspoon
ginger powder	1 teaspoon
cassia powder	generous ¼ teaspoon
nigella seeds	1 teaspoon
cumin seeds	2 teaspoons
fennel seeds	1 teaspoon
turmeric powder	½ teaspoon
green cardamom pods	5, husks cracked
black cardamom pods	3, husks cracked
jaggery pow	2 pinches
mustard oil	2 tablespoons
ghee	1 tablespoon
tomatoes	2 fresh, diced
coconut milk	1 cup (250 ml)
fresh curry leaves	8–10

One of the ways to re-settle pitta once we've tapped into the energy of fire and heat is to create unusual tastes that engage the drive and curiosity inherent in this energetic body type. You also have to start big. Tapping straight into fire with red chilli powder catches the body's attention. We immediately intensify this with two types of white salt before diving headlong into acidity – sumac a little dark and salted; and then amchur with a softer, fruity acidic taste. Once we've captivated the sensory body with charismatic and fiery messaging, we can begin to bring it down. Ginger powder offers a bridge between heat and warmth. Cassia powder carries the heat further into more benign sensory body territory.

Now pacified, we can introduce earth spices. Nigella seeds for grounding with a little windy movement. Then cumin seeds, more truly of the earth. Fennel seeds for fluidity and sweetness. Turmeric powder to settle in and solidify the changes we've made before taking that tangent that pitta finds so irresistible – with green and black cardamom pods for depth and interest. Jaggery powder's sweetness provides an illusion of heat. We bed this in two types of fat – mustard oil and ghee – to keep things interesting. The finishing trio of fresh tomato, coconut milk and curry leaves is a seal of sweet and gentle acid, cooling richness, and a fresh, nutty finish. It's the kind of wild ride that resonates with pitta, but one that's sustainable.

Use as a masala to make a baingan (eggplant/aubergine) sabji or fish curry. See Baingan bharta (page 79) or Ashok's marron masala (page 172) for a guide to the vegetable and seafood methods to use respectively.

A riff on panch phoron

Unlike garam masala, panch phoron can be used as a blend on its own (with the addition of salt) to create coherent masala. This is rare – that a masala weighted into one category still feels whole. But that's the nature of earth aromatics – the contrasts in texture between these spices create the illusion of completeness.

In the case of panch phoron, we have cumin seeds and their profile of fulsome brackish menthol, fennel seeds and their sticky sweet wetness, fenugreek seeds with their maple appleseed bitterness, kalonji or nigella seeds with their charred and sulphurous spaciousness, and finally the warm toasty cleanse of sesame seeds.

I call this a riff on panch phoron because along with the classic five whole-seed spices used to make this blend, I've included a few additions that give this masala a less obviously regional shape (see Regions and masala ownership, right). The salt seasons. The turmeric powder stabilises. The chilli powder heightens.

You could use this masala with any of the aloo preparations on pages 126–29. A little with butter on barbecued crustaceans would be divine. Temper the masala through ghee to make the nigella seeds appear softer, through mustard oil to draw out kalonji's astringent and more aggressively windy quality, or through coconut oil to increase its flavour dominance in the masala.

Panch phoron blends raw spice – not toasted seeds – and is not ground to powder, unlike garam masala.

- 1 teaspoon fennel seeds
- 1 teaspoon nigella seeds
- 1 teaspoon cumin seeds
- 1 teaspoon fenugreek seeds
- 1 teaspoon sesame seeds
- ½ teaspoon fine pink salt
- ½ teaspoon red chilli powder
- generous ¼ teaspoon fine white sea salt
- generous ¼ teaspoon turmeric powder

Mix the quantities listed and use as is.

Regions and masala ownership

The first comment on my YouTube video for this recipe was from a viewer who told me in no uncertain terms that my inclusion of sesame seeds makes the recipe wrong. As an Indian, talking with any confidence about the masala of a region other than one's own is fraught. We care so much that our culture is correctly represented. Which is why in my own listings of Kashmiri Hindu recipes, I'll refer to our own Ganju traditions – even within small ethnic groups, there can be vast differences in our approaches to technique and taste. I'm always willing to be corrected.

What I will say here is that, like garam masala, panch phoron is a classic masala with multiple representations. Fennel, nigella, cumin and fenugreek seeds are standard inclusions, but that fifth seed can change. I've used sesame seeds here because that's what my cousin-sister Shivani uses in her home, and I love its contribution. But other recipes may use mustard seeds – black normally – or sometimes celery seeds.

CORIANDER POWDER
DHANIA

Category: Earth spices.
Form: Light and very pollen-like powder.
Colour: Pale silvery sand.

I surprised myself by putting coriander as the first of the powders in the earth category, even before cumin powder. But there's something recognisably inclusive about coriander powder as an aromatic. Subtle. Herbaceous. Raw tastings have me immediately recalling chamomile – it's very pretty like that. Many people get it mixed up with fresh coriander (cilantro) leaves.

Because of its subtlety, coriander powder is generally used, by those unfamiliar with its character, as a 'just because' addition. Folks can be unsure of what it does, but they figure it contributes to the idea of what curry should be. As someone once said to me: 'I don't really know what to do when I make Indian food, so I sort of just add every spice that starts with "c" ... it works sometimes!'

I loved that honesty.

What you need to know about coriander powder is that it responds ecstatically to being freshly ground from dried seeds. Its ephemeral texture – that pollen-like character – translates aromatically, and so if you want flavour as well as volume, it's best to add it towards the end of the cooking time. Masala relies on subtle single aromatics like coriander powder to create bridges between charismatic tastes and angular contrast (see Use in masala, below).

Unlike its divisive close cousin fresh coriander (cilantro), coriander powder is derived from the dried seeds of the coriander (cilantro) plant, and it takes acuity to detect its taste in masala.

Tasting notes

The **gritty** and **pollen-like** texture of coriander powder hits first. What follows is a **lightly herbaceous** taste with **soft lemon** and **chamomile** qualities. It has secondary notes of **soft loam** and **light dust**.

Use in masala

There are two key uses for coriander powder in masala. The first is as a spice that creates volume or thickness in an otherwise thin sabji. The second is as the 'girl/guy next door spice'. Wholesome. Gets along with everyone. *Kind of* easy to overlook for more glamorous aromatics – until you realise the work it does to create cohesiveness in spaces where cohesion is challenging: its texture and subtlety work like mortar in a brick wall, softening the connection points between disparate tastes.

Emotive content

Gentleness. Not many spices can create such body of texture and density in such a quiet and unassuming way.

Matar sabji

Sabji can be challenging when you're growing up – cabbage, capsicum (pepper), tomato, gourd ... not exactly high on the list of kids' favourite vegies. But peas! How good are peas? I actually spent years trying to write a book in my early twenties based on a memory I have of shelling peas with Ammi in the sunshine out the back of her Defence Colony kitchen in New Delhi on a cold December morning in the early 1980s. I haven't shelled peas for years, but I still think of that moment whenever I make this dish.

Peas are a great vehicle for showcasing coriander powder because – much like green beans – they're not carriers of flavour. Rather, peas require a masala that will stick to their skin, which is why it's so apt to think of dhania as mortar.

I'll generally make this sabji as a filling for samosas when I want something that cooks faster than aloo (potato). But it can also be nice tossed through a salad of butter lettuce with fresh ricotta, finished with thin rings of pickled red onion.

Serves 4 as a salad or side
(or provides stuffing for 12 samosas)

2 cups (300 g) fresh or frozen peas

Masala

1 heaped tablespoon ghee
2 teaspoons coriander powder
1½ teaspoons cumin seeds
1 teaspoon fine pink salt
½ teaspoon turmeric powder
½ teaspoon Kashmiri chilli powder
½ teaspoon ginger powder
1 × 4 cm piece of jaggery

Boil or blanch your peas until just cooked, about 2 minutes. Drain and set aside.

Combine all the masala ingredients in a large frying pan. Place over medium–low heat and, once the ghee has melted, temper the spices until aromatic.

Add the peas and stir until well coated in the spices. Reduce the heat to low and cook for about 5 minutes, to ensure the coriander powder preserves its aroma and contributes that vital textural volume.

You can serve this with rice and dal for a light lunch, toss it through a lettuce and ricotta salad (see left), or use as filling for samosas.

> '... uniquely for a powder, it brings intensity and a propensity for stealing the limelight.'

CUMIN POWDER
JEERA

Category: Earth spices.
Form: Slightly gritty powder, heavier than coriander but less dense than fennel.
Colour: Muddy sand, like you'd find in a mangrove.

Ashy cleverly described cumin powder as a hallmark spice. Just like coriander powder, it tends to get a pretty heavy-duty workout in the kitchens of those who aren't quite sure how to work with masala but have a feeling that those kinds of gritty/earthy tastes are important. Funnily enough, cumin powder isn't an aromatic I use without careful consideration: uniquely for a powder, it brings intensity and a propensity for stealing the limelight. This is thanks to its textural impact on masala's underbelly.

Tasted raw, cumin powder's profile is short-lived and flat – it lacks the resonance of whole cumin seeds. What it doesn't lack is a natural ability to draw dark, pungent and heavy tastes towards it: a great visual would be of cumin powder as a villainous conjurer in a Marvel movie, calling in the shadow energy from the spices around it in order to increase its own weight, presence and power.

Cumin powder has this capacity for a couple of reasons. The most obvious is that, in masala, like attracts like, so cumin powder draws out the 'dirty' quality in any aromatic it sits with. A masala of ginger powder, Kashmiri chilli powder and fennel powder, for example, will create a warm floral bloom. Add cumin powder and from that floral bloom emerges a weight of dark and dirt, like when you're repotting a plant and a dump of soil spills over the flowers.

Less obvious is that the dark centrifugal pull of cumin powder owes itself to *cultural* weight. The Indian regional character can be forceful. Not all the time. But the characteristics are there – aspects of arrogance, and an argumentative and strident nature. I hear Dad's 'strict' voice when I write those words, and also mine – though I've worked hard to skin myself of the worst of it. Cumin powder in particular is a container for these aspects of the Indian psyche. Texturally, it brings the same intensity to masala.

And lastly, the very familiarity of cumin powder increases its intensity. When we taste, intensity of flavour is only partly determined by how much of a spice we use, or how we use it in combination with other spices. A less considered influence is how well we *know* a taste (see page 157).

Easy skinless chicken thigh burritos

Chicken's inherently light meat makes a great combination with cumin powder: the 'whiteness' of the chicken balances out the dark and heavy quality of the cumin. I wrap these chicken thighs in soft tortillas and top them with guacamole, pickled jalapeños, sour cream and Tabasco sauce.

Serves 4

600 g (1 lb 5 oz) boneless, skinless chicken thigh fillets, cut into 2 cm (¾ inch) strips
1 green capsicum (pepper), cut into strips
corn kernels from 1 corn cob
½ zucchini (courgette), cut into thin strips

For browning

1 tablespoon vegetable oil
1 tablespoon mustard oil
1 teaspoon fine white sea salt
3 dried bay leaves
1 small cassia stick
1 star anise

Masala

2 teaspoons cumin powder
1 teaspoon fine pink salt
1 teaspoon dried oregano
1 teaspoon cumin seeds
½ teaspoon dried red chilli
½ teaspoon red chilli flakes
scant ½ teaspoon turmeric powder

To finish

425 g (15 oz) tinned black beans, drained
2 tablespoons tomato paste (concentrated purée)

Start with the ingredients for browning. Combine the vegetable and mustard oils and the spices in a large kadai or heavy-based saucepan over high heat. Toss in the chicken and cook for 5–7 minutes, until a little browned on the outside but not cooked through.

Add the masala, along with the capsicum, corn and zucchini, and stir through. Cook over high heat for about 3 minutes. (If you taste it now, you'll find complex flavour that sits lightly atop the chicken. Cumin powder keeps the chilli grounded and the oregano still.)

Add the black beans and tomato paste and cook for a further 5 minutes. Serve with fresh tortillas and your choice of accompaniments.

Ammi's garam masala

I felt like I had to check with Bui before including this recipe. Traditionally, a family's garam masala recipe is kept secret – sometimes even by mothers from daughters.

Regionally, the ingredients of garam masala vary. A simple recipe may contain just six spices. A complex recipe could contain twelve or more. Practically, it supplies both bells and whistles: a great garam masala can be the difference between delicious and transcendent when it comes to a finished dish. That said, we use garam masala selectively. In our Kashmiri Hindu tradition we say yes to garam masala with any yellow dal, all variations of rogan josh – from mutton/lamb or chicken, through to cauliflower – and often in dum cooking (see Bui's dum aloo on page 255).

From an aromatic perspective, finishing with garam masala reinvigorates masala's base: the spice mixture is made by grinding and mixing many of the whole aromatics that are classically introduced early in the cooking process – such as black cardamom pods, bay leaves, green cardamom pods and cinnamon sticks, among others. Finishing with a powdered blend of these aromatics refreshes the dish.

Its secondary purpose – that of sealing a dish – is thanks to garam masala's textural density: in any style of cooking, dense spice added towards the end of cooking can create an aromatic 'lid'.

The interesting thing about this recipe – other than it being a Ganju family heirloom – is that it allows you to experience the benefit of cumin powder's centrifugal capacity (see page 154). The striking power of this garam masala wouldn't be communicated without cumin powder to draw it in tight.

This recipe makes enough garam masala to use for a little while. If you don't think you'll use it much, then make a half-quantity. You really don't want to keep freshly ground whole spices for longer than a few months.

And yes, although this recipe calls for cumin seeds, it does its work once it's ground, which is why it appears in the cumin powder section of this book.

Makes 1½ cups (150 g)

- 1 cup black cardamom pods
- ½ cup green cardamom pods
- ⅓ cup cumin seeds
- 1½ tablespoons cloves
- 1½ tablespoons mace flower
- 4 large dried bay leaves
- 2 nutmegs
- 1 cinnamon stick

Grind together. (Do not toast; see page 131.) Store in a dark place in an airtight container.

Off the shelf: a note on Kashmiri garam masala

When it comes to garam masala, the Kashmiri Hindu version is distinct. What makes it so is the absence of black pepper. Black pepper is a muscular spice. In Western kitchens it's not given much thought. But black pepper in the regional Indian tradition is used sparingly because its impact is so great. You can read more about black pepper on page 225. For now it's enough to say that regional recipes in the Ganju family tradition aren't built to hold that style of garam masala. For that reason alone, it's worth making up a batch of this recipe to have on hand.

'Traditionally, a family's garam masala recipe is kept secret – sometimes even by mothers from daughters.'

Tasting notes
Cumin powder is **gritty**, **cranky**, **soil-like** and **flat**. Texturally, it's heavy, its secondary and tertiary notes sensations rather than tastes. Cumin powder **muffles** and **tamps down** hot and acidic spices in the way dirt does a fire. It deepens the effect of pungent taste.

Use in masala
Cumin powder isn't a leader spice when it comes to masala – dishes built around its profile tend to fall into the category of snack foods and side dishes. Outside of regional Indian cooking, I use it to deepen chicken-based meals: cumin powder gives this light meat a sense of gravitas. All of that being said, it's the secret ingredient in Ammi's Ganju-family garam masala (page 156).

Emotive content
Cumin powder creates an undercarriage of earthy weight. It can be used to call forth the fortitude required to get a difficult task done.

The role of familiarity in taste
I once had a conversation with a female diner about truffles – the fungi, not the chocolates. It was late winter in Margaret River and this diner had ordered a main course highlighting in-season truffles. When I asked if she'd enjoyed her meal she said she had, but her tone suggested otherwise. I persisted. She admitted that while the meal had been lovely, it was her first experience of truffles and she was really disappointed. After hearing so much about their rarity and taste she'd been expecting more.

I sympathised and shared with her that my first experience of black truffle at La Maison Blanche in Paris back in the early 2000s had left me feeling similarly underwhelmed. But it can often be the case with new aromatic experience, particularly as it relates to produce like truffles: their subtlety and our lack of recognition of that aroma makes its taste elusive.

The same happens in reverse with familiar tastes. The soil-like taste and texture of cumin powder is so universally familiar that our acuity to its aroma is almost unmatched in the world of spice. It's one of the reasons it can be so easy to overdo cumin powder in masala. When we know a taste very well, it draws our focus. Not only that, but its familiarity is highlighted by any unfamiliar spice with which it's paired. The emphasis that comes with contrast works across all aspects of taste: salty emphasises sweet, pungent emphasises pretty, a quality of the unknown emphasises the known. As a rule, I would rarely use more than ½ teaspoon cumin powder in any regional Indian dish unless a recipe specifically calls for more.

DIGESTION AND LONGEVITY

Any Hindu kid who grows up cared for by an Indian householder of even moderately traditional belief is instructed from pretty early on not to count their life in years, but in breaths. We're told that we come into the world with a certain number, and when that number is counted ... thud! We hit the floor. Or that's how I always imagined it. I never found this idea disconcerting, maybe because at least it seemed to contain rhythm and a reason. But likely also because in our Hindu home death was always a natural part of our conversations. It sort of has to be – energy expenditure is a precursor to teachings about digestion and longevity.

This is because domestic Ayurveda views digestion as the most energy-consuming process that the physical body pursues every day. Within the framework of Ayurveda, energy expended is breath breathed, and the breathing of breath determines the length of life. The act of feeding ourselves in that very traditional and watchful sense then becomes an act of life extension – stoking our digestive fire so it burns *just right* and our moments are multiplied. The symmetry is quite beautiful.

Panning right back to poetic ideas about digestion and longevity helps us appreciate the lyricism of masala. Maybe we believe the premise of numbered breaths and maybe we don't. But touching upon metaphysical, esoteric or even fanciful messaging somehow relieves the tension that can build up when we attempt to understand how a concept like masala relates to us. It also draws us closer to that central tenet – spice is about more than taste, because masala is about more than food.

WARM SPICES

Function in masala: Offering warmth and density as points of contrast to pungent and angular tastes.
Emotive quality: Providing simple pleasure within the complex and sometimes challenging frame of masala.

Both Dad and Mum have passed away in the past four years, Mum just six months ago at the time I was drafting this book, which makes writing the overview of this category a little tricky. I tell people new to masala that warm aromatics are those thought of as baking spices in Western kitchens: cinnamon powder, cassia powder, ginger powder, nutmeg powder and clove powder. Indian householders, however, use these aromatics in savoury contexts to tell the stories of our families. And I miss my parents, which makes it feel a little hard to talk about using these spices.

At the most basic level, warm spices are all powders, and all are the ground and dried version of whole spices that largely belong in the structural spices category (page 283). Aromatics in this category are pretty and front-palate-centric, and generally require anchoring by grittier back-palate spices in order to show their true length and clarity.

One of the common mistakes made by newcomers to regional Indian cooking is forgetting this category. Not because it's not beautiful, but because it *is*. They tend to think that masala means shouldering into challenge and exoticism. But not allocating space in the pan for the aromatic signature of pleasure and comfort is problematic for a few reasons. On a purely sensory level, it results in cacophonous masala: without the experience of pleasure offered by spices from this category, the aromatic angles and contrasts are too loud (see Why pleasure matters, right). On a storytelling level, a masala without the intimacy of meaning offered by warm aromatics becomes too broad to decipher. Or if a message can be deciphered, at the very least it's less delicious for its impersonality.

But I also think that, culturally, Western kitchens undervalue the savoury aspects of these spices. When I'm teaching people about masala, they're often surprised to find how wooded cinnamon powder is when they taste it raw. Or how dusty and sharp ginger powder is. Or the strong presence of salt and soil in aniseed powder. Calling these spices warm doesn't just mean that they're easy or friendly aromatics. It's also about the shape they make in the mouth: the density of these powders and the beauty of the memories they evoke gives them a roundness of form that feels pleasurable to the sensory body. This is because roundness as a shape signifies completion. You know when things come full circle? For that one moment in time everything feels *good*.

On a less emotive front, this category brings density and front-palate weight. It doesn't matter how much complexity and length you build into the back or base of a dish if the front palate is left sparse – imagine a fish out of water doing that thing with its mouth as it tries to 'breathe' in the air. That's what masala feels like to the mouth without a full front palate.

How spice stows feeling

Our ability to function well relies upon our ability to digest our experiences. It's a big ask – every day brings new things, old things, repetitive things, surprising things, things we don't want to deal with. We have to sort through it all. One of the ways we do that and lessen the effort is to allocate certain bodily resources to certain tasks. And one of the ways we do this is by assigning emotional experiences to eating.

This natural process is too complex to explain here – you can read more on page 161. What I'll say now is that the biological connections between taste, smell and memory mean that aromatics work as receptacles of emotion and memory – the experiences in our lives that make us, us.

When we decide to place ourselves emotionally in our kitchens, we give ourselves access to a daily form of awareness therapy. We give ourselves permission to notice how we're behaving with our consumption, and to think about how that reflects our emotional state. I know, for example, that during difficult times I drink more alcohol and eat less food. It happened after Dad's death, and after Mum's. But because I know this pattern, I don't panic when it happens. I understand that all I'm doing is trying to make my insides fit what feels like the chaos of my outside.

Eventually I work through the crises and return to masala. I make dal makhani during recipe testing. I wake up to a kitchen that smells deliciously like a roadside dabba. I feed people. I stock my pantry. And I put myself back in my life again.

Why pleasure matters

Most Eastern cultural and faith traditions legitimise the importance of pleasure. From an Indian perspective, the most obvious example is that we have our own god of pleasure, Kama. Ayurveda views pleasure as an important component of wellbeing across the three body states. In all cases, 'pleasure' has a larger scope of meaning than is conveyed via contemporary usage.

The short story is that it's deeper: pleasure in a traditional regional Indian sense means more the spark of new life or new ideas, and the refined artistry of creative pursuits. The longer story is that, within the context of masala and the sensory body, pleasure is a necessary point of relief from complexity and contrast.

Acknowledging pleasure as part of our lives lends a permissiveness to the experience of consumption as a whole, just as grounding the idea of pleasure in philosophy and faith corsets it with a natural restraint. Permission and restraint are contrasts that co-exist in the Indian householder's ideal of a life well lived.

MASALA AND EMOTIONAL EATING

When I give masala masterclasses, women often start to discuss issues with feeling good around food. Many of these women want to find ways to handle emotional eating.

Emotional eating in this context is shorthand for bingeing or for bad habits. The way we see the things we put in our mouths as personal faults. For an Indian householder, however, there's an alternative way of looking at emotional eating that has its roots in Ayurveda.

Within Ayurveda, knowing how to eat emotionally is an indicator of wellbeing; it's understanding how to scaffold spice in order to build upon strength or de-escalate anxiety (see page 146). This perspective means that emotional eating ceases to be code for 'I have an issue with food' and instead becomes a starting point for understanding ourselves within our lives. And the great news is that the starting point is exactly where you are.

Say you're unhappy and so you reach for a beer and a bag of crisps, which is you responding to sadness by attempting to elevate your emotional state. That unconscious act shows understanding. You're reading your own play. The only issue is the actual choices you make – alcohol will transmute your state, and salty, crispy chips are an edible experience of breezy feeling, but neither will offer you anything more than temporary distraction from a state of being that's asking for deeper treatment. Just becoming aware of that – experiencing that internal conversation – is profound. You don't have to change your actions right away. But by ceasing to deny that eating *is* emotional, we open ourselves up to awareness and forgiveness of the patterns we'd like to shift. Breaking down denial means breaking down self-sabotage: it's harder for us to creep up on ourselves and trip ourselves up when we're willing to admit that we know and can see where we are.

Getting to this point means getting to know masala, which means getting familiar with identifying uncomplicated switches. For me, crispy, light and salty might mean golden-fried, crunchy gobi – cauliflower florets – tossed through a masala of amchur, fine pink salt, Kashmiri chilli powder, fennel seeds and a little turmeric powder in a pan of ghee. The alcohol has no replacement, other than that of understanding that feeling something is better than *not* feeling something: at least that way the emotion has more freedom to move through with less delay. But that's emotional eating, too. As with everything masala, the absence of produce or aromatics or (in this case) alcohol is also seen to have impact on our experience.

For every aromatic in this book, I discuss its emotive impact. Use these as starting points, if you like, for learning how to flip the paradigm – to eat emotionally, but to do it well.

FENNEL POWDER SAUNF

Category: Warm spices.
Form: Dense and soft powder.
Colour: Pastel khaki.

Culturally, fennel powder is a vital choral aromatic in the traditional Kashmiri Hindu kitchen. The taste of Kashmiri Hindu cooking is like that of the culture itself: regal, and dense with history (see From the mountains to the stars, opposite). On a day-to-day basis, the spicing is relatively simple: masala includes hing, cumin seeds, chilli powder or Kashmiri chilli powder, salt and perhaps turmeric powder. Fennel powder in the dabba is the vital addition of ballast and depth.

Kashmiri Hindu cooking is unique in that it almost always uses fennel and ginger powders together. Much like fats and salts, they have an impact on each other that magnifies the contributions of both.

Tasting notes

Fennel powder is relatively subtle aromatically – it's flatter than the vibrant and textural fennel seeds. The primary aroma is **Dutch licorice** with a back note of **dusty cumin**. A tertiary characteristic of **minced onion** lends fennel powder a quality of **recessed sulphur**.

Use in masala

Fennel powder creates depth and comfort in masala. Without the husk intact, the earthy licorice sweetness associated with fennel seeds falls back into a warmer and gentler soft aniseed quality that tucks itself into the depths of a dish. Its impact is discreet: in some ways, the full mouthfeel created by fennel powder is more apparent than its aromatic contribution.

Fennel powder is a bridge between earth and warm spices, which is why we're looking at it first here. As a taste, it's a little sweet and dark, like a warm Dutch licorice, but tamped down by the texture of the powder itself – all powdered aromatics contain a taste of soil, even if it's recessed (see below).

Emotive content

In the kitchens of my family, fennel powder is like a goodnight kiss on the forehead – it settles into masala like a blanket. This is not peculiar to us, but results from the aromatic's binding warmth.

Texture and its impact on taste

When we feel into the texture of powdered spice, we'll experience various textural references to grit, soil or dust and sometimes pollen. With cumin powder the soil connection is obvious. But even aromatics like cassia powder and mace powder will hold a recessed taste 'of the earth' simply because they are in powdered form. This is because the palate recognises soil-like textures as having soil-like tastes.

But it's not only powders that offer textural points of connection to the natural environment. Spices like cassia bark and cinnamon sticks have a wooded quality, in part derived from their point of origin. The hessian-like husky pod of both green and black cardamom can be tasted as a quality of dried straw.

The impact of nature on aroma opens a window into yet another perspective on taste. It can become a tool as we develop closer relationships to masala – a reference point that helps us identify aromatic qualities of individual spices more easily. It can also help us allocate function to spices when we're unsure of where they sit. Although I cover these aspects for each aromatic, it's nice to be introduced to the idea that our experience of nature makes each of us experts in understanding the character of spices.

FROM THE MOUNTAINS TO THE STARS

The world's changed a lot since my siblings and I were kids, and language with it. Dad was very proud to let us know that we were Kashmiri Brahmans. Thrice born, he would say, and already three turns around the Karmic wheel. Talk of the Brahmanic class harks to the caste system, now outlawed by the Indian government for good reason: caste for many years across India determined the scope of possibility of a human life. Brahmans like us were entitled to reach for the stars, but lower castes were held down and in place by cultural laws. We called ourselves Pandits, and that one word, like masala, tells the story of who we are to those who know the language. And yet one can't look away from the fact that a Pandit or Brahman is held in position by a fleet of humans clustered below in 'lesser' groupings.

I was in Delhi to see Mum in early 2023 when Shyam suggested I refer to our family as he does – Kashmiri Hindu. It tells the same story of us without the human scaffolding. I like that.

My Kashmiri Hindu story is from Dad's mouth – pieces of family history fed to me over the years like a child offered prized bites from a parent's thali. The Gamkhars, Ammi's family, were at one point scribes in Kashmir for the Persian royal family. Persia and Kashmir have a long history, which is reflected in the food: soft and complex spicing, and a great love of mutton and offal, combine to create the cuisine for which Kashmiri Hindus are famed.

But further back than Persia were the mountains, the Himalayas, and our family at the foothills. The Himalayas hold a special place in the imagination of Hindus as the abode of the gods. The river Ganga that flows from the Himalayas is where our parents and grandparents are returned – both Dad and Mum were given back to the river by my brothers and me after their deaths. Once returned they go on a different journey. Dad said we trace our lineage back to the Seven Rishi Saints, known now as the constellation Pleiades. That's where I look to say goodnight and to chat to them both when I'm feeling lonely for them. It's valuable family mythology for me: to be in relationship with ancient geography was a beautifully romantic notion to me as a girl, and it remains so now.

Just in these few paragraphs, a connection is condensed that folds back through generations of my people to the start of the world. Or at least that's how it's always felt. When I'm with my family, that strength is what I feel. And it's that cohesion that finds its way into our masalas.

Thool zamboor

A thrice-cooked egg sabji, thool zamboor is Kashmiri Hindu to its bootstraps and has become one of my favourites: rich, dark, warm, but also simply executed with minimal produce. This is one traditional recipe I never alter. It's already perfect.

Serves 6 as part of a shared meal

8 eggs

For deep-frying

2 cups (500 ml) vegetable oil
1 cup (250 ml) mustard oil

For the kari (sauce)

¼ cup (60 ml) mustard oil
1 teaspoon red chilli powder
2 tablespoons cold water
3 tomatoes, diced

Main masala

2 teaspoons fennel powder
1½ teaspoons fine pink salt
1 teaspoon ginger powder
1 teaspoon cardamom powder
½ teaspoon turmeric powder
2–3 pinches of hing (asafoetida) powder
6 cloves
4 black cardamom pods, husks cracked
3 dried bay leaves

Place the eggs in a medium saucepan, cover with cold water and bring to the boil. Boil the eggs for 7 minutes. Remove from the heat, drain the eggs and set aside to cool completely. Shell the cooled eggs, taking care not to tear them – the end result needs to taste and *look* delicious.

Heat the oils for deep-frying over high heat in a kadai, stable cast-iron wok or heavy-based saucepan large enough that the oils come up no more than halfway. Fry the eggs one or two at a time, turning them to make sure they blister and brown evenly. Drain on paper towel until cool enough to handle, then pierce each egg with a skewer all the way through about half a dozen times. This will allow the masala to penetrate.

For the kari or sauce, heat the mustard oil in a medium heavy-based frying pan over medium–high heat. Stir the red chilli powder into the cold water in a small bowl. When the mustard oil is hot, pour in the chilli water and stir through – take care, it will spatter. This creates a savoury fat base for the masala. Add the tomato to the pan and stir through for 2–3 minutes. The tomato should start to break down, providing a lush and dark filter for the masala, like a velvet curtain.

Add the main masala to the pan. Reduce the heat to medium and stir until the tomato has cooked, thickened and reduced, and the spices are rich and fragrant. (Fennel powder is integral in this stage – it's the bridge between earthiness, warmth and sweetness, creating coalescence between produce, masala and technique. It also contributes textural density, which is one of the key storytelling characters in this dish.) Simmer the masala over medium heat for 15–20 minutes, stirring frequently to ensure it doesn't stick and burn.

Add the deep-fried boiled eggs to the kari, reduce the heat to medium–low and stir for a further 15–20 minutes, until the masala forms a rich gravy on the outside of the eggs. Serve with chapatis and pickles.

GINGER POWDER
SAUNTH

Category: Warm spices.
Form: Heavy powder.
Colour: Sand through to golden tan.

Ginger powder is like cumin seeds and turmeric power in that you'll find it in every masala dabba, at least across the northern regions of India. But we know by now that with masala, ubiquity is an amplifier of aromatic importance.

In India's south, ginger plants bloom in the dry winter months. Some flowers are like a cluster of hanging toucan beaks. Others are torch-like. Others still look like a tight bud of flame. Ginger powder comes from the dried and ground rhizome of the plant. It's related to turmeric and has a cousinly character of recessed earth. But in masala the two perform vastly different roles. Where turmeric powder is structure and stabilising weight, ginger powder is an aromatic scout, driving the palate to look towards what's coming.

Cailean got hugely into mountain biking as a pre-teen, and so I took it up to keep us connected. I was never that good or that fast, but I *was* pretty scared of falling, and so I learned quickly that the art of not falling on fast downhill trails while navigating rocky terrain is to tilt the gaze just slightly forward – that way you can feel where you are on your seat and on your trail, and still see ahead to what immediately could throw you off your line or off your bike. Waking the palate and turning the sensory body to what lies just ahead is a key to digestive health – forward enough to keep the system moving, but not so far removed from what's occurring in the moment that we disconnect from its process.

Until this halfway point in the book, masala has been reliant on knowing where we are. But now it also needs to have an indication of where we're going – with taste and with intention. Ginger powder is the first of a series of spices that introduce this forward gaze.

Because ginger powder is a key spice in Kashmiri Hindu masala, it appears throughout this book. There is only one specifically ginger recipe (see page 168), but ginger also appears in the following recipes, where it performs these functions:

- **Turmeric chaaman** (page 45), where ginger powder tempered through water works with the fennel powder to square up and support the strident message of the dish
- **Matar khoya** (page 180), where ginger powder softens the impact of the combined mace powder and mace flowers by shading in the aromatic texture of softer warm spice.

Tasting notes
Ginger powder is a subtler and rounder spice than fresh ginger. **Wood** and **sand** are the strong primary notes, followed by **rose** and **oil**. There is a secondary **orange rind** quality and a fragrant tail of **fine white pepper**. But maybe what's most striking about ginger powder is how spicy it is – hot spicy. I always say that ginger powder

could technically be classified as a hot spice were it not for its function: unlike a chilli powder, which lengthens aroma by virtue of its upward draft (see page 206), ginger powder retains that round, front-palate-filling quality of all warm spices.

Use in masala

Ginger powder functions in masala primarily as a moderator or amplifier of style and intensity of heat. Hot spices (page 206) are about creating height as much as heat, but it's ginger powder that determines in large part the *texture* of heat within masala. Add it to a masala containing fresh red chilli and black pepper, and a heat that would otherwise be two-pronged, direct and aggressive becomes single, dispersed and resonant – less 'punch in the face' and more 'built to height over time'. Use it in masala with fresh chilli, and it will give that bright-light heat a subtle coat of dust.

Emotive content

Ginger powder has the most get up and go of the warm spices. It's a practical kick up the backside when a practical kick up the backside is needed.

Traditional medicinal impact

Ginger powder has been used in Ayurveda to treat nausea, migraines and motion sickness, and to stoke *agni*, the digestive fire. It's believed to destroy *ama*, or toxins.

'It's a practical kick up the backside when a practical kick up the backside is needed.'

Gajar matar sabji

Gajar matar in the Ganju family style is earthy, warm and just a little sweet. It's all the best tastes of childhood – with a hitch: ginger powder. Ginger powder is included in this sabji as awareness of maturity: it propels the cosy child in us forward into the world (see page 170). The Indian householder uses a spice like this in a sabji to introduce young palates to increasingly adult tastes.

Serves 4 as part of a shared meal

- 2 tomatoes, roughly chopped
- 3 carrots, peeled and finely diced
- 2 cups (300 g) fresh or frozen peas, blanched

Masala

- 2 tablespoons ghee
- 3 teaspoons coriander powder
- 2 teaspoons cumin seeds
- 1 teaspoon fine pink salt
- 1 teaspoon ginger powder
- ½ teaspoon Kashmiri chilli powder
- scant ½ teaspoon turmeric powder
- 3 cloves
- 3 cm (1¼ inch) piece of jaggery

To finish (optional)

- ½–1 cup (125–250 ml) whey

Combine all the masala ingredients in a large frying pan over medium–low heat. Once the ghee is melted and bubbling and the spices are aromatic, remove from the heat and add the tomato. (Taking it off the heat ensures the masala won't burn when the sizzle of fresh tomato hits the pan.)

Return the pan to medium–low heat and cook for as long as it takes for the ghee to split and the tomato to break down a little, 10–15 minutes. (Taste the masala: it will be warm and delicious and a little sweet from the jaggery, but the ginger powder will combine with the Kashmiri chilli powder to propel the palate gaze forward and provide a bit of adult sizzle.)

Add the carrot and peas and cook for a further 10 minutes or so. Once the carrot has softened a little, add the whey if you have any. The whey allows us to simmer the gajar matar over low heat for 45–60 minutes, creating a masala that is simultaneously rich and nurturing.

If you don't have whey, add water or vegetable stock instead and keep cooking over low heat until the carrot has completely softened and the vegetables have taken in the ghee, tomato and masala and then let go of the excess. This process takes 25–30 minutes.

Working with whey

There's little that's traditional about using whey in masala. I started reserving it to cook back down into my paneer (see Matar paneer, page 230) and I've gradually expanded its use to other dishes (see page 276). Whey is also delicious with chicken stock in a chicken noodle soup.

Whey brings a lot to the table. It has protein, soft acidity and a subtle dairy imprint. When a single ingredient has multiple facets, it's an instant asset in making masala. When you don't have whey handy, a 50:50 mixture of water and yoghurt makes a good replacement. Watered-down buttermilk can work, too.

How children understand taste

Lots of parents have lamented to me that their kids won't eat spices. One woman told me how disappointed she was that, while at daycare, her preschool daughter would eat anything and everything, but once she got home she reverted to being the least adventurous eater possible.

A young child can be very brave out in the world. And for many kids it does take bravery to walk out of the home and into different care settings. In that new setting, if they are comfortable enough, it makes sense to the child to be open to new things – new tastes, exotic ingredients, different food preparations. In fact it's logical: if you're somewhere different, being someone different, then eating something different is cohesive. But when our children walk back in their front doors, they're not different people any more. And after a long day of bravery, the simplicity of non-adventure feels restorative. They don't to want to hop on the 'new and exciting' train again. They want nursery food.

That mother and I did talk a little about how to satisfy her daughter's need for an emotional security blanket of a dinner while also fulfilling her own adult desire not to feel trapped in an unimaginative kitchen space. For an Indian householder, the energy goes both ways; in order to keep giving out we have to feel at some point that our needs are also being catered for, even if that's as simple as not having to cook steamed broccoli and potatoes every night. A sabji like gajar matar (page 168) is a nice halfway point – vegetables that are very familiar, with spicing that's subtle and soft.

Obviously, a child raised in a culinarily Western household might find a masala like this too much. But take the idea and play around with it: use familiar ingredients that your family loves for their simplicity, and trick them up just a bit with elements of spice that entice young palates to explore.

CINNAMON POWDER
DALCHINI

Category: Warm spices.
Form: Very fine powder.
Colour: Dusty clay.

Cinnamon powder is the chameleon of this category. Depending on how it's used, and with what, it can present as either woody and 'masculine' or warm and 'feminine'. (Gender tropes can allow us to draw an immediate and detailed aromatic picture.)

In a traditional regional Kashmiri Hindu context, cinnamon powder contributes savoury warmth. It's quite straightforward – cohesive but strong. Its texture means it disperses differently to its warm spice companions – ginger, cassia, mace powders and so on – which are generally dense and weighted. Perhaps contrarily, the lightness of cinnamon powder makes it more pervasive.

When shopping for cinnamon powder in chain supermarkets, make sure the label says 'true cinnamon', otherwise you might be buying cassia powder – its cousin spice with radically different aromatic impact, as you will see opposite. Cinnamon powder is a common ingredient in Kashmiri Hindu masala, so apart from the recipe on page 172, it also appears in:

- **Simple aloo gosht** (page 67), where cinnamon powder provides the warmth of family
- **Matar paneer** (page 230), where cinnamon powder acts as a scaffold for cinnamon sticks, impregnating the masala with deep and wooded warmth, without the shadow brought by pungent–warm aromatics such as clove. And even when it doesn't appear in a Kashmiri Hindu recipe, adding about half a teaspoon will contribute seamless elegance.

Tasting notes
Tasted raw, cinnamon powder surprises because it's subtler than expected. It has a **tight** and **woody** aromatic quality that precedes its **sweetness** and **warmth**. Aromatically **restrained**, its character is released through tempering. Cinnamon powder's tertiary element is a **tree trunk height** through the mid-palate, like a long-lost memory that harks back to its time as a stick.

Use in masala
Cinnamon powder is a classic inclusion in so many regional Indian masalas. The way it's used – alongside ginger and fennel powders in Kashmiri Hindu cooking, with black pepper and fresh ginger as we head further south, or with red chilli powder in the central deserts – gives masala regional context.
As an aromatic it's very tight. Without heat or fat and consumed on its own, cinnamon powder is a little difficult to get to. Even in powdered form, it retains the tightly whorled element of its stick or quill, with tastes that circle in on themselves. It's this very restraint that allows cinnamon powder to express such clearly different messages in different regions. Its every facet can be experienced with clarity.

Emotive content
Elegant restraint. Cinnamon powder is a reminder that we can be warm and caring without losing track of our personal boundaries and our own needs.

Traditional medicinal impact
In Ayurveda, cinnamon powder is seen as a warming spice that improves respiratory conditions, disperses bodily cold and generates *prana*, or life energy.

Delineating cinnamon from cassia
Cinnamon powder is relatively structural, lending masala an elegant turn of phrase. It contributes a queenly notion of nurture, comfort and maternal care. It adds a dryness to hot spices and exposes the texture of earth aromatics.

Cassia powder is all round front-palate weight, and gives masala a blousy appearance, contributing a sensual earth-mother vibe. It lends humidity to hot spices and softens any brackishness in earth spices.

Ashok's marron masala

The texture of restraint is what makes cinnamon powder and marron a match. Building this masala around cinnamon powder ensures a tight flavour corset for a delicate seafood within a beautifully stitched fabric of spice. 'Loose-hanging' flavour would enunciate the undesirable, recessed elements of the marron – a flaccid, bottom-of-the-river, muddy quality.

Ash sat with me at the kitchen bench and pulled this masala together. He knew we wanted cinnamon powder to star, so he combined it with other powdered spices to ensure there were no distracting textures. The coriander powder is a nice touch – it has that hint of lemon that seafood loves.

If you're using langoustine, the masala will need a quarter of a teaspoon of cassia powder for extra sweetness. Lobster or crayfish are less delicate seafoods that need a stronger masala; they can cope with the addition of a cinnamon stick and a small piece of cassia bark.

Though mustard oil is strong, the density and richness of the crustacean tails, and the nature of cinnamon powder, call for a stronger fat: mustard oil gives the flesh the appearance of more structure, and cinnamon powder a slightly hotter and harder character. Together these changes ensure the dish has distinct shape.

Serves 2–4

3–4 marron or langoustine tails or 2 lobster or crayfish tails

Masala

- 1 tablespoon mustard oil
- 2 teaspoons coriander powder
- 1½ teaspoons fennel powder
- 1 teaspoon fleur de sel
- 1 teaspoon fine pink salt
- scant ½ teaspoon Kashmiri chilli powder
- scant ½ teaspoon turmeric powder
- 1 cassia stick

To finish

- 135 ml (4½ fl oz) coconut cream

If your crustacean tails are still in their shells, they will need blanching. Fill a bowl with ice and place it beside the stovetop. Bring a large pot of heavily salted water to a rolling boil over medium–high heat then add the tails. Blanch for 20–30 seconds (for smaller marron or langoustine) or 45–60 seconds (for larger crayfish or lobster). Remove the tails from the water and plunge them straight into the ice to stop them cooking. While the tails are still wet, cut them open with kitchen scissors – front and back – and gently remove the shell by pulling it away from the flesh. Blanching frees up the thin membrane between the shell and the flesh. I then cut the tails into medallions so that they cook through.

To prepare the masala, heat the mustard oil in a large frying pan over medium–low heat. Add all masala spices and stir through. (Taste at this point and you'll see how much wooded, warm strength is expressed, with a pleasing tail of heat.)

Add the crustacean chunks and cook over medium–low heat for 2–3 minutes, until not quite cooked. Add the coconut cream, then cook for 2–3 minutes more, until the tail meat is cooked through. Serve immediately with basmati rice and a light salad.

CASSIA POWDER
JANGLI DALCHINI

Category: Warm spices.
Form: Dense powder that's a little oily to the touch.
Colour: Rich clay.

Cassia powder is rich, a sultan of spice. It tastes like cinnamon sugar, but throw it into masala and suddenly that sweetness becomes sultry humidity. Luxurious, yes, but there's also hot steel beneath the silk.

In the interest of creating warm density, I will often use cassia and cinnamon powders together. In combination, they offer more than the sum of their parts – an intensified 'cinnamon' flavour that can't be achieved through using only cinnamon or cassia on its own.

As we saw on page 170, cassia powder and cinnamon powder are close cousins, and so supermarkets often sell cassia powder labelled as cinnamon.

Tasting notes
Cassia powder is distinctly sweeter and more robust than cinnamon powder. It really is like eating **cinnamon sugar**, though with overtones of **wet cedar** (that's the humidity) and a tail of **honeyed chilli**. It's worth keeping in mind that – like cinnamon – it has **recessed bitterness** that stands out when added in excess to masala.

Use in masala
Cassia powder is a heavier warm aromatic, and so can help to 'hold down' prettier spice, making it appear bolder. It can also be used to create humidity in heat, which goes a long way to telling the story of India's tropical southern states.

Emotive content
Sultry heat. Cassia powder speaks of date-night excitement at a relationship's beginning and the frisson of the unknown. When things get scary through change, cooking with cassia powder can remind us that – at some point in our lives – the unknown was thrilling.

A hand-to-mouth experience
Touch. Hands. Food. These are vital components of masala. Eating with our hands creates links to aroma and to consumption. The experience of touching tells us things about texture, and whether or not a dish is familiar or unfamiliar. In a very literal way, it connects us to the person whose masala we're eating – just as you might touch an ancient wall in Rome and marvel at bridging the time between you and the one who built it.

Kaddu

Dad made this sabji for Ash all the time when he was a toddler. By the time Ash was born, Dad was working less and had driven his energy into the kitchen. He found joy there, and a relationship to masala focused on finding new ways to show nurture. The dishes he'd cooked for us as a dad still appeared in the food he brought to me, Scott and the boys once a week, but kaddu was a dish for his *baba* or grandfather phase.

In true Kashmiri Hindu style, Dad's kaddu is complex and 'adult'. The cassia powder, cinnamon stick and Kashmiri chilli powder combine to create resonant heat. Whenever Ash ate this dish, he'd cry two ways – first because the masala was a lot for his little palate, and then when I'd move to take it away. An emotional warrior, our Ash. Love him.

Serves 4 as part of a shared meal

- 2 tablespoons ghee
- 1½ teaspoons fine white sea salt
- 1 teaspoon cumin powder
- ½ teaspoon turmeric powder
- ½ teaspoon cassia powder
- scant ½ teaspoon Kashmiri chilli powder
- 1 mace flower
- ½ cinnamon stick
- 500 g (1 lb 2 oz) pumpkin (winter squash), cut into 2 cm (¾ inch) cubes
- ½ lime (optional), to finish

Heat the ghee in a large kadai or cast-iron wok over high heat. As the ghee is warming, add all of the spices at once and stir them through.

Before the masala reaches the point where it looks like it might burn, add the pumpkin. Toss it through the masala to coat, then spread the cubes evenly, in one layer if possible. Cook until the pumpkin browns on one side, taking care not to move it too much. Turn carefully and cook as before until the pumpkin is completely browned on all sides and cooked through. The entire dish should take no more than 20 minutes from start to finish.

Serve with a squeeze of lime juice, if you like, alongside dal, rice and your meat curry of choice; as a side with grilled fish; or to spice up a poached chicken summer salad.

Masala and the texture of cultural wisdom

In Kashmiri Hindu culture, spices like mace flower, cinnamon sticks and cassia powder – though undeniably warming and maternal – are used for their secondary and tertiary qualities. These are the textures we get to know through repeated usage.

Mace flower is strongly reminiscent of nutmeg (not surprising, given it is derived from the waxy covering of the nutmeg kernel), and has latent qualities of orange rind and saddle – leathery qualities with a flat pungency. Cinnamon sticks, though warm, have an empty wooded authority: straight, tall and a little dispassionate. Cassia powder, while ostentatiously aromatic, is simultaneously ambitious: it has a strong internal stamp of heat.

Working from these deeper characters creates a masala grounded in a deliberate authority. This is how a dish so redolent of warmth also expresses complexity and strength.

MACE POWDER
JAVITRI

Category: Warm spices.
Form: The weightiest powder of all the warm spices.
Colour: Apricot.

If cassia powder is the steel beneath the silk, then mace powder is the anvil of warm aromatics – bold, beautiful, weighted. Ground from the dried 'flower' – in truth a waxy coat (aril) that embraces the nutmeg kernel – its taste profile is floral but with that pungent, hot, deeply shadowed quality of its sister, nutmeg powder. Unlike nutmeg powder, mace powder has an undeniable prettiness. It's an unusual spice to see in Western kitchens, but it's a hallmark taste of Kashmiri Hindu cuisine. We commonly use both whole and ground forms, but rarely, if ever, in the same masala. Mace is too discernible to be scaffolded, except when it comes to Matar khoya (page 180).

Eaten raw, mace powder will numb the tongue, betraying its anaesthetic quality. Texturally, it has a quality of saddle leather.

Tasting notes

Mace powder packs a punch. Primary characters are **saddle leather** and **orange rind**, chased by a secondary **stripe of mint**. Its tertiary character offers an anaesthetic quality that faintly **numbs** the tongue.

Use in masala

Using mace powder means working with a warm spice corset – its inherent astringent, citric and leathery overtones create a front-palate 'waist' for masala. It's a concise aromatic counterpoint to blousier warm spices.

Emotive content

The astringent quality of mace powder contracts our attention inward. The warmth it instigates is an emotion we have the strength to direct back towards ourselves.

Mornay sauce

Mornay sauce is a béchamel sauce with added cheese. Mum taught me how to make it. She was famous for her cauliflower cheese, and the sauce was key. It was one of the first dishes that taught me about kitchen alchemy – the way that butter and flour create a roux that's then transformed through the addition of milk and cheese into a creamy, cheesy delight. The alchemy of the Indian householder generally occurs out of sight, as it were, contained within the invisible aromatic body of masala. Seeing the roux come together was something else: I still love the feeling of accomplishment its creation brings. Small pleasures.

Seasoning for a mornay is relatively light. Salt and pepper. Nutmeg is a classic, but I prefer mace powder – it has the not-so-subtle astringency of freshly grated nutmeg but it's brighter, floral. If you have your own recipe or go-to technique for béchamel that you love, just add a quarter of a teaspoon of mace powder to a quantity of béchamel that you would make to feed an average family of four. If you double the recipe, don't double the mace powder but instead aim for around one and a half times.

This is a broad-brushstrokes recipe. If you need more, the internet is awash with tips for making this French classic.

Makes 1½ cups (375 ml)

- 2 tablespoons butter
- 3 tablespoons plain (all-purpose) flour
- 1 cup (250 ml) milk, plus extra to taste
- ½–1 cup (50–100 g) grated sharp cheese (I use mixed cheddar, pecorino and parmesan)
- ground black pepper, to taste
- ¼ teaspoon mace powder
- fleur de sel (optional), to taste

Melt the butter in a medium saucepan over medium heat. When it begins to bubble, stir in the flour, a little at a time to ensure there are no lumps. When the flour is evenly incorporated and the mixture is bubbling, gradually whisk in the milk, a little at a time, whisking well after each addition to ensure minimal lumps.

Stir over medium heat until the sauce begins to bubble and thicken. Once it has the consistency of a slightly gluey paste, whisk in the cheese. Season with the pepper and mace powder, taste, *then* add the salt. Cheese has a pretty high salt content, which the black pepper and the mace powder will draw forward. If it's feeling a little underdone at the end, turn up the volume with fleur de sel.

Matar khoya

Khoya is condensed milk solids made by boiling down milk, so it's an intense process. We didn't eat it growing up because we couldn't source it in Australia back then. But by the time Cailean and Ash were born, Indians had become more commonplace even in regional Australia. Dad found fresh khoya at the Indian grocer he favoured in Werribee, an urban outpost between Melbourne and Geelong. And because Dad found khoya, he made us matar khoya. Dad and I had a difficult relationship back then, but no matter what was going on between us, I always ate that dish with relish. It was sweet, but savoury with masala.

To test this recipe I made my own khoya, chiefly because it hasn't yet found its way to Margaret River as a grocery item, and I've provided the recipe on page 110 if you'd like to try it yourself. Without mace powder, I find khoya too rich, too sweet. This is the one recipe where I scaffold mace – the raw density of khoya itself can handle the intensity of both forms of mace at once, and together they provide texture.

Note: See the QR code on page 300 for a video of making khoya. You could cook this dish in a kadai rather than a frying pan, but the masala and khoya will show a square edge. Also watch the heat, as a kadai works at a drier intensity than a frying pan.

Serves 4–6 as part of a shared meal

300 g (10½ oz) Khoya (page 110)
1 cup fresh or frozen peas, blanched

Initial masala

1–2 tablespoons ghee
pinch of hing (asafoetida) powder
3 cloves
1 mace flower

Main masala

1 tablespoon mustard oil
2 teaspoons fennel powder
1 teaspoon fine pink salt
1 teaspoon Kashmiri chilli powder
1 teaspoon ginger powder
½ teaspoon mace powder
½ teaspoon cinnamon powder
½ teaspoon cumin powder

Heat the ghee in a large frying pan (see note) over medium heat until melted. Add the initial masala spices, reduce the heat to medium–low and stir until aromatic, 2–3 minutes.

Reduce the heat to low, add the khoya and stir it through, using a wooden spoon to break it up. Cook until the khoya absorbs the ghee and spices, then softens and expels its own liquid, 10–15 minutes.

Once the ghee splits a little, add all the main masala ingredients and stir them through thoroughly, using the wooden spoon. (The mustard oil introduces fat through which the masala can be expressed, along with aromatic texture.) Continue cooking over low heat for a further 20–30 minutes, stirring constantly, or until the mustard oil has been absorbed and expelled by the khoya.

Serve with flaky paratha and Bhavna's mum's winter carrot pickles (page 100) for a decadent lunch.

SECOND-TIER WARM SPICES

These are the warm aromatics that exist – for the most part – outside my centrally used dabbas. This is particularly true of nutmeg and clove powder, which I rarely add to my Kashmiri Hindu family dishes. The order here is deliberate, from most to least used.

ANISEED POWDER

Just as side-by-side raw tastings indicate the difference between aniseed and fennel seeds, the same can be said of aniseed and fennel seed powders. The differences are a little less obvious when the aromatics are in powdered form, however. Aniseed powder is ostensibly the darker of the two. In masala, it has a deeper anchor and a downward warmth. When used to replace fennel powder, it will shift the overall tone from 'domestic' towards 'regal'. Clearly I like my Ganju recipes friendlier, so I won't say they're interchangeable. But I will say that aniseed and fennel powders are perhaps the most closely aligned of any two individual spices.

CARDAMOM POWDER ELAICHI

I barely use cardamom powder – sometimes just as a last-minute accent to create a bit of extra textural warmth in a dish I fear might be heading towards bitter or overly pungent. Cardamom powder is the most ephemeral of the warm spices – if added at the beginning of cooking it fades out. And yet more than half a teaspoon in any masala becomes unpleasant. Across the Indian regions, elaichi is typically used in desserts, or with extreme subtlety in savoury dishes. If you want to try it in a Western dessert, add half a teaspoon to an eight-egg pavlova (page 222) when you fold in the cornflour (cornstarch), rosewater and vinegar. It will intensify the textural richness of the meringue.

NUTMEG POWDER JAIPHAL AND CLOVE POWDER LAUNG

I'm breaking my own rules here and putting two very different spices in the same descriptive basket – but for good reason. I use neither of these spices as individual aromatics in Kashmiri Hindu cooking, and never in Indian sabji. I find that these pungent spices are better used in their whole form, which provides a natural container – seed, bark, flower or pod – for pungent aroma (see below). In their powdered form they become too pervasive.

What we mean by pungent

Pungent is like umami. It's a word used in cooking by people who know what it means, but for everyone else it seems like a meaningless catchall. 'Pungency' is one of Ayurveda's six tastes or *rasas*, along with sweet, salty, bitter, astringent and sour. We've spoken a lot about whole taste, whole experience, whole caregiving for ourselves and others. Without pungent tastes, there's a hole in the whole. And what we miss is the dry and hot intensity that this bracket of taste brings.

Emotively, pungent taste is important because it plays into the expression of strong experience. Human nature makes it difficult to see the benefit of difficult experience when we're in the midst of it. Pungent aromatics don't *explain* anything, but they do mean we can embroider their difficult tastes through masala in order to present those feelings as a reality.

ACIDIC SPICES

Function in masala: Providing the frisson that focuses the attention of the palate on the eating experience.
Emotive quality: Electrifying and stimulating high-tone sensory body feeling.

There is a simplicity to acidity that's made it a challenging category to write after the complexity of earth and warm spices – masala sees magnetic interplay between these two, encapsulating familiarity and family, stability and storytelling. Writing about earth and warm spices is like writing about love, which has made it an exacting task.

And then comes acidity.

Acidic spice is the frisson. The lightning strike. It's the taste that alerts us. While hot spices stimulate, and salts drive, acids electrify. They are independence. The 'i' in team. Acidic aromatics pucker the palate – drawing focus in but not inward. More than semantics, this phrasing tells how acidity is sharp and not ponderous. It is concise because it acts on its own: aromatically, acidic spice doesn't integrate so much as delineate.

Spice like this has to be handled cautiously. Zeroing in on acidity too early alters the course of masala, at least in Kashmiri Hindu cooking. In the right context, acidic spices light it up. But in the wrong context their impact is too great, breaking down the community of aroma that masala requires to tell its story.

TAMARIND
IMLI

Category: Acidic spices.
Form: The pulp of a fruit pod either in a block or processed into a syrupy concentrate.
Colour: In block form, glossy brown. As a concentrate, almost black.

My first experience of tamarind was eating the fruits fresh from the trees in the jungle at my Bengaluru high school. It was a Krishnamurti school – an anti-institution that purported to raise students without rules and with free minds. Of course, we just took our free minds and walked right out of chemistry and into the hundred acres of treed grounds. The tamarinds were as sweetly tart as our daily taste of rebellion.

Tamarind is unique as an aromatic in that it's a fresh spice that works in the way of a dried aromatic. Wet spice is generally divisive: it splits masala, whereas dried spice tends to work more cohesively, even if that cohesion is used to achieve contrast or dissonance. Tamarind is unique because its pulpy nature mimics the density of dried spices: its fibres draw the acidic structure of the fruit tight and inwards. Taste fresh tamarind then take a lick of fresh lime and you'll instantly experience what I mean.

There are two common forms of tamarind – the fruit pulp compressed into a block, or a concentrate. The recipes that follow will help you to understand the impact and function of each.

Tasting notes

Tamarind has a strong primary character of **sour grass**. The pulp has tertiary characters of **wood** and **husk**. As a concentrate, its **sweet** and **high acidic notes** push forward, before being toned down by a tail of **tamarind fruit**.

Use in masala

In traditional regional Indian cooking, tamarind lends beauty and texture to sabjis requiring a tart bite. Tamarind adds a striking element to South-East Asian noodle dishes; works as a meat tenderiser in marinades; and gives an extra zing to chutneys. In Kashmiri Hindu cooking specifically, tamarind creates a sassy right-angle contrast to the dense weight of fennel powder, ginger powder and Kashmiri garam masala.

Emotive content

Just like the joy of those high-school walks in the jungle that spoke of independent decision-making, tamarind is a youthful taste of illicit independence. It creates a freedom and brightness that leavens masala's weight without serious disruptive consequences.

Masala: hyper regional and hyper personal

One of the commonalities of masala across all regions is that when it comes down to it, most of us only know the dishes we know – the ones that were served at our family tables and celebrations, cooked by (normally) mothers, grandmothers and aunties. The scope of regional Indian food is largely misunderstood – it's exponentially more diverse than korma, vindaloo and jalfrezi – and so I can't possibly know it all. Even as it relates to Kashmiri Hindu cuisine, my breadth of knowledge is limited. Of course, the beauty of limited knowledge is that it allows for continual learning.

Tamarind eggplant

I never knew tamarind was an ingredient in Kashmiri Hindu masala until I discovered this dish. Somehow I imagined that so far north, neither the fruit nor the spice would be accessible. But in the cookbook I have that was written by an aunt, more than one recipe finds its aromatic axis in tamarind pulp, this sabji included.

This recipe uses the tamarind most commonly bought in blocks – it's fibrous, with a textured sourness. The density and subtlety of its acidity means it feeds into the masala and takes the tone higher without corroding its structure.

Serves 4–6 as part of a shared meal

2 cups (500 ml) vegetable oil
⅓ cup (80 ml) mustard oil
500 g (1 lb 2 oz) eggplants (aubergines), cut into thin batons

First stage

¼ cup (60 ml) mustard oil
1 teaspoon Kashmiri chilli powder
1 tablespoon cold water

Main masala

2 tablespoons tamarind paste
1 tablespoon finely grated fresh ginger
2 teaspoons fennel powder
1 teaspoon ginger powder
scant 1 teaspoon fine white sea salt
scant ½ teaspoon hing (asafoetida) powder
scant ½ teaspoon kala namak
2 fresh red chillies, halved lengthways

Final touch

1 cup (250 ml) cold water

Start by deep-frying the eggplant. Heat the vegetable and mustard oils over high heat in a kadai, stable cast-iron wok or heavy-based saucepan large enough that the oils come up no more than halfway. (Using the two oils creates instant texture right at the beginning of the dish.) Fry the eggplant strips in small batches until well browned and softened. Drain on paper towel and set aside.

To begin the first stage of cooking, heat the mustard oil in a medium heavy-based saucepan or pot (I use a Le Creuset casserole) over medium–high heat. While the oil is heating, stir the Kashmiri chilli powder into the water. Add the chilli water to the hot oil and stir through for 1–2 minutes, taking care to avoid the spatter. If you taste it now, you'll experience a tiered heat through the oil and water.

While the chilli water and oil are still sizzling, add the fried eggplant. Stir through for 1–2 minutes, until the eggplant starts to soften and leach out its oil. Once you see the oil building and becoming richer, add the main masala. Stir through for 5 minutes, until the eggplant reduces further and begins to break down into the masala.

Add the cold water and stir over medium–high heat until the eggplant has completely broken down and thickened, and the water has evaporated, about 15 minutes. Reduce the heat if the eggplant begins to stick to the pan.

I love how the fibrous acidity of tamarind paste is a textural match for the eggplant when cooked in this way. The end result will be rich, oily and satisfying. Serve with Simple aloo gosht (page 67), Simple yellow dal (page 39), basmati rice and Mum's tangy raita (page 229).

Imli chutney

In a recipe like this, the benefit of working with tamarind concentrate is twofold. Texturally, the concentrate is easier to work with in a dish that's liquid. And aromatically, its sharp acidity chimes with the street-food vibe of this chutney. This is the only recipe in the book that uses acidic spices in such high volume – the vinegar, sumac and amchur are there to push the tamarind concentrate forward and add acidic texture that's grounded in the cumin powder and dispersed through the volume of oil. It's not an approach that would work with a sabji, but condiments and pickles in the regional Indian tradition operate from a different subset of rules.

Makes about 200 ml (7 fl oz) or enough for 12 samosas

⅓ cup (80 ml) peanut oil

¼ cup (60 ml) tomato paste (concentrated purée)

Main masala

¼ cup (60 ml) sweet rice vinegar

1 teaspoon fine white salt

1 teaspoon amchur

1 teaspoon sumac

½ teaspoon ground cumin

scant ½ teaspoon hot ground chilli powder

scant ½ teaspoon Kashmiri chilli powder

1 teaspoon tamarind concentrate

2 pinches of jaggery powder

Combine the peanut oil and tomato paste in a small saucepan over medium heat and whisk together until the oil splits the tomato and the tomato begins to turn a richer, darker red, about 5 minutes. (This step is about creating a body with enough integrity to hold onto the volume of acidic spice in this dish.)

Add the sweet rice vinegar and all of the spices except the tamarind concentrate and jaggery powder. Continue whisking until the sauce thickens, 3–4 minutes. You might need to reduce the heat a little so it doesn't keep splitting.

Once the sauce is thickened and cohesive, add the tamarind concentrate and jaggery powder. Whisk them through and taste to ensure the balance is right for you. You can add a little more salt, chilli powder, jaggery or tamarind concentrate, depending on how you feel the masala has progressed. Once it's to your taste, remove from the heat and continue to whisk as the sauce cools, to ensure it comes together effectively.

Turn out into a cool bowl and serve with samosas.

AMCHUR & SUMAC

Category: Acidic spices.
Form: Amchur is a dried powder with a dense texture akin to partially wet sand. Sumac is a granular dried and ground spice.
Colour: Amchur is a soft and sandy khaki. Sumac is a dark berry–grape purple.

It's unusual to combine the explanations for two spices with different cultural origins and different aromatic profiles. But they are united by their functionality.

Amchur is made from green mangoes, dried and powdered. Sumac is made from berries, dried and powdered. Amchur finds its home in regional Indian cooking traditions. Sumac commonly belongs to the food of the regions across the Middle East. Sumac is the emo – it's a little dark, and salty and brooding. Amchur is gentler and happier. But both have a soft and textured acidity that is subtler than tamarind (page 184). And both work upon masala in the same way: functionally, powdered acidic spices bring subtle shape.

This effect comes from the way these powdered acidic spices stimulate the inner cheeks – like a fingertip touch to a Venus flytrap, the palate contracts without the strong pucker created by fresh tamarind, lemons or limes.

A key quality of both amchur and sumac is persistence – both maintain character no matter the cooking heat and time.

Tasting notes

Amchur is the definition of an unusually delicious acid. It's unusual because its sour notes are so pretty. Amchur's aromatic body is redolent of **sweet lime** and **sherbert**. It has secondary notes of **flat cola**, and a very subtle herbaceous quality akin to **coriander seeds**. Amchur exhibits a **soft acidity**.

Sumac's granular texture creates a tactile acidity. You can taste it *and* feel it. The initial gritty experience gives way to **coriander powder**, **cardamom** and **sweet lime**. It has a secondary character of **salt** that gets less subtle the more familiar I become with the spice.

Use in masala

Amchur pops up in a few traditional contexts: as an addition to Fresh nimbu soda (nimbu pani, page 75), and as the spice to provide tang and accelerate kala namak's sulphurous quality in chaat masala. Outside of traditions, amchur is a sassy foot-skip of acidity in dishes where an inherent prettiness can be undone by overly rich tastes.

Sumac is useful in situations when acidic texture is required.

Emotive content

Finding a degree of autonomy within a large Indian family is challenging, particularly as a daughter. I presume the same must be true of many traditional cultures where the idea of community cohesion is built into every aspect of life *and* identity. The individuation represented by acidity pertains to more than just masala. Like most information about spice, it doesn't take much to shift the concept from kitchen instruction to allegory. At some point, I was the vinegar inside the Ganju family masala: for whatever reason, my need to be seen as I was meant to be became a sharp disruption to those to whom I was closest. Amchur is more the individuation that comes with age. Or if not age, then at least the softness of experience.

Emotively, of all the aromatics within this category, sumac is the shadiest, with that profile of salt, and its beneath-the-bramble coarse texture.

Three ways with acidity as seasoning

Thinking of sumac and amchur as salt-and-pepper-style seasonings opens up a world of easy flavour. Try using either (or both) when making spiced roasted nuts or when prepping roasted cauliflower to toss through a salad of butter lettuce, peas and fresh ricotta. I do the same for roast lamb. In each case, use the following masala. There are no quantities. Use your fingers to pinch and scatter.

For the masala, try a little fine pink salt and fleur de sel, combined with turmeric powder and perhaps fennel seeds. I like Kashmiri chilli powder for subtle floral heat, and one or two peppers – maybe fine white and cracked black – with sumac or amchur or both. If you're doing spiced nuts, I'm all for a little honey as well. In all cases I use olive oil as the carrier. Although it's not a match with traditional regional masalas, in this case it does the job of deconstructing some of the cultural messaging, allowing these dishes to appear as being 'seasoned' rather than as pseudo curries.

Fish kebabs

Sumac or amchur with fish kebabs is about working with acidic aromatics that can be used to give seafood a sour texture. Sour texture is quite different from acidic taste. It's more subtle – powdered sour spices won't cure seafood proteins the way fresh acids do, so you get the benefit of acidic spice – the aromatic waist, and the brightness – without cooking the flesh.

Serves 2 as a meal, 4 as a snack

For poaching the fish

- 250 g (9 oz) semi-firm, white-fleshed fish
- ⅓ cup (80 ml) milk
- ⅓ cup (80 ml) water
- ½ teaspoon fenugreek powder
- ½ teaspoon fine white salt
- ½ teaspoon ground red chilli
- 2 cassia sticks

Main masala

- 1 tablespoon mustard oil
- 2 teaspoons finely grated fresh turmeric
- 1 teaspoon sumac or amchur
- ½ teaspoon fine white sea salt
- ½ teaspoon cracked black pepper
- ½ teaspoon cayenne pepper
- scant ½ teaspoon kala namak
- 1 small handful of fresh coriander (cilantro), chopped
- 1 egg, lightly whisked
- ½ small white onion, finely diced
- ½ cup (80 g) rice flour

For deep-frying

- 1 cup (250 ml) vegetable oil
- ½ cup (125 ml) mustard oil

Combine the fish with the other poaching ingredients in a medium saucepan over medium–low heat and poach gently for about 8 minutes, until slightly undercooked. Poaching the fish and spices in milk softens the aromatic input.

Remove from the heat and carefully lift the fish out of the liquid and spices and into a medium bowl.

Add all the main masala ingredients except the rice flour. Stir in the rice flour a little at a time, breaking up the fish, until the mixture holds a firm shape when rolled. Roll pieces of the mixture into golf ball-sized kebabs. Pop any remaining rice flour in a separate bowl and use it to lightly coat the kebabs.

Heat the vegetable and mustard oils until hot but not smoking in a kadai, stable cast-iron wok or heavy-based saucepan large enough that the oils come up no more than halfway.

Fry the kebabs in small batches, turning them with a metal slotted spoon so the rice flour crust browns evenly.

Drain on paper towel and serve hot with Turkish bread, pickled vegetables and Toasted cumin powder raita (page 130).

Sticky lamb ribs

This can be made with pork ribs, but I'm a sucker for the sweetness of lamb. The umami of the lamb fat polishes the acidity of both the sumac and amchur versions of this masala. The key difference is that sumac takes the tone lower while amchur keeps things bright.

If you do decide to use pork ribs, use the same method with the alternative masala. Replacing the salt and chilli creates the right kind of drive for the pork meat and fat. Pork is a broader and flatter meat than lamb.

Serves 4 as part of a shared meal

800 g (1 lb 12 oz) lamb or pork ribs, cut into individual ribs

Masala for lamb ribs

2 teaspoons honey

2 teaspoons kecap manis (Indonesian sweet soy sauce)

1½ teaspoons fine pink salt

1 teaspoon peanut oil

1 teaspoon sumac or amchur

1 teaspoon fennel powder

1 teaspoon fennel seeds

½ teaspoon Kashmiri chilli powder

Masala for pork ribs

2 teaspoons honey

2 teaspoons kecap manis (Indonesian sweet soy sauce)

1½ teaspoons fine white sea salt

1 teaspoon peanut oil

1 teaspoon sumac or amchur

1 teaspoon fennel powder

1 teaspoon fennel seeds

½ teaspoon red chilli powder

Preheat the oven to 180°C (350°F) fan-forced (200°C/400°F conventional).

Place the ribs in a roasting tin then sprinkle or drizzle the masala ingredients over them. Using clean hands, massage the masala into the ribs, moving them around and turning them over to ensure they're well coated.

Roast for about 20 minutes, until browned, bubbly and sticky. Turn halfway through if you like, but it won't be a big deal if you forget.

Serve as is with rice and coleslaw, or strip off the bone and use as a succulent filling for leavened flatbreads along with hummus, rocket, pickled jalapeños, and thin onion rings.

SECOND-TIER ACIDIC SPICES

Most second-tier acidic aromatics in my kitchen fall into the category of wet or fresh spices: they have a harder impact on masala than dried and powdered acidic spices. The propensity of acidic spices in liquid form to 'split' flavour is magnified. This is precisely why, in my kitchen, they are second-tier aromatics.

LEMONS

It's relatively common domestic cooking lore to use a squeeze of lemon juice on a completed dish as additional seasoning, particularly in South-East Asian cuisine. But it's worth pointing out that this can be counterintuitive. Lemon juice has the ability to deconstruct complex aromatic structure.

When used deliberately in cuisines that rely on dark and dense spice, lemon juice carries a high-tone message of the simple joys of the land and community connections – think, for example, of the traditions of the Levant and the Mediterranean rim. In these dishes, the weight of spice or produce is dense enough that lemon juice is a delicious and intelligent foil and counterpoint as opposed to a disruptor.

LIMES NIMBU

The sweetness and acidic subtlety of limes means they're not as disruptive to masala as lemon juice. It's possibly why limes or some variety of nimbu are sometimes used in regional southern Indian or Sri Lankan cuisine. Limes in my kitchen find their way into Fresh nimbu soda (nimbu pani, page 75), or become an essential ingredient in Butter chicken (page 209). In the latter, the lime juice in the masala-rich yoghurt marinade tenderises the chicken before it hits the tandoor, unoiled kadai or flat barbecue grill. At home in India, we squeeze lime over a salted raw cucumber and onion salad – standard lunchtime fare when served with Channa sabji (page 102) and chapati.

POMEGRANATE MOLASSES

I've needed to find a reliable substitute for tamarind because where I live, my preferred form isn't always available. Like sumac, pomegranate molasses belongs to the canon of Middle Eastern cuisine. But it fits pretty seamlessly into masala, too. Pomegranate molasses is unique in that it's tart, acrid and sweet – a pretty irresistible combination. Given its intensity and complexity, the quantity should be kept light. The one caveat with pomegranate molasses is that it can thin masala's texture. In the Tamarind eggplant recipe (page 188) in particular, it doesn't work effectively as a substitute.

A word on vinegar

I haven't singled out vinegar in this book, even as a second-tier acidic spice, but that doesn't mean it's not used at all in regional Indian cuisine. Vinegar has always been essential in Mum's raita recipe (page 229), but other than that – in the Ganju kitchen at least – it was reserved for salad dressings.

VADA PAV
TAVA PULAV
GOBI
MANCHURIAN
Mob: 8722363634
20
100
125 Mbps
@ ₹749
GO COLO

SWEET SPICES

Function in masala: Smoothing out discordance, mollifying heat and softening pungency.
Emotive quality: Adding an element of youthful ease and joy.

For the Indian householder, sugars play a part in masala when parenting young children. Introducing toddler palates to spice requires coaxing – we use gentle spice with familiar foods to create soft tastes. Adding a small amount of sugar ensures that those new to masala receive the mouthful with less difficulty.

Sugar in this context refers largely to jaggery – that less refined version of cane sugar that's known in many parts of regional India as gur. As it's less refined, its taste is more complex and broader, making it a better fit for masala. Even on its own, jaggery is texturally satisfying: tasted raw it has a quality of caramel fudge.

It can be bought in block or powdered forms and each has a different aromatic profile. In block form it's buttery – Ash and I love to shave off bits to eat with a little ghee and flaked salt. In powdered form it has that flat and 'brown' sweetness of rapadura or coconut sugars ... only powdered jaggery is sweeter than both.

Outside of childhood, sweetness takes on a different appearance. As we age, our emotional states are fed by sweet experiences that are broader, more complex and more elegant. These emotive experiences are best transcribed by the round and weighted quality of warm spices, or the grounded familiarity of earth spices. That's why we're moving on to sweet spices only now – we have already seen the other ways we can use masala to taste, express, transmute and reinforce affection, love and tenderness in all its textures. But still the child in us remains.

The first taste: a *sattvic* emotion

Sweet is our first taste. Breastmilk – or if not, formula – is the first thing we all have in our mouths. It signifies connection, care, nurture. Whenever someone tells me they crave sweet foods when they're under stress, it feels pertinent to point out that considering our entrance to the world, it's pretty natural to crave sweet things in response to shock, high emotion and anxiety.

Emotively, formal Ayurveda labels sweet tastes as those that arouse *sattvic* emotions. *Sattvic* comes from the Sanskrit word *sattva*, which means 'complete'. Not just complete but also vital, clean, conscious, of balanced mind, of balanced state, harmonious, pure, strong and of the essence. Like masala, like Ayurveda, *sattvic* is a Tardis word that opens the door to a multiverse of meaning.

According to the sweet *rasa*, love, joy, bliss, contentment and compassion are flavours. It's hardly the first time in this book that we've spoken about taste having emotive content. But there's something exceptionally beautiful about a culture that formally and deliberately writes emotional expression through food into culinary scripture.

JAGGERY
GUR

Category: Sweet spices.
Form and colour: In block form, from light to dark tan. In powdered form, from burnished bronze to reddish copper.

Aromatically, jaggery is a classic sweet spice in that it offers a black-and-white expression of love. It's the happiness of childhood; it tastes like a toddler laughs. We add it to masala as that carefree top note.

From a sensory body perspective, jaggery is warming. Ayurveda views it as an energy support for the bodily systems, particularly through the winter cold. I explain this a little more in the recipe for peanut chikki (page 202). Block jaggery addresses this function better than the powdered form, which is 'thinner' in texture and taste.

Knowing which form of jaggery to use when relies on understanding their contribution. Block jaggery will be richer and sweeter, with a heavier or more 'visible' taste. Powdered jaggery disperses more evenly throughout masala, and so hides better – its sweetness is more completely incorporated.

While jaggery has a function within the framework of Ayurveda, it's a stretch to call it a healthy sugar. Like all sugars, jaggery is high in energy. It's a 'sometimes' spice and it also needs to be a 'sometimes' food.

Tasting notes

The interesting thing about jaggery is how varied and tonal its sweetness is, depending not only on its form, but also the batch. I've had blocks of jaggery that are super fudgy, and others with a less assertive caramel-butter taste. The colour will give some indication – the 'fresher' the block looks, or the lighter its colour, the fudgier it will be. Normally, primary characters are **caramel**, **butterscotch** and **butter**. **Molasses** and **honey** secondary characters add texture and complexity.

Use in masala

Jaggery is a great addition to masala when cooking for children. The old adage of 'a spoonful of sugar' holds up with spice: using a little jaggery in a simple masala that's meant for kids will help a young palate acclimatise to complex flavour. Reduce the quantity of jaggery gradually as the child becomes more comfortable with aromatic contrasts. When using jaggery in its block form, add the cut pieces to the base of the masala: the heat and fat will soften the jaggery enough that it will break apart at the press of a wooden spoon and can be stirred through evenly. Jaggery powder is simpler to use, but that one extra step of refining the sugar reduces some of its dimension.

Emotive content

Jaggery tastes like the sweetness of a child's giggle.

Traditional medicinal impact

Jaggery is used in Ayurveda to lift a weary body state, to warm the body in cold climates, and to help combat both anaemia and anxiety.

Chikki

'Jaggery tastes like the sweetness of a child's giggle.'

Chikki is made from jaggery block or powder and peanuts (pictured on page 205). In India it's a winter treat – high in energy and warming. It's the kind of food in which Ayurveda sees benefit, when consumed in the right season and in small and occasional quantities. We had it all the time as kids in Delhi when December got super cold. Australians might liken it to a more bombastic version of the skinny sesame bars sold in blue packets at every 1980s health food shop and corner store next to the coconut-coated apricot delight.

There's not too much in the way of recipe. We're using jaggery in its block form because it's rounder and fudgier.

Serves 12

Pan 1

¼ cup (50 g) ghee

500 g (1 lb 2 oz) jaggery, roughly chopped

Pan 2

1 tablespoon ghee

4 cups (560 g) skinless raw peanuts

a few pinches of fine pink salt

Line a baking tray with foil.

Heat the ghee in a large frying pan over medium heat. Once the ghee is melted, lower the heat and add the jaggery, stirring constantly until the jaggery and ghee are fully combined and the mixture is golden.

In a second frying pan over medium heat, melt the ghee then add the peanuts and salt. Once the peanuts are a little golden, add them to the ghee and jaggery mixture and stir through. Reduce the heat to low and cook for 2–3 minutes.

Spread the peanut chikki evenly over the prepared tray and set aside to cool and harden. Break it into small pieces to serve. It will keep in an airtight container in the fridge for 5–7 days.

SAFFRON
ZAFRAN or KESAR

Category: Sweet spices.
Form and colour: Bright orange threads, the stigma and styles from the flower of the saffron crocus (*Crocus sativus*).

Saffron, according to Ayurvedic taste or *rasa*, is a sweet spice. Which is why we find it here. Not such a stretch if we consider the joy its use brings. Fragrant and complex, it is deeply telling of an intimate connection to Kashmiri Hindu culture.

Saffron from Kashmir has its own variety (*Crocus sativus* 'Cashmirianus'), and is widely regarded as the world's best. Its harvest – like saffron harvest anywhere – is labour-intensive and constrained to a tight seasonal window. Its rarity, its seasonality and the human effort required to bring it to our kitchens makes it a precious spice. In the Kashmiri Hindu tradition, saffron (zafran or kesar) is reserved for use in 'highlight' masalas, preparations that produce moments of quiet elegance – kahwa tea, the Kheer (rice pudding; page 204) served following *havans* (ceremonies), a pulao in which the inclusion of saffron flags the dish as one of celebration. For all of these reasons, it's not a common ingredient for Indian householders (see Use in masala, below).

Tasting notes

The first time I tried saffron all I smelled was Ammi. Its primary notes of **dry floral heat** through to **sandalwood**, and an aroma of **fresh pressed cotton** are all of the scents that trailed her. Ammi was a tailor and she worked in a room upstairs in her New Delhi home full of printed cottons and incense.

Use in masala

Kashmiris have an intensely romantic and nostalgic relationship to their landscape – even those of us who, like me, have rarely had the opportunity to spend time on home soil. We refer to ourselves as Kashmiri, not Indian. There is a staunchness in our allegiance to Kashmir, as if that particular geographical patch encompasses everything we are and anyone we'd ever need to be. Saffron in masala expresses this connection. When saffron *is* in the mix, it doesn't form part of the circle of masala but stands apart as a spotlight on the specialness of the occasion.

Emotive content

Saffron is a sophisticated expression of joy. It also carries an ancestral anchor within.

Kheer

As a dessert, kheer appears on Kashmiri Hindu tables at all the significant *havans* – weddings, funerals and annual *pujas*. Saffron isn't always included, but when it is, it changes kheer, embedding a deeply traditional taste. It's absolutely worth starting with the best long-grained basmati rice you can find. And the pot matters quite a lot. Mum used to make it in our rice pot. I did too ... until I discovered how beautifully my Le Creuset casserole conducts heat for this type of longer, low-temperature cooking.

Serves 6

- 150 g (5½ oz) basmati rice
- 5 cups (1¼ litres) milk
- 50 g (1¾ oz) slivered almonds
- 4 green cardamom pods, husks cracked
- pinch of saffron threads

To finish

- 1¼ cups (330 g) caster (superfine) sugar
- edible silver leaf (optional), to decorate

Start 3 hours before cooking by rinsing the rice a few times with cold water, then leaving it in a bowl of cold water to soak. Soaking allows the rice to release its flavour profile.

When ready to cook, heat the milk in a large heavy-based saucepan over medium–high heat, stirring constantly, until it begins to boil.

Reduce the heat to medium and add the slivered almonds, cardamom pods and drained basmati rice. Cook, stirring constantly with a wooden spoon, for about 20 minutes, until the rice has softened. (We're cooking the rice starch and milk protein into a sweet foundation that will create weight and structure. The aromatic body of green cardamom is structural reinforcement.)

Spoon 2 tablespoons of warmed milk from the pan into a small bowl. Crush the saffron threads just a little, then stir them through the warmed milk until they release their colour. (Smell it now and you'll get all of that incredible sandalwood, pressed-cotton, hot dry flower aroma. For a fragrant and delicate spice, saffron has incredible integrity.) Stir the saffron milk into the kheer.

Add the caster sugar, still stirring constantly. (The overt sweetness creates density and richness, but if you taste it now, you'll feel why this kheer is not about the sugar. Instead, the lasting impression is an entrance into green cardamom and then a step up to the strong elegance of saffron. It feels like rice pudding, but grown up.)

Now replace the wooden spoon with a metal one – it keeps the sugar notes tighter – and continue cooking over medium heat, stirring constantly, until the rice has thickened and yellowed, 20–30 minutes.

Remove from the heat and spoon into small bowls. Decorate with silver leaf if you like. Refrigerate for 2–3 hours, then remove from the fridge about 30 minutes before serving.

Opposite: Left: Chikki (page 202). Right: Kheer.

HOT SPICES

Hot spice is unique as categories go, in that it splits into two distinct aromatic groupings – spices from the chilli family and aromatics from the pepper family. Although both chillies and peppers contribute heat, to the Indian householder each has different functional and sensory body utility:

- **Chilli family hot spices** elongate masala, arouse the central nervous system and stimulate wit and courage.
- **Pepper family hot spices** anchor masala, bracket the central nervous system and stimulate grit and perseverance.

We'll cover these two families in two subcategories.

CHILLI FAMILY HOT SPICES

Function in masala: Creating length. Dried and fresh chilli both draw aroma upward and disperse its weight.
Emotive quality: Offering excitement in the way of new beginnings.
Traditional medicinal quality: Stimulating the metabolic system.

When I used to teach kids about masala, they would fall into two distinct categories: those who wailed about not wanting to try chilli, and those who (cutely) chest-thumped about their love and tolerance for it. To be honest, adults are pretty much the same.

There's something *about* chilli. Just talking about it arouses emotion. Chilli is a natural stimulant. It's fire and excitement. When a group of people tastes raw chilli, their volume skyrockets. Everyone chatters, exclaims, yelps, dives for a drink or dives in for more. Tasting chilli raw feels like taking a risk.

Masala loves chilli for the same reasons we do. While pretty much everyone views chilli as a way to drive heat, what's more important is its natural propensity to drive excited engagement in all three bodies – sensory, emotional and metaphysical. This is due not only to the arousal that chilli's heat brings throughout our bodily systems, but also to chilli's capacity to connect us with weightlessness and light.

This functional capacity works like the literal energy of a flame: chilli family hot spices create an upward draft like hot air rising, lifting heavy, textural and dense tastes from the palate floor and central palate and licking them up through the palate roof. This sensation elongates masala, lending length – where length refers to the pull of flavour. Flavours that linger feel elegant, even when they are pungent or dark. The gradual fading of any sensory experience suggests subtlety, and a body convinced of a subtle presence will respond with curiosity and openness.

We can learn to use chilli family hot spices differently by plugging into different regional Indian traditions. Once, on a family holiday with my cousin-brothers and cousin-sisters, our parents had organised a minivan driving trip from Delhi to Siliserh Lake and Sariska Tiger Reserve in Rajasthan. One of our drivers was from the south, and was super proud of his chilli heat tolerance. We were northern Kashmiri babies, and so heat in masala for us was always subtler. One lunchtime, we dared the driver to eat as much chilli as he could. He couldn't resist, chomping down on hot, raw green chillies – seeds and all – until sweat was pouring from his forehead. It left us in awe. He was outrageous to watch. That's the lure, the dare and the excitement of chilli.

The geography of hot spice

The regional storytelling of masala is obvious in the use of hot spices. In the desert states – Rajasthan and Punjab – the dishes display a regional character of dry heat. In the mountain areas of Kashmir and Himachal Pradesh, the heat of masala is broad and resonant – the deep warmth demanded in cold climates. In the south – Kerala and Goa – the heat of masala is as humid and encompassing as the weight of the tropical jungle climates. The obviousness of the connection is due in part to the body's need to be in harmony with its external environs. Ayurveda says that having our body at odds with our external environment results in needless energy consumption. Hot spices, then, are a vital element of internal regulation via masala.

KASHMIRI CHILLI POWDER
KASHMIRI MIRCH

Category: Hot spices.
Form: Fine powder that's neither granular nor dry, unlike most other dried chilli powders.
Colour: Vermilion red.

Kashmiri chilli powder is an aromatic that garners people's attention. It's unusual for a chilli to be so pretty – floral, smoky, subtle, even a bit sweet. Its heat builds slowly.

I use Kashmiri chilli powder to showcase the ways heat can be manipulated via masala. During raw spice tastings, we chase Kashmiri chilli powder with a little turmeric powder, which spreads and subdues its heat. Or with cassia powder, which creates a blooming humid heat. Or with cinnamon powder, which yields a dry, runaway-grassfire heat. It's a great way to understand that chillies are complex and that heat with masala can mean a multitude of things.

Kashmiri chilli powder is used in many of India's better-known international favourites – including Rogan josh (page 302) and Butter chicken (page 209) – to create that 'curry red' colour.

It's my preferred chilli and the one I use as a default unless a recipe instructs otherwise. This is a consequence of being a mum, the Kashmiri Hindu penchant for less focus on chilli in general, and the ways this chilli suits my usual selection of spices (see right).

Tasting notes

Whereas other dried red chilli tends to be hot, less subtle, sometimes dry and often inflammatory, Kashmiri chilli powder has none of that in its nature. To its core, this chilli has a **humid** and **floral** heat with a strong brush of **smoke**. It's a classic, pretty chilli, with recessed **salt** and a **soft** but **'red' heat**.

Use in masala

Kashmiri chilli powder is prized for its beautiful colour, but I'm more concerned here that you absorb the notion that it possesses all the useful functionality of this category. It lengthens, lightens and elongates masala, and has an inherent flexibility that makes it easy to manipulate depending on the heat requirement of a dish. Though every spice can be manipulated – in fact, that's the whole premise of masala – the subtler aromatics within each category display the most facets and as a result show the greatest nuance.

Emotive content

Hot without challenge. Floral without being cloying. Smoky but not charred. Kashmiri chilli powder is the Goldilocks chilli. It's balanced stimulation, moderated drive, directed passions. An arousal of the senses without loss of equilibrium.

Different folks, different strokes

As your relationship to masala deepens, you'll find yourself preferring to use certain spices over others. This is particularly true for salts and for the spices within the hot category as a whole. That's because salts, chillies and peppers have multiple varieties. There are hundreds of types of chillies, dozens of peppers, multitudes of salts.

What's interesting to note as you develop your preferred stash of chilli, pepper and salt, is how this determines which other spices you use, and what underlying message you're turning and returning to in the kitchen. Dad preferred to cook with red chilli powder rather than Kashmiri chilli powder, cassia rather than cinnamon. I'm the opposite in both cases. His masala was drier, mine is warmer. That doesn't mean that he was harder and I'm softer, just that we chased different aspects of ourselves through our food.

It's good to notice these things about the way we cook – to become more interested in the ways *we* are affected by masala, not just the ways we're manipulating *it*. Reversing our viewpoint can result in insights into who we think we are.

Butter chicken

We never once ate butter chicken growing up, and I never cooked it until I started my YouTube channel and thought it might get me a few subscribers. I also wanted to see what all the fuss was about. My recipe didn't go viral, but I did come to appreciate the dish.

Charring the marinated chicken on a dry surface is key to the success of this dish. As is working twenty-four hours ahead – it makes a noticeable difference if the chicken is left to marinate in the fridge overnight.

I went to the original restaurant (now franchise) for butter chicken in Delhi, Daryaganj. The story of butter chicken is that the restaurant owner, Kundan Lal Jaggi, threw some leftover tandoori chicken into a tomato gravy rich with butter to make a more filling meal for a guest dining at his restaurant. I think my version is tastier.

Serves 6–8 as part of a shared meal

1.3 kg (3 lb) boneless, skinless chicken thigh fillets, cut into 5 cm (2 inch) cubes

Marinade

500 g (1 lb 2 oz) plain yoghurt
2–3 tablespoons water
2 tablespoons lime juice
2 tablespoons Kashmiri chilli powder
1 tablespoon finely grated ginger
1 tablespoon crushed garlic
1 tablespoon hot red chilli powder
2 teaspoons coriander powder
1½ teaspoons cumin powder
1 teaspoon fine white sea salt
1 teaspoon garam masala
½ teaspoon turmeric powder

Butter chicken sauce

600 g (1 lb 5 oz) tomato passata (puréed tomatoes)
1 teaspoon garam masala
½ teaspoon fine pink salt
½ teaspoon red chilli powder
¼ teaspoon fine black pepper
125 g (4½ oz) chilled butter, finely diced

To finish

¼ cup kasoori methi (dried fenugreek leaves)
¼ cup (60 ml) cream
finely diced red onion, to garnish
lime wedges, to serve

To make the marinade, whisk the yoghurt with the water in a large bowl. This thins the yoghurt and draws forward its acidity, one of the power players in chicken. Add all of the marinade spices and the lime juice and stir them through. (The Kashmiri chilli powder is key here: a standard chilli powder would reach into the char of the chicken and create a driving and drying heat that would overwhelm the rich makhani sauce, the floral/herbaceous element of dried fenugreek leaves, and the end drizzle of cream. The subtlety of Kashmiri chilli powder keeps the masala pretty.)

Add the chicken pieces to the marinade and mix well. Marinate in the fridge overnight. If you forget to start the day before, marinate for as long as possible before cooking.

The best cooking vessel is a large cast-iron kadai or wok. You could also use a flat indoor grill plate or barbecue (grill) plate. It needs a cast-iron surface that will conduct high heat and char the chicken without oils or fats. I work in batches, spreading the chicken pieces in a single layer on the bottom and up the sides of the kadai and cooking them over high heat on the stovetop, without moving them, until they start to char. I then flip them and char the other side. This takes about 5 minutes per batch. When the chicken pieces are charred but not cooked through, I set them aside in a bowl. The charring makes this dish grown up and smoky. It also makes the creaminess of the makhani sauce pop.

Reduce the heat to medium, pour the leftover marinade into the kadai and cook for 1–2 minutes, scraping in any charred pieces from the bottom and side.

Add the tomato passata and the butter chicken sauce spices to the kadai and stir through for 2–3 minutes, until the passata heats and the masala is no longer raw. It should bubble just a little. Return the charred chicken pieces to the kadai and stir through. Simmer for 5 minutes over medium–low heat.

Add the butter and stir it through, then increase the heat to medium. Once the sauce is bubbling evenly, reduce the heat to medium–low and simmer until the chicken is cooked through, about 10 minutes.

Add the dried kasoori methi and cream and stir through until hot. Serve immediately with naan or rice, garnished with diced red onion and with a wedge of lime on the side.

Lal paneer

The nice thing about lal paneer is that it's simple. Kashmiri chilli powder is very much used here for colour. *Lal* means 'red' in Hindi, and the red of this dish really is beautiful, as is the creamy end texture.

It's best to make the paneer the day before cooking this dish, so that it has plenty of time to hang.

Serves 4 as part of a shared meal

2 cups (500 ml) mustard oil
500 g (1 lb 2 oz) Paneer (page 110)
½ teaspoon turmeric powder
½ teaspoon fine white salt

Main masala

6 small tomatoes
1 tablespoon mustard oil
1 teaspoon Kashmiri chilli powder
2 teaspoons coriander powder
2 teaspoons fennel powder
1 teaspoon ginger powder
½ teaspoon cumin seeds
½ cup (125 ml) paneer water, from frying (above)
2 teaspoons fine white sea salt

Tadka

⅓ cinnamon stick
4 green cardamom pods, husks cracked

Heat the mustard oil in a kadai, stable cast-iron wok or heavy-based saucepan large enough that the oil comes up no more than halfway. Heat the oil to smoking point, then remove from the heat and let it cool. This reduces the pungency of the mustard oil, which is vital for a subtle dish like lal paneer.

Meanwhile, cut the paneer into 2 cm (¾ inch) cubes. Fill a large bowl with cold water and set it beside the stovetop.

Reheat the mustard oil over high heat until very hot but not smoking. Add the turmeric powder and salt to prevent the paneer from sticking to the kadai. Fry the paneer in small batches until just browned. Remove the fried paneer from the oil with a slotted spoon and place carefully in the bowl of water, taking care that your cooking implement doesn't touch the water, so it won't spatter when you return it to the oil. The water keeps the paneer soft and helps it to slip out from beneath the oil.

To begin the masala, remove the top of the tomato cores and score the bases with a cross. Place in boiling water until the skin starts to split and lift. Remove from the water and peel off the skin. Purée in a food processor or with a hand-held blender. The tomatoes need a smooth texture, to provide a silken carriage for the masala.

Heat the mustard oil in a medium saucepan over high heat. Add the Kashmiri chilli powder and stir through for 2–3 minutes, keeping the heat high. Add the puréed tomatoes and stir them through for another 2–3 minutes.

Reduce the heat to medium–low. Add the coriander powder, fennel powder, ginger powder and cumin seeds. Stir through for 1–2 minutes, then add the drained paneer and the paneer water. Add the salt, stir it through, then continue cooking for a further 10 minutes.

To finish, add the cinnamon stick and cardamom pods and stir them through. Keep at a low simmer for 10 minutes, then serve immediately with Haakh (page 252), Simple yellow dal (page 39) and basmati rice.

SECOND-TIER CHILLI FAMILY HOT SPICES

I don't cook using high-heat chilli, which is why my list of second-tier chillies is so long. I do know, however, that there are more than a few fans of super-hot masala out there, which is why I go into more detail here than for other second-tier spices.

GROUND RED CHILLI POWDER LAL MIRCH

Heat character: Dark and earthy, feeding intense flame.

Emotive content: Brooding and intense.

Ground red chilli powder is the chilli powder most people think of and are familiar with. But red chilli powders can be hot, medium or mild. They vary in texture, too, but most are a little granular and contribute a desert heat to masala – a heat to match the brick-red colour of the powder itself. Dad kept his lal mirch in a glass jar with a cork lid by the stovetop on timber shelves he built himself – Dad's dad was a carpenter. I keep mine in my masala dabba alongside chilli flakes, Kashmiri chilli powder and a few peppers of varying texture – cracked black, fine white and Szechuan.

Functionally, red chilli powder performs the same role as Kashmiri chilli powder – it elongates and lengthens masala. But it does so in a less refined, shorter and heavier way. Its earthiness means that it will leave a little bit of its weight behind on the palate floor even as it reaches towards the roof of the mouth.

FRESH RED CHILLIES MIRCH

Heat character: Fresh, bright and hot.

Emotive content: Bright and stimulating.

Fresh red chilli is the other commonly used chilli in many cuisines, but Kashmiri Hindus use it subtly. I only use it a little – primarily whole, slit lengthways, and removed from the dish before eating. This way, my dishes reap the benefit of a gentle, tingling hum of heat without anything too aggressive. That aggressive heat in fresh chilli is found within the seeds, so the choice to include the seeds or not has a big impact. And yet, what's interesting about fresh chilli is that it doesn't lengthen and elongate masala in the way dried chilli does. It's more like throwing little red *patakhas* – firecrackers – into the masala mix.

Other regions of India have a different relationship to fresh chilli. The variety of chilli changes from region to region, altering and personalising masala.

FRESH GREEN CHILLIES HARI MIRCH

Heat character: Savoury and textured.

Emotive content: A little odd-bod.

Fresh green chilli is quite different from red. No matter how much heat it has, it will always retain a savoury 'bell pepper' element. That savoury element works to lower the tone of masala, even as it flames the palate. It's an unusual aromatic contradiction. For me it's also a rare one – I use it even less than fresh red chilli, and that's saying something. But I do love its contribution to the no-soak dal (page 219) made from masoor lentils, where ajwain is the star spice. Yes, it uses three dried red chillies, but these are relatively mild and their dried quality beds them into the dish. It's the fresh green chilli that builds a savoury step-up in the power of ajwain's stage presence. In this instance, fresh green chilli really makes the dish.

Sapna's auntie's ready-made masala

The story of this masala goes to the heart of this book. While the ingredients of the masala are Sapna's, the ratios are mine. Sapna, my younger brother's landlady in Goa (see page 102), was vague in her recollection of spice quantity. It's the way of Indian aunties everywhere: key pieces of information are tossed in at the last minute, and you can never be sure that some secret isn't being withheld. With a smile, of course. The key piece of information that Sapna has given with this one is that everything happens around the whole dried red chilli: that ratio is decided first, and then the masala is built from there.

Makes about 2½ cups (300 g)

- 50 g (1¾ oz) whole dried red chillies
- 40 g (1½ oz) fenugreek seeds
- 25 g (1 oz) fennel seeds
- 25 g (1 oz) dried turmeric root
- 25 g (1 oz) cumin seeds
- 20 g (¾ oz) black peppercorns
- 20 g (¾ oz) star anise
- 15 g (½ oz) cassia bark
- 15 g (½ oz) cloves
- 15 g (½ oz) white poppy seeds
- 15 g (½ oz) black cardamom pods
- 15 g (½ oz) nigella seeds
- 10 g (¼ oz) nutmeg
- 10 g (¼ oz) mace flower
- 7 g (¼ oz) dried bay leaves

Toast all the spices together, and then grind to a fine powder. Sapna says there are shops in India that do this, because a domestic grinder or mortar and pestle can't grind the spices finely enough. I tested it in a Thermomix and it worked, though it did take some time. Store in an airtight jar in a cool, dark place.

Sapna adds the mix to recipes as one would a garam masala – as a final addition in the last minutes of cooking, after beginning with fresh aromatics. But it also works beautifully when tempered in fats at the beginning of cooking and used as the primary masala.

No-soak masoor dal

The key to deliciousness here is threefold: using the right quantity of water, skimming off the scum as the dal cooks, and including the green chilli. In this dish, the chilli waves its green capsicum (pepper) flag higher than it does its heat.

Serves 6 as part of a meal

1⅓ cups (300 g) masoor dal (split red lentils)
2½ teaspoons fine pink salt
½ teaspoon turmeric powder
4½ cups (1¼ litres) cold water

Tadka

2 teaspoons ghee
1 teaspoon ajwain seeds
3 dried red chillies
1 fresh green chilli, chopped

Thoroughly rinse the lentils under cold water. Drain.

Transfer the lentils to a large saucepan, then add the salt, turmeric powder and water. Place over high heat, bring to the boil and continue boiling for about 5 minutes, skimming off the scum that rises to the surface. This will allow the masala a cleaner and brighter expression. Once the scum diminishes, reduce the heat to medium–low and simmer gently for about 20 minutes, until the lentils have softened and lost their shape. Keep an eye on the pan and stir occasionally to prevent the dal sticking.

For the tadka, heat the ghee in a small frying pan over medium heat. Add the ajwain seeds and the dried and fresh chillies. Use your own discretion in your kitchen when handling the fresh chilli – you might want to remove the seeds to reduce the heat. Cook the spices until aromatic, 2–3 minutes.

Once the tadka is ready, stir it into the cooked dal. Serve immediately, with basmati rice and Tamarind eggplant (page 188).

PEPPER FAMILY HOT SPICES

Function in masala: Anchoring flavour, drawing aroma into the back palate and holding it there.

Emotive quality: Representing grit and determination.

Traditional medicinal quality: Stabilising heavy and erratic energies.

It took me a while to explore the possibilities of peppers because they are ubiquitous in Western kitchens, but pepper manages to seem both ordinary and completely removed from my experience.

It's worth considering peppers in relationship to chilli as a way of establishing that the concept of heat is nuanced. Heat from peppers has a slower burn than chilli, and a deeper drag because of the way it anchors aroma into the back molars. It's persistent. It's often black pepper that makes Sri Lankan cuisine so fiery, and the same is true of certain regional cuisines from India's south, where the pepper bush is endemic.

In an everyday capacity, think of peppers as a T-junction – their aromatic intensity means they work as axis points, rerouting masala. Adding pepper family hot spice to a chilli-led masala will drop the tone. In a masala led by warm spices, it will engender grit. In a masala dominated by bright acidity, it will introduce a corrosive note. In each example, the pepper provides a distinct change of direction.

FINE WHITE PEPPER

Category: Hot spices.
Form: A gritty powder – peppers have a particular texture that differentiates them from other powdered spices.
Colour: Off-white.

I love white pepper for its 'sun-dried' aromatic quality: a raw taste transports me to Mum's vegetable garden on the Victorian south-west coast where we grew up. Her plot smelled of dried hay, paper flowers and sun-hot herbs. That's white pepper. Used in masala, white pepper serves as a lighter anchor than black pepper. It brings out the floral quality of chilli powders and isn't as brackish as black pepper when paired with cumin seeds.

Though it's not a traditional inclusion in Kashmiri Hindu cuisine, there are times when I use it to create tiered or floral heat. It's become a natural thing for me to use it in tandem with cracked black pepper from day to day. I find it evens out some of the black pepper's rough and boulder-like heat.

I always use white pepper in a 'fine' form – I feel like its delicacy is better experienced that way.

Tasting notes

As we've already established, white peppercorns are different from black in terms of aromatic presentation. This is the softer, less angular expression of dried peppercorn heat. White peppercorn as a finely ground spice has notes of **warmed earth** and **dried hay**. Secondary aromas reach into **flint**, and the end taste leaves a faint and fine **metallic residue**.

Use in masala

Fine white pepper is so uncommon to masala as to be practically unused in a traditional regional Indian capacity. That said, I do reach for it when working with masala that weighs into the astringent, hot and earth categories. I find that a small addition of fine white pepper sits underneath chilli, and draws astringent and earth spices closer together, introducing subtlety.

Emotive content

If black peppercorns are about grit and weight, fine white pepper is the deceptively athletic cheerleader – smilier and brighter, but still offering determination and persistence.

White pepper pavlova

Adding fine white pepper here isn't about making the pavlova peppery. Neither is it about offering a simple contrast to all of that sugar. Even in small amounts, white pepper draws out a savoury element from egg white and brings forward a woodiness in the rosewater. And it makes the pavlova richer. A word of warning: adding white pepper to a pav naturally restricts how much it's possible to eat. It's up to you to decide whether that's a good or a bad thing ;)

This recipe is derived from Nigella Lawson's pavlova in one of her earliest books, *How to be a Domestic Goddess*. I've made it just about every Christmas for more than twenty years.

Serves 12

- 8 egg whites
- 450 g (1 lb) caster (superfine) sugar
- pinch of fine white sea salt
- 1 tablespoon cornflour (cornstarch)
- 1½ teaspoons apple cider vinegar
- generous ¼ teaspoon fine white pepper
- 2–3 dashes of rosewater

Preheat the oven to 180°C/350°F fan-forced (200°C/400°F conventional).

While the oven is heating, whip the egg whites to stiff peaks in a clean steel bowl using electric beaters. Add the caster sugar, a little at a time, beating well after each addition to ensure the sugar is mixed through and dissolved. Don't rush this step. Doing it well means your pavlova will be silken.

Add the remaining ingredients and fold them through carefully using a large metal spoon. You want the meringue to stay super light. Working with metal utensils helps prevent contamination of the egg white, ensuring the meringue will cook to a crisp outside with a sticky, fluffy inside.

Trace the outline of a dinner plate on a sheet of baking paper. Lay the sheet, tracing side down, on a baking tray. Spoon the meringue into the middle of the circle and use the outline as a guide for spreading it into a round, ensuring it retains height.

Put the pavlova in the oven and immediately reduce the heat to 150°C/300°F fan-forced (170°C/325°F conventional). Bake for 90 minutes to 2 hours, until the meringue is set and well crusted but not browned. Turn the oven off and leave in the oven, with the oven door slightly ajar, until it cools. This is meant to prevent cracking, but to be honest it's never actually worked for me. I persist, however, just in case.

Dress your pav as you like. I love cream whipped with a touch of caster sugar and topped with fresh mango if it's summertime: the mango sweetness is a foil for the white pepper that shines through with notes of hay and sun-warmed vegie patch – in the best possible way.

SECOND-TIER PEPPER FAMILY HOT SPICES

In Western kitchens peppers are treated as a compulsory table seasoning, but in Eastern kitchens they are used to define a dish or they're not used at all. For me, finding a middle ground has meant stepping away from both traditions. Generally, I tier my peppers, using them for back-palate weight, and to give pretty masalas grit and depth.

CRACKED BLACK PEPPER KALI MIRCH

Heat character: Blooming, gritty and hard.

Emotive content: Determined and blunt.

There's a widely held belief that turmeric powder needs to be paired with black pepper for the turmeric to release its benefits. I can't speak for the chemistry, but I can speak as an Indian householder and say that Ayurveda uses *fats* to ensure turmeric powder's aromatic release. I do use cracked black pepper in my Turmeric Masala retail blend, though – not only to anchor flavour into the back palate, but also to texture the aromatics it accompanies.

In taste terms, cracked black pepper increases the felt presence of the other spices in a masala. The more we feel the presence of a collection of aromatics, the more our sensory body is able to draw out the information it needs from the mouthful. In effect, black pepper bullies us into paying closer attention.

On its own, cracked (freshly ground) black pepper offers a synchronised aromatic experience – its taste is as gritty as its texture. Taste it raw, and I promise you'll still be picking bits out of your teeth hours later.

FINE BLACK PEPPER KALI MIRCH

Heat character: A flare-up in hot coals.

Emotive content: Mildly short-tempered.

Fine black pepper is my second-reach black pepper. Its fine form results in a lesser impact. In some ways, fine black pepper is secretive: it holds things back and displays a passive black-pepper heat. This is due entirely to its form: ground to a fine powder, the peppercorns lose their obvious character. I always use this spice as part of a triumvirate – cracked black pepper, fine white pepper and then a little fine black pepper to round out the shape. Using this combo on even the simplest of dishes – fried eggs, avocado on toast – or to season meats before roasting, adds a depth and complexity to any seasoning.

SZECHUAN PEPPER

Heat character: Rose meets hot sandalwood.

Emotive content: Proud beauty.

Szechuan is the flamenco dancer of the pepper berry family – striking, impactful and bold, but also soft, subtle and disciplined. This is because Szechuan pepper is an aromatic bomb-drop that occurs in two parts. First is that pretty and fresh floral rose hit. The pause is a held breath before a rush of cool fire. Unlike black and white peppers, Szechuan pepper has a menthol aspect that heightens its heat bloom.

Johnson Ebenezer's milagu tanni

(mulligatawny)

It took less than a second for Johnson Ebenezer to nominate the spice and the dish that goes to the heart of his connection to masala – milagu (black pepper), and the reclamation of the traditional regional Tamil dish the English bastardised and turned into mulligatawny. Johnson Ebenezer is the chef patron and co-founder of Farmlore, a restaurant and farm on the outskirts of Bengaluru in Karnataka state, in India's south. Writing this book gave me an excuse to finally visit and eat there. I wanted to include one of Johnson's recipes, but I didn't know just how much that recipe would mean.

It can be easy to forget that chilli isn't an origin aromatic for the Indian regions, particularly for those of us from the north who no longer use black pepper in regional masala. Johnson brings this up straight away – that reminder of the way time works on cultural landscapes: how change grows roots, and the valley of old wisdom is filled by the landslide of time and ceases to be remembered. This dish is a reminder of that valley. Milagu tanni – pepper water. A form of rasam, a soup-like southern dish.

Make sure you use short-grain rice, which holds its shape and gives the dish a creamy texture.

Serves 2

- 2 tablespoons ghee or sesame oil, plus extra ghee (optional) to serve
- 1 teaspoon whole black peppercorns, or to taste
- 1 teaspoon cumin seeds
- ½ teaspoon finely grated fresh ginger
- 1 cup (220 g) short-grain rice (preferably ponni or sona masoori), soaked in water for 30 minutes, then drained
- 2 cups (500 ml) water, for boiling
- salt, to taste
- fresh curry leaves, to garnish

Heat the ghee or sesame oil in a large saucepan over medium heat. Add the peppercorns, cumin seeds and ginger and let them sizzle for a few seconds, until fragrant. Add the rice and stir to coat in the pepper-infused oil. Add the water and bring to the boil, then reduce the heat to low and simmer, covered with a tight-fitting lid, for 15–20 minutes or until the rice is cooked and fluffy.

Season with salt, garnish with fresh curry leaves and, if you like, finish it in the traditional way with a dollop of ghee on top. Serve hot.

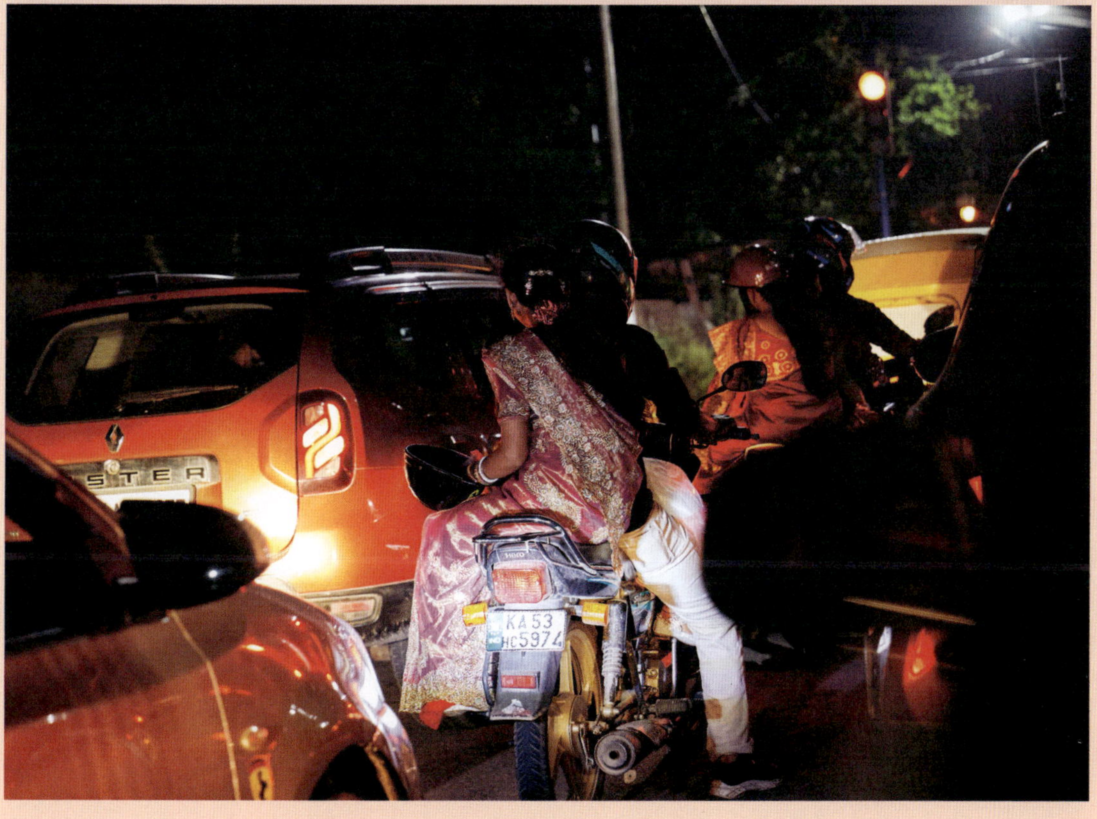

TOMATOES
TAMAATAR

Tomatoes are so integral to Kashmiri Hindu dishes that I almost forgot to include them. Shame on me!

Tomatoes are used to create body in masala. That whole idea of wet spice pastes suspended in vegetable oil and sold in jars in retail outlets has – for many outside of regional Indian traditions – created an erroneous view of masala texture: very rarely does it appear in that paste-like format. More often than not we use pastes of garlic and onion; skinned, parboiled and diced tomatoes; or a body of yoghurt to provide that rich, paste-like texture. In this way, tomatoes offer an aromatic bridge between masala and produce in recipes where such a bridge is required.

Of course, as always with masala, there's more than one way to tell the story of any aromatic. Aloo tamaatar ki sabji (page 245) showcases tomato as a last-minute textural addition to simple aloo sabji. The Matar paneer on page 232 is all about the beauty of tomato's wet sweetness.

And while it is true that tomatoes, like chillies, are an introduced ingredient, the fact that tomato *wallas* sell the fruit piled high on wooden carts or in the trays of small trucks on Indian roadsides everywhere shows their complete assimilation into regional Indian kitchen culture.

Mum's raita

This is the first masala I ever made. I make this raita now with the ease of almost forty years of repetition. Don't worry too much if you don't achieve the taste you're looking for the first, second or even third time round. The type of yoghurt, the batch of salt, small alterations in quantities of vinegar and sugar – all will have a larger impact than seems reasonable.

Makes about 1½ cups (500 g)

- 1⅓ cups (355 g) plain yoghurt
- 100 ml (3½ fl oz) apple cider vinegar
- 1 teaspoon caster (superfine) sugar
- 1 teaspoon fine white sea salt
- 1 teaspoon cracked black pepper
- scant ½ teaspoon fine white pepper
- 2 small tomatoes, finely diced
- ⅓ large onion, finely diced

Whisk everything together in a medium bowl, tasting as you go. Refrigerate for at least 1 hour before serving, to allow the aromas to coalesce.

Matar paneer

No one in my family ever gets tired of this dish. Part of what makes it so sweet and warm to eat is the diced tomato tossed in to thicken the masala and bring a fresh and bright character. I always make my paneer the day before and leave it to hang for 24 hours. I love it so much that I still make it once a week, despite the effort required. Make sure you save the whey.

Serves 6 as part of a shared meal

- 3 cups (750 ml) vegetable oil
- 2 cups (150 g) fresh or frozen peas
- 2 roma (plum) tomatoes
- 1 quantity of Paneer (page 110), whey reserved, cut into 5 cm (2 inch) pieces

Main masala

- 2 tablespoons ghee
- 3 teaspoons cumin seeds
- 2 teaspoons coriander powder
- 1½ teaspoons fennel powder
- 1 teaspoon fine pink salt
- 1 teaspoon ginger powder
- ½ teaspoon turmeric powder
- ½ teaspoon Kashmiri chilli powder
- ½ teaspoon cinnamon powder
- scant ½ teaspoon amchur
- scant ½ teaspoon fine white salt
- generous ¼ teaspoon mace powder
- 4 green cardamom pods, husks cracked
- 3 cloves
- 1 cinnamon stick
- 2 × 2 cm (¾ × ¾ inch) piece of jaggery

Heat the vegetable oil over high heat in a kadai, stable cast-iron wok or heavy-based saucepan large enough that the oil comes up no more than halfway. While the oil is heating, parboil the peas for 3–4 minutes and dice the tomatoes. Set both beside the stovetop, along with 3 cups (750 ml) of the reserved whey. Fill a large bowl with cold water and set it beside the stovetop.

Once the oil is hot, fry the paneer in small batches. When slightly browned, carefully remove from the hot oil and drop directly into the cold water. Once all the paneer is fried, drain it and set it beside the stovetop.

In a large frying pan that is off the heat, combine the ghee and all of the spices except the jaggery – if you add the spices while the heat is on, you won't be able to work quickly enough and they will burn. Place the frying pan over medium heat and add the jaggery. Stir until aromatic and tempered. Taste the masala – it will be delicious, a little salty, very warm and ripe, with woody, tangy and embroidered spice.

Add the tomato and taste again – it freshens the masala. The complexity is lifted by a bright and sweet acidity. Cook for 5–7 minutes, until the oil begins to split and the tomatoes form a rich and spicy slurry.

Add the peas and the fried paneer, then gently stir them through the spices. Immediately add enough of the whey to not quite cover the paneer cubes – think of them like icebergs, with 70 per cent of their surface area below the waterline.

Increase the heat to medium–high and cook for 2–3 minutes, until the sauce begins to bubble. Reduce the heat to medium–low and cook, without stirring, for 45–60 minutes, until the paneer is fluffy and there is just a small amount of richly spiced sauce left in the pan. If the simmer gets too strong during cooking, reduce the heat to low.

Serve with basmati rice, Simple yellow dal (page 39) and Simple aloo gosht (page 67).

3

MOVEMENT

POTS & PANS

In this last part of the book we look at two of the remaining three categories – astringent–sulphurous and forest-floor spices. Both bring movement to masala, each in a different capacity. We then have a final interlude, if you will, where we examine structural spices – those that provide pillars of support for other spices within masala.

What movement in masala means

Movement affects masala because it changes the way we experience taste.

The meaning contained within movement is broader than that contained within the categories of spice we've already encountered – in masala's foundations, or in the information related by shape and form. The foundation of masala establishes context. Shape and form are about perspectives. Movement creates overall shifts.

These shifts are deliberately built into traditional masalas so that sabjis align with regional identity. There are lots of examples of this. Use of garlic and/or onion moves food out of alignment with Brahmanic traditions (see right), just as replacing garlic and onion with hing (asafoetida) can move those dishes back into that Brahmanic frame. Use of mustard seeds – both black and yellow – shifts sabji out of the context of the northern states (where these aromatics are used less) and into India's south, where these two closely related spices serve as defining profiles. Replace those mustard seeds with fennel and cumin seeds and we're back up in the northern regions.

Obviously these examples are simplified, but that idea of movement within masala is what prevents it from being a fixed concept. In the kitchen of a modern Indian householder this is especially important as we work to keep traditions relevant. One thing I appreciated about Dad was the way he kept his kitchen moving with where he was – by the time he died, he'd pulled in threads from France and had become curious about other Western culinary techniques. Far from diminishing his relationship to masala, it imbued his time at the stovetop with vibrancy, and his relationship to me with continued relevance.

Garlic and onion in the faith traditions

Certain aromatics are pivotal in understanding Indian regional faith traditions and how they relate to masala. Garlic and onion are big ones. In simple terms, they're the aromatics most representative of the division between karmic callings. In the Hindu faith tradition there is a definitive connection between food and god, just as there is a definitive connection between the nature of our actions and our consumption. Onion and garlic are heating to the system, and so according to Ayurvedic thought disrupt the connection between spirit and body for one whose calling is prayer. And yet those same aromatics drive action when action is one's karmic responsibility.

Poetically, I think of the desert, of Rajasthan, and of the warrior caste – the Kshatriya – whose cuisine included garlic and onion because their spiritual duty was to fire their system for the protection of the good. I think of the pandits of Hindu Kashmir – the Brahmans – who replaced garlic and onion with hing because their spiritual duty was to perform the rites and rituals of their community.

These faith-based understandings go to the heart of why masala doesn't operate within systematic or blanket rules. Different rules exist for different social groups. Reliance on rules simultaneously removes our curiosity about the nuances and truncates our understanding of an ancient concept.

ASTRINGENT–SULPHUROUS SPICES

Function in masala: Opening up the palate and creating space for more complex masala.
Emotive quality: If hot spices are about excitement and determination, astringent–sulphurous spices shake us up and shift our perspective.
Traditional medicinal purpose: Garlic is used for respiratory issues and viewed as life-enhancing, onion for fever and what's referred to as blood purification.

Astringent–sulphurous spices open the trapdoor (see pages 22–23) from the palate floor to the gullet, the throat area that takes in the internal space from the chin to the base of the throat. If you're not sure how to find it, take a break from reading and go snack on a small piece of raw onion: you'll soon feel that space of the throat bloom and open.

Functionally, we engage the gullet for strong or pungent masalas in order to make the mouthful palatable. Engaging the gullet means opening it to alleviate the work of the central palate: once that palate floor trapdoor is opened, heavier flavours that feel like too much if held within the central mouth space drop down into the gullet. The end result is masala with consumable, digestible depth.

Emotively, the gullet is what we could call a secondary palate space – it is one of the last areas of the mouth that we think about when we consider flavour. In this way it aligns with secondary aspects of our emotional and sensory experience of ourselves in the world – our deeper thoughts about the way we affect the people around us, or our habitual patterns in relationships. Stimulating the gullet allows us to move our attention to hidden patterns of emotions, and to notions that require thought away from the immediacy of action and reaction.

You might notice that there are no second-tier spices within this category. This is because astringent–sulphurous spices are strong and incapable of subtlety. We use them with deliberation or not at all.

Two bodies in one

Astringent taste and sulphurous taste are two distinct aromatic expressions, but I've compressed them into one category for several reasons. One of the most significant is that the aromatic impacts of these tastes on masala are similar – both are stripping, hard, gullet-opening and heating. Spices from both groups open up space in meats for masala to penetrate. They increase sensations of bitterness and slice breathing space into dense dishes. They are so closely aligned that even separating them into two subcategories (as we did with chilli family and pepper family spices) is difficult.

Nevertheless, there are a few pertinent differences. If pushed, one could say that sulphurous spices – such as onion, garlic and hing (asafoetida) – are less bitter, have a weightier gullet impact and are more disruptive. Astringent spices, on the other hand – such as fresh ginger, black and yellow mustard seeds and bay leaves – can accelerate bitterness, build more into the body of masala and be less stripping.

In a similar vein, you might notice that I group two individual spices together more than once in this section. Yes, every spice is still unique, but for any Indian householder, there is a hierarchy of importance. Astringent–sulphurous spices are less detailed in Kashmiri Hindu cooking because they are, in large part, used less. They have an 'otherness' quality (see page 249).

ONION & GARLIC

Onion and garlic are the default inclusions in curry for many a home cook, but Kashmiri Hindu tradition doesn't use them at all. Somewhere in the middle is the sweet spot for use of these aromatics across the breadth of regional Indian culinary traditions.

ONION PYAZ

Category: Astringent–sulphurous spices.

Form: Generally round or oval, with layers.

Colour: Ranging from brown, yellow or white to red or purple.

I once spent Afghan New Year, Nowruz, with Zarifa Hameed and her family in an outer suburb of Melbourne. Of all the dishes she prepared, it was her korme kofta (page 239) that altered my view of the aromatic possibilities of onion. She'd used barely four aromatics in this dish, including salt, but then pressure-cooked one kilogram of seasoned mince with *two kilograms* of finely diced onion. Her handling of onion showed the power of purpose.

Onion as the central aromatic fundamentally shifts masala. In Zarifa's case, it was the directive, transmuting mince from a little-thought-of cut to a celebratory feast centrepiece. But even in lesser quantities, onion can move the Geiger counter on masala.

Tasting notes

The sensation of onion is more powerful than its aroma. Its **vaporous** fumes enter the nose and throat, before dousing the palate with a **slicing wet heat**. There is a **nutty** quality to brown onion, and a **sweet** note to purple or red onion that blooms once those initial sensations settle.

Use in masala

Onion use in masala should be deliberate. It has two primary actions. When used in moderate quantities with heavier meats or complex masala, onion has a carving action, opening the gullet trapdoor so that darker and heavier elements of masala can drop down into the throat and make more space for accompanying spices to penetrate. When used in sparse masalas, with vegetables or lighter seafood, onion becomes part of the body of masala, sitting below the other flavours and providing a strong foundation.

Emotive content

Onion drives emotional content into areas of our sensory body that receive less attention.

Traditional medicinal impact

In Ayurveda, onion draws down fever when rubbed on the soles of the feet. Raw onion is thought to have laxative properties and cooked onion antimicrobial qualities.

GARLIC

Category: Astringent–sulphurous spices.

Form: Bulb that is a cluster of individual cloves.

Colour: From papery cream through to pink or purple-tinged.

Garlic is distinct from onion in that its sulphurous quality affects the opening of the cavity behind the back and top palates. It's why using these two aromatics together has such an impact upon masala, dispersing flavour down into the throat but also releasing aromatic intensity into the airy upper space behind the bone structure of the nose. Masala is built upon complexity, and introducing two ports for aromatic dispersal means that garlic and onion need careful consideration to ensure that masala's messaging is not diminished.

Garlic has an obvious earthy quality that makes it a commonplace pairing with fresh ginger across the regional Indian cooking traditions. In these cases, garlic gives roots to fresh ginger's slicing heat, bringing a provocative energy and drive to accompanying spice.

Tasting notes

Garlic is a tamer raw spice experience than onion. Of course it's strong. But fresh, young garlic has a **sweetness** and a **nuttiness** that serves as counterpoint to its more **stripping** aromatic qualities. Unlike onion, in-season garlic takes on subtleties – you'll notice **earth**, **recessed apple** and, to my mind at least, the **colour pink**.

Use in masala

Garlic offers a balanced experience of astringent–sulphurous tastes. Its body of earthiness is a strong connection point to the mid-palate. This means that, when garlic enters the fray, the opening of the gullet and the nasal cavity retains an anchor. From a functional viewpoint, garlic creates space with less overall disruption. Taste-wise, it's bright and enthusiastic.

Emotive content

Garlic is spirited, but rooted in physicality. It feeds the state of happy purpose.

Astringent–sulphurous masala: grouping the disruptors

Astringent–sulphurous aromatics are disruptor spices that shift masala's tone and meaning in wholesale ways. In masala, they're the switch to flick the stage lighting from white to red.

Zarifa Hameed's korme kofta

I think this is the most fitting recipe to illustrate the power and beauty of onion when it's used deliberately and with diligence. The experience of eating this dish is like nothing else – it's rich, soft and simple, but deeply touching. Even ten years after my first time, I can still taste it. Which brings me to an important point – the large amount of onion used means that you will continue to taste this dish well into the next day. I woke the day after feeling as if my insides had been gently scoured. It was resonant.

Serves 10 as part of a shared meal

Meatballs

- 2 kg (2 lb 4 oz) onion, finely chopped
- 1 kg (1 lb 2 oz) minced (ground) lamb
- 1 tablespoon tomato paste (concentrated purée)
- 1 teaspoon sweet paprika
- 1 teaspoon cracked black pepper
- ½ teaspoon turmeric powder
- 1 large handful of fresh coriander (cilantro) leaves, chopped
- 1 egg

Sauce

- 2 tablespoons olive oil
- 2 onions, finely chopped
- 2½ cups (625 ml) water
- 1 tablespoon tomato paste (concentrated purée)
- ½ teaspoon turmeric powder
- ½ teaspoon fine white salt

To finish

- 4 potatoes, cut into quarters

Combine all the meatball ingredients in a large bowl and mix well. Shape the mixture into small even balls, about the size of a table-tennis ball. Set aside. (At this point you'll notice how hard and driving the sulphurous aroma is. The lamb mince is really the only source of sweetness – even tomato paste is rich and dark when used in this type of masala. This is why it's important not to replace the lamb with beef or pork – pork will be too light to carry the volume of onion, and beef too flat and muscular to allow the onion to express sweetness once cooked.)

To make the sauce, heat the olive oil in a large flameproof pressure cooker or broad, heavy-based saucepan over medium heat. Add the onion to the hot oil and cook for a few minutes until translucent, then add the remaining sauce ingredients and bring to the boil. This is the base for the meatballs, an aromatic bed that they can cook into.

If using a pressure cooker, add the meatballs and set the pressure cooker to high. Once it emits one or two jets of steam, turn down to medium – the pressure cooker should be sputtering constantly but not whistling. Cook for 45 minutes, then turn off and leave the pressure cooker to depressurise on its own, about 20 minutes. If using a saucepan, either transfer the sauce to a pressure cooker and add the meatballs, then continue as above, or add the meatballs to the saucepan, put the lid on and simmer for about 90 minutes.

Add the potatoes and simmer gently over medium–low heat for a further 30 minutes, until the potatoes are tender.

Serve with a simple pulao of rice made with salt and a touch of saffron.

Karima's fattoush salad

There aren't a lot of salads in this book, but nothing quite explains the possibilities of garlic like fattoush salad. I reached out to Karima Hazim Chatila for this recipe, because she has a strong sense of story and place, shared with her mother – Sivine Tabbouch – and her daughters, in her kitchen. Karima, who runs Sunday Kitchen in Sydney with Sivine, is a powerhouse of a woman. I love her book, *SOFRA: Lebanese Recipes to Share*.

The muscle of garlic is beautiful when used to communicate matriarchal lineage.

Serves 4–6

- 3 Lebanese cucumbers
- 3 tomatoes
- ½ yellow capsicum (pepper)
- ½ red capsicum (pepper)
- 1 cos lettuce
- 5 spring onions
- 1 bunch small radishes
- ¼ small white cabbage
- ¼ small purple cabbage
- 1 bunch fresh parsley, leaves picked
- 1 bunch fresh oregano, leaves picked
- 1 bunch fresh purslane (optional), leaves picked
- ½ bunch mint, leaves picked
- 1 loaf Lebanese talami bread (or Turkish bread)
- seeds from 1 pomegranate

Dressing

- ¼ cup (60 ml) pomegranate molasses, or to taste
- ½ cup (125 ml) lemon juice
- ½ cup (125 ml) extra virgin olive oil
- sea salt, to taste
- 1 tablespoon sumac, plus extra to serve
- 2 garlic cloves, crushed

The fattoush (minus the tomatoes and the dressing) can be prepared the day before and kept in an airtight container in the fridge. The dressing can also be mixed and refigerated in an airtight jar or container.

Cut the cucumbers and tomatoes into 1 cm (½ inch) dice and transfer to a salad bowl. Cut the capsicums and lettuce into 1 cm (½ inch) pieces and the spring onions into 1 cm (½ inch) lengths and add to the bowl. Slice the radishes then cut into matchsticks and add to the bowl. Shred the cabbages finely and add to the bowl.

Preheat the oven to 180°C (350°F) fan-forced (200°C/400°F conventional).

Combine the parsley, oregano and purslane, if using, and add to the bowl. If the mint leaves are large, cut or tear them in half. Add the mint to the bowl and set aside.

Place the bread in the oven and bake until crisp, then use clean hands to crush lightly into a separate bowl. Set aside as a garnish.

Combine the dressing ingredients in a small bowl and mix well with a fork.

Add half the pomegranate seeds and the dressing to the salad bowl and toss using clean hands. Scatter the crushed Lebanese bread and the remaining pomegranate seeds on top, and sprinkle with an extra pinch of sumac.

Serve immediately.

BAY LEAVES
TEJ PATTA

Category: Astringent–sulphurous spices.
Form: Large, classically shaped leaves.
Colour: Deep forest green when fresh, a dusty and dark khaki when dried.

Bay leaves are complex. Their astringent character, which is soft enough to act as a tenderiser of meats in the early stages of the cooking process, is combined with a quiet volume of aromatic 'skirt' that offers smoke, bitterness and pungency. Their herbaceous and astringent qualities are loud enough to attach their message to other spices across a wide spectrum of masala. All this and yet they're still modest enough not to dominate.

Both aromatically and functionally, bay leaves have a chameleon quality that sees them used across almost all culinary cultures, thanks not least to the hardiness of the plant itself – there are few climates where a bay tree won't thrive. Similarly, no single culinary framework 'owns' bay leaves' aromatic message. They don't shout Middle East like sumac (page 191) or India like kala namak (page 72). Because of this, they allow harmonious use across a broad spectrum of dishes.

I haven't included any recipes specifically for bay leaves, not only because so many are already scattered throughout the book, but also because bay leaves will never lead a recipe. When it comes to masala it's not an aroma we build around. To see bay leaves' impact, take a look at:

- **Kabargah** (page 135), where it provides light movement in the base of a heavy masala
- **Shivani's mutton yakhni** (page 107), where it gives a subtle shadow to the masala's nursery softness
- **Ammi's garam masala** (page 156), where it gives aromatic movement to a dense and weighted masala.

Tasting notes
Bay leaves are difficult to taste, primarily because chomping down on dried leaves is unpleasant and doesn't do much more than release bitterness. In masala, bay leaves impart a subtle **bitter** and **sharp** flavour. They have a distinct herbaceous element, with taste notes reminiscent of **oregano** and **thyme** wrapped around a **pungent leaf bite**. Secondary notes approach **eucalyptus**.

Use in masala
Bay leaves see a lot of the stovetop in Kashmiri Hindu households because they form an element of the whole garam masala used to begin a lot of our mutton dishes (see page 242). Bay leaves are also used in ground garam masala. What's interesting and little understood about bay leaves is that they will tenderise meats if added at the beginning of cooking – courtesy of their astringent nature.

Explaining whole garam masala
Whole garam masala is like the North Indian bouquet garni, a group of whole spices used together to create a familiar baseline profile that provides structural support *and* familiarity to dishes.
For a Kashmiri Hindu, whole garam masala normally consists of black cardamom pods, bay leaves, cinnamon stick or cassia bark, and quite often green cardamom pods and/or cloves. But given every family has its own recipe, there are as many variations as there are kitchens.

MUSTARD SEEDS

Mustard seeds can be a bit like cumin seeds for those unfamiliar with regional Indian cuisine. Folks know they're part of the framework for 'curry' but aren't always certain when to add them and in what quantity. With cumin seeds this partial knowledge isn't a big deal, because cumin seeds are friendly. But mustard seeds – whether black or yellow – aren't so amenable. Their unique combination of astringent, bitter and savoury can cause aromatic disruption.

If you're unsure exactly what you're doing, go a little easy and use both, which will reduce the chance of things going awry. That's the beauty of scaffolding or tiering spice: while it seems counterintuitive to use more variations of a thing we don't understand, it's as if the aromatics work together to create their own cohesion. If you do choose to scaffold, know that while black mustard seeds are aromatically milder than yellow mustard seeds when tasted raw, the opposite is true once they hit heat and fat.

BLACK MUSTARD SEEDS RAI

Category: Astringent–sulphurous spices.

Form: Tiny round balls, like very miniature marbles or, for Australian readers, spicy hundreds and thousands.

Colour: Charcoal black.

Tasting notes

Black mustard seeds are known for their pop when they hit heat and oil. Primary aromas segue from **raw pea** through to **rancid hazelnut**. Their secondary character goes deeper, into **green pea shoot** and **light soil**. Their tertiary character is that sensation of **oral spaciousness** facilitated by astringent–sulphurous spices in general. The application of heat and fat draws out black mustard seeds' **heating** quality. Tasted raw, they're **restrained**.

Use in masala

Black mustard seeds are a taste blueprint for much of India's southern regions. Not all the time or in every dish, but they appear in the primary dabba of most South Indian householders (see page 243). When they're not used to translate regional character, black mustard seeds iterate nutty tastes, contribute to texture and apply an undercoat of shadow and black-skivvy intensity – character-wise, they're definitely a little Beatnik. Classically, they are paired with garlic, turmeric powder and cumin seeds. Fresh curry leaves, too. They are a natural inclusion in seafood-based curries and with coconut milk, cream or flesh.

Emotive content

Black mustard seeds are odd in that they are both difficult and weirdly moreish. Whenever I chew them, I feel both intrigued and repelled, as if at the entrance to a dark room, and the part of me that wants to enter is more compelled than the part that wants to flick on the light. Emotively, it's a mature suggestion – that we're strong enough to face an emotion or a circumstance that some other less secure part of us finds frightening. Perhaps that's why mustard seeds in general are difficult for younger palates not quite ready for that experience of the world.

What's in a name ... and a dabba

One of my friends at Valley School in Bengaluru was a Parsi (Persian). Her name was Anu Batliwalla and she was beautiful: porcelain skin, large hazel eyes, light brown curls – like an early era Marilyn Monroe, only prettier.

The Parsi community came to India in medieval times to escape religious persecution by Muslims: Parsis are the descendants of Persian Zoroastrians. They arrived in India without surnames, so when British rule established census laws that required registration of citizens, the Parsi community came up with surnames that took their cue from professions, the foods they loved or the places they lived.

Anu's family must have been involved with bottles in some way: *walla* refers to any merchant and *batli* means bottle. A *batliwalla*, then, is a trader or vendor whose stock in trade is bottles. No other community in India has such a whimsical approach to surnames.

Parsis are representative of all communities across the Indian region in that, historically, it's nearly always possible in India to know someone's family origin if you know their surname. Ganju is definitively Kashmiri. Singh is Punjabi. The surname Fernandes indicates Goa. And just as it's possible to tell where someone is from by hearing their surname, it's equally possible to guess someone's origin by virtue of what's in their masala dabba.

Masala dabbas indicate regions because as we've seen, masala is traditionally defined by regional considerations. We've spoken about this a lot – the way geography influences masala through the lens of Ayurveda (see page 26) and how regional character is expressed through masala. So while a Kashmiri Hindu householder's dabba would feature cinnamon powder, for example, that of a householder from Bengaluru might instead contain black mustard seeds. When travelling India or spending time in a desi household, these are small details for the masala-curious to notice.

YELLOW MUSTARD SEEDS
SARSON

Category: Astringent–sulphurous spices.

Form: Tiny round balls, like very miniature marbles or, for Australian readers, spicy hundreds and thousands.

Colour: Tan yellow.

Tasting notes

Yellow mustard seeds have a subtler profile than black mustard seeds. They're also in some ways more commonly known, as they're used in European cuisines to create mustards. They are, however, less used in masala than black mustard seeds. Primary taste notes of **summer hay** and **toasted bread** evolve to secondary characters of **fresh almond**. The finish of yellow mustard seeds has a gentle, **young green onion** quality.

Use in masala

I use yellow mustard seeds as a softening agent in a masala that has heavy astringent or sulphurous overtones. As we know, astringent–sulphurous spices are inherently disruptive, which is not a characteristic of Kashmiri Hindu cooking. Tiering spices from this category lessens their disruptive impact.

Emotive content

Yellow mustard seeds offer a feeling of distant connection – like the person in the supermarket whose face you recognise but can't place.

Cabbage sabji

Cabbage, like cauliflower, is an acquired taste. While we tend not to love it as kids, we learn to do so as a vehicle for masala as we age: that bitter earthiness of cabbage makes it a natural companion for mustard seeds.

This dish is a good example of the use of black mustard seeds in traditional south Indian regional cuisine. I love this kind of sabji at lunchtime with Poori (page 140) and pickles – Bhavna's mum's winter carrot pickles (page 100) would be perfect.

This recipe makes a small quantity because this dish doesn't reheat well.

Serves 2

- 1 tablespoon mustard oil
- 2 teaspoons black mustard seeds
- 1 teaspoon fine white lake salt
- ½ teaspoon red chilli powder
- generous ¼ teaspoon fine white sea salt
- 4 garlic cloves, crushed or finely chopped
- ¼ cabbage, thinly sliced

Combine all the ingredients except the cabbage in a large frying pan over medium–high heat until popping and aromatic. Taste it – it will be salty, hot, driving and striking.

Toss in the cabbage and cook for about 15 minutes, until soft and redolent of masala. Serve immediately.

Aloo tamaatar ki sabji

Serves 2 as a snack

⅓ cup (80 ml) vegetable oil
3 small–medium potatoes, cut into 1 cm (½ inch) cubes
2 small tomatoes, finely diced

Masala

2 teaspoons black mustard seeds
1 teaspoon fine white lake salt
½ teaspoon red chilli powder
¼ teaspoon fine white sea salt
4 garlic cloves, crushed or finely chopped

To finish (optional)

pinch of fleur de sel

Dad was the inspiration for this sabji. When we were kids, he used to spend days travelling on sales runs up to Melbourne from our home in Jan Juc, Torquay, on the Victorian south coast, at that time about a ninety-minute drive from the city. Mum and Dad made and designed textiles. Those were long and stressful days pushing merchandise and writing orders, and he'd walk in the door late, not having eaten breakfast or lunch, and fall on a thali of fried potatoes tossed with salt and chilli powder. This sabji is a riff on that memory. It shows how aggressive tastes can healthily address a demanding appetite.

Heat the vegetable oil in a large kadai, cast-iron wok or heavy-based saucepan until almost smoking. Toss in the potatoes and fry until tender, stirring frequently to fry them evenly. Taste a piece. It should be crispy on the outside and tender on the inside.

Toss in the main masala and stir through until the potatoes are well coated and the masala is no longer raw, 2–3 minutes. The black mustard seeds should pop and sizzle and the aroma should be strong.

Add the tomatoes, being prepared for the sizzle. Stir for a few minutes, until the tomatoes are fried, the initial sharp sizzle has died down and the sauce looks rich. This stage is key to the recipe – as the tomato fries with the skin on it becomes a little leathery, like jerky, and rich with umami. The potatoes will continue to brown and soften. Cook until the oil is minimised. Taste. If it needs a little more kick, add the fleur de sel.

Over the page: Left: Cabbage sabji (opposite). Middle: Aloo tamaatar ki sabji. Right: Simple gobi sabji (page 290).

HING ASAFOETIDA

Category: Astringent–sulphurous spices.
Form: Powder or resin. The powder is a little gritty but fine. The resin is soft like wax when fresh but hardens over time.
Colour: Hing powder ranges from dirty cream to pale canary yellow. The resin is toffee brown.

There's a lot of curiosity around hing (asafoetida). Hing is the Hindi name, asafoetida is its botanical name – *asa* is the Persian word for resin and *foetida* is Latin for strong odour. I've described it elsewhere as a combination of pineapple, blue cheese and sweaty feet. One person took offence, but it's pretty accurate.

Common use focuses on hing's digestive function.

In a cultural context, hing signposts a dish as belonging to specific cultural groups whose ethnicity prevents their consumption of garlic and onion based on faith traditions. This includes small pockets of Hindus, from the mountains in the north to the jungles in the south, who subscribe to Brahmanic traditions. It is a unique and deliberate marker.

A couple of recipes featuring hing appear in the pages that follow. But hing also appears in other recipes in the book, particularly:

- **Tamarind eggplant** (page 188), where there's a lot going on and hing forms an understorey
- **Matar khoya** (page 180), where hing provides an astringent break from the weight of mace.

Tasting notes

The tasting notes of hing differ depending on its form – the resin can be carried by water, and so it's broader, softer and it sits a little lighter within masala's framework. The powder has a blunt edge. In both cases, the primary character is **overripe sweet sulphur**, which is where that trio of **pineapple**, **blue cheese** and **sweaty feet** kicks in.

Use in masala

Those for whom hing has cultural connection use it in masala as a claiming of identity. I've loved watching Chachi repeatedly reach for the bottle of hing water by her stove when she makes mutton, for example. Unlike the powder, which is added once, the resin dissolved in water is normally added a little at a time throughout the cooking process. Perhaps like saffron, that intimate relationship with hing is a marker to indigenous users of the uniqueness of what it feels to be us. For non-indigenous users, the easiest way to consider hing is as a garlic and onion replacement.

Emotive content

For those without a cultural connection to hing, its emotive content is like the thrill of the circus sideshow – that feeling of being seduced by something strange and strangely attractive. For native users, it is a representation of the occasional comfort of otherness (see page 249).

A note on powdered asafoetida for coeliacs

It's worth checking the ingredients listing on packages of powdered hing – it's hard to find brands that don't add gums, wheat starch and even turmeric. I'm not super pedantic about this, but obviously a coeliac would need to take note. In terms of taste, the additives can make hing blunter. There are online products available labelled as pure asafoetida powders. Even just as an experiment, it's worth taking the time to compare powdered types alongside each other in raw tastings. Noting differences is always useful in the art of masala.

Hing water: a softer option

The softest option is to buy hing resin and dilute it in water. I've never looked for the resin in Australia, but I have bought it in New Delhi – the Ganju family heads to INA (Indian National Airways) Market for what is apparently the best-quality fresh hing in Delhi, and then brings it back through customs. It's beautiful to use. A piece of resin the size of an average pinkie fingernail can be dissolved in a 275 millilitre (9½ fl oz) jar of water and set in the fridge, lid on, ready to pull out at any time. Hing water can be applied throughout the cooking process. It has all the aroma of powdered hing, but with a rounder and broader impact.

AYURVEDA AND OTHERNESS

In the early stages of this book we talked about the barrier that exoticism erects in front of understanding masala, and the ways we can familiarise ourselves with certain spices by integrating them into known recipes. Like using fenugreek powder in Osso buco (page 54) or seasoning avocado toast with kala namak (page 72). But at some point – once our skill levels increase – we can draw more from an experience by letting the aromatic we're handling retain its 'otherness'.

Otherness is an important idea in Indian culture. In the way of many ancient cultures, it allows us to believe in the simultaneous existence of a material and a metaphysical world. The Himalayas, for instance, can at once be a climber's mountain range and the literal seat of the gods. Or Kurukshetra can at once be the mythical and ancient battleground upon which the story of the Bhagavad Gita is set, and a modern Indian municipality in Haryana state.

The feeling of otherness was my favourite part of the stories of the gods Dad told us when we were kids. I remember him once telling me about Parvati. I must've been in my early adolescence: a young teenage female with all the usual insecurities, compounded by the feeling of being a fuzzy brown girl in a shiny white-girl world. We were living in the small Victorian coastal town of Torquay. My friends all seemed smoother than me. They didn't have bushy eyebrows, frizzy curls or downy dark hair covering their arms and legs.

Dad said Parvati approached her husband, Shivji, asking for money to buy a new dress. As the god of destruction, Shivji is the blue-skinned ascetic. He and his consort wife lived in a cave in the Himalayas without ostentation: in Hindu mythology, destruction and death refer to the annihilation of ego and material identity as much as any literal end. Parvati wanted a new dress for a night out with Lakshmi and Devi. Lakshmi, as the goddess of wealth, and Devi, as *shakti* or pure universal energy, are typically depicted as fair-skinned, bejewelled beauties. Parvati was of course beautiful – all the goddesses are – but dark-skinned. She felt the insecurity of that and, like so many women, looked to raise her confidence with a new outfit.

Being the god of destruction, Shivji was derisive of his consort's material concerns and so reached into his loincloth and produced a small drawstring pouch. Parvati opened it to find not gold, but powdered *vibhuti* – sacred ash. At her expression of dismay, Shivji reminded her that any of his disciples would value such an offering more than life. That, as his consort and in her own right as the archetypal mother goddess of fertility, abundance, food and nourishment, Parvati was intrinsically of value. And in fact, that pouch of *vibhuti* was hardly equal to her standing, fair skin, bejewelled saris or no.

I loved that moment with Dad.

The obvious moral is to be proud of who you are. That what's inside matters more than a polished exterior. But more subtle is the understanding that a broader sense of who we are comes when we accept the otherness within us. That the feeling of not belonging to an external environment is but a reflection of the ways we feel at odds with ourselves. And becoming familiar with our internal otherness isn't about rectification, or even about acceptance. It's about peacefully coexisting with difference or dichotomy, even when we don't like what it says.

In domestic Ayurvedic practice, knowing this sense of otherness is important chiefly because so much of Ayurveda and masala is about understanding patterning rather than striving for balance. We might always be a little off kilter – the bell curve of normalcy says that indeed we will be, much of the time. Emotional, physical or spiritual limps don't always require crutches. These concepts allow us to see that, in life, we will frequently move with an uneven gait. Recognising that is about touching our otherness inside from time to time.

சுயம்பு அருள்மிகு ஆதிபராசக்தி

Sandeep's hing haakh

I met Sandeep Pandit the same night that many Australians did – during his first appearance as a contestant on Australian *MasterChef* in 2019. It was huge for me to see another Kashmiri Hindu in the flesh: even in India we're considered a relatively niche ethnic group, let alone in Australia (see opposite). I'm really happy he's contributed a recipe to this book, and I love the one he chose, and his words about why.

'In India,' he says, 'when someone talks about having enough to eat, the most basic is "dal-roti". But *haakh* and *bhata* is the equivalent of dal and roti for Kashmiris. *Haakh* is a bitter green, *bhata* is rice. It's the commoners' food, just as it's the food of the rich folk.

'This simple dish and this style of cooking appears in almost all of Asia: just about every culture has a stir-fried green dish. But they use the ingredients that are known to them. In China you'll see it with sesame oil, chilli and garlic. In Kashmir, instead of sesame oil we use mustard oil, and instead of garlic we use hing. (Because Kashmir was right at the confluence of branches of the silk route, Kashmir and China have the same way of making this type of dish – whether it went as a tradition from China to Kashmir, or Kashmir to China.)

'In Ayurveda we have *katu* foods that bring pungency, so in order to add that pungent flavour, that *rasa*, we use hing. Hing is used to bring that flavour profile even in meat. I chose *haakh* as my recipe here because it shows hing more clearly than, say, rogan josh. Hing is part of our cultural identity. And it's this dish that I prepared for the judges in round one of *MasterChef*. It's such a testament to that land and, in its simplicity, hing transforms *haakh*.'

Serves 4 as part of a shared meal

600 g (1 lb 5 oz) Chinese broccoli (gai larn) or bok choy

2 tablespoons mustard oil

Masala

½ teaspoon hing (asafoetida) powder

2 green chillies, split and deseeded

sea salt, to taste

Separate the broccoli or the bok choy leaves, trimming away any thick stems, and wash well under cold running water. Gently pat dry with a clean tea towel (dish towel).

Place a wok (choose a wok that has a lid) over high heat. Pour the mustard oil into the hot wok and heat until it smokes.

Add the Chinese broccoli and stir immediately until wilted.

Add the masala and mix well. Cover with a lid and simmer for 2–3 minutes.

Serve with basmati rice.

Seeing ourselves reflected

Until I saw Sandeep on *MasterChef*, I had no idea that Pandit cuisine and Kashmiri Hindu culture was a bona fide ethnicity. I mean I knew, but I didn't know. Growing up, whether in India or in Australia, my only experience of that world was inside my family. When I heard Sandeep's story on *MasterChef* I felt – not legitimised – but a spark of drive that what I had to share was an actual part of a broader conversation, one that exists beyond the Ganju family kitchens.

But equally transformative has been the way it has felt to see other pockets of regional Indian cooking spoken about: Mischa Tropp's Keralan cuisine, Helly Raichura's Gujarati food, Kishwar Chowdhury's Bengali thalis. And that's just Melbourne. Suddenly India is on the map not as a mass subcontinent of whitewashed exotica, but as a nuanced, real-life landscape where people are people and we all have unique things to say. I've liaised hard to include recipes from others, when fitting, so that this book can reflect the joy and the relief I have felt at writing during an era of increasing representation.

Bui's dum aloo

I thought I made a decent Kashmiri dum aloo until I made it with Bui. I got *schooled*. It was great. This recipe has a lot of tips, but for the full bonanza I have a video of Bui making it on my Spirit of Spice YouTube channel (see link below). The presence of hing (asafoetida) is a cultural reflex – when it comes to Kashmiri Hindu food, few spices say more without explanation.

You'll need to start a few hours before you intend to eat – or even a day earlier – as dum aloo responds well to being left for a few hours to soak in the masala, then gently reheated to serve. It's important to use new potatoes that are very close to the same size, so that they cook evenly.

The dum cooking tradition

Broadly, dum means oven. More specifically it's 'warm breath'. Cooking in the dum tradition involves a pot with a sealed lid – the seal is traditionally created with a ring of wheat flour or atta dough. The warmed breath refers to the steam used in this method of cooking. Masala is nothing if not poetic.

Left: Bui's dum aloo, served with Sandeep's hing haakh (page 252).

Serves 6 as part of a shared meal

- 800 g (1 lb 12 oz) evenly sized new potatoes
- 1–2 cups (250–500 ml) mustard oil
- 1 teaspoon fine white sea salt
- ½ teaspoon turmeric powder
- ½–¾ cup water

Chilli yoghurt

- 1 tablespoon plain yoghurt
- ⅓ cup (80 ml) water
- 1 teaspoon Kashmiri chilli powder

Chilli water

- 1 teaspoon red chilli powder
- ½ cup (125 ml) water

Masala

- 2 pinches of hing (asafoetida) powder
- 1½ teaspoons cumin seeds
- 1 tablespoon plain yoghurt
- 3 teaspoons fennel powder
- 2 teaspoons coriander powder
- 2 teaspoons fine white sea salt
- 1 teaspoon ginger powder

To finish

- 1 teaspoon Ammi's garam masala (page 156)

Pop the potatoes in a pressure cooker and just cover with cold water. Cook under pressure for 4–5 minutes. You want them to be not hard but also not falling apart – they still have a long cook ahead of them. If you don't have a pressure cooker, cook the potatoes in a large saucepan of boiling water for 7–10 minutes, taking care not to boil them so much that they become soggy. Drain the potatoes, allow to cool, then peel them carefully: part of the beauty of this dish is lovely-looking potatoes.

Using a toothpick or fine skewer, poke about 30 holes all the way through the potatoes. It's a lot and takes ages, but it's important because it prepares the potatoes for the next stage.

Heat the mustard oil in a kadai, stable cast-iron wok or heavy-based saucepan large enough that the oil comes up no more than halfway (this is very important), using enough of the oil so that you can fry all the potatoes at once without them popping above the oil surface. Once the oil is very hot, add the salt and the turmeric powder. This prevents the potatoes from sticking.

Put in all the potatoes at once. With so much produce, the oil will cool a little and the potatoes have the chance to cook all the way through. The temperature should be hot enough that the potatoes bubble and boil, but not so hot that they break right down. Bui's stirring technique is important here: using a large flattish slotted spoon, she rolls them gently, not too frequently, through the oil to tip them over and make sure they cook on all sides, never disturbing them too much so they won't break apart.

At 10-minute intervals during the frying process, which takes about 30 minutes, briefly turn down the heat slightly (this is important) and carefully add 2–3 tablespoons of the water to the boiling oil and potatoes. Pop a lid on so that the steam from the oil and water mix is contained. (This steam bath pushes the oil through the potatoes, making them more delicious but also ensuring that the potatoes are very tender on the inside and crisp on the outside. Beautifully cooked dum aloo jets masala like a volcano when you bite into it.) Be very careful here – if the pan is too small and the temperature too high, the oil can climb up the pot, run over the sides and catch alight. The water has to be added to the oil three times throughout the 30-minute frying time.

Remove the cooked potatoes from the mustard oil using a slotted spoon, and drain on paper towel. Reserve the mustard oil.

Make the chilli yoghurt by whisking all three ingredients together. Make the chilli water by stirring the chilli into the water. Set both aside near the stovetop.

In a large frying pan, heat ⅓ cup (80 ml) of the reserved mustard oil (which already has so much flavour) over medium heat.

We will add the masala in parts rather than all at once. First add the hing and cumin seeds, along with the chilli yoghurt, and stir through for 2–3 minutes. Add the chilli water and stir through for another 2–3 minutes. Now add the remaining masala ingredients, reduce the heat slightly, stir them through and bring to a simmer. Taking time to stir after adding liquid components gives the masala a chance to cook off the spice and create subtle structural tiers of taste.

Add the drained potatoes and gently stir them through the masala. Simmer over low heat for 2–3 minutes. Transfer gently to a large pressure cooker, if you have one. The water in the masala should almost cover the potatoes, leaving a small circle of their topside exposed. If there isn't enough water, just add a little more. Stir in the garam masala and set to pressure-cook until it emits one or two whistles or until soft, about 10 minutes. The potatoes shouldn't break apart at this point, unless you really overdo it, because the oil and extended frying period have built in a very strong structure. If you don't have a pressure cooker, add the garam masala and continue cooking in the frying pan over medium heat, with the lid on, for about 30 minutes, until the potatoes are soft but not breaking apart.

Set aside for a few hours to let the dum aloo really absorb the masala before gently reheating to serve. Serve with roti or chapati, dal, a raw cucumber and onion salad, and pickles, or with Sandeep's hing haakh (page 252).

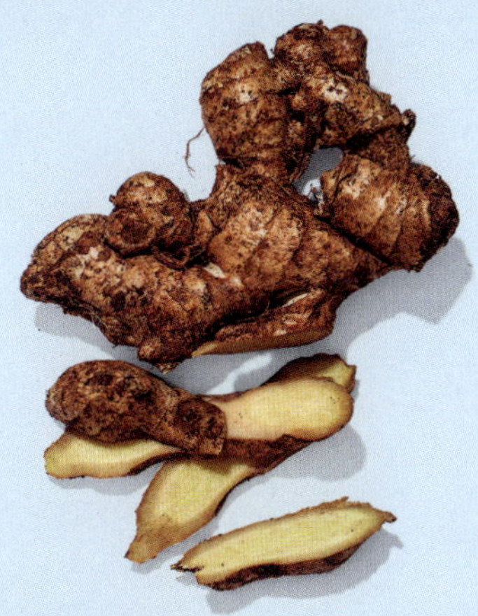

FRESH GINGER ADRAK

Category: Astringent–sulphurous spices.
Form: Thin-skinned rhizome.
Colour: Pale, pretty beige.

Culturally, fresh ginger is a unifying aromatic, not just across the regions of India, but the regions of Asia as a whole. Like turmeric, it belongs to the householder medicine cabinet as much as it does the kitchen.

Fresh ginger introduces a precise ray of light to masala. For Kashmiri Hindus, it is slicing contrast to dense, warm, powdered and heavily textured aromatic combinations. Whereas onion and mustard seeds hit the gullet, and garlic opens the space behind the nasal cavity, fresh ginger blooms into the olfactory space. It's prettier. Brighter.

While astringent and sulphurous spices are generally considered to be heating, and moderate consumption is advised for most body types and environments, fresh ginger is considered a *sattvic* spice (see page 200). A knuckle of fresh ginger in the fruit bowl is a kitchen constant. Added to any recipe in this book, it will find a way to harmonise, and it's the rare spice in our dabbas to make that claim.

Tasting notes

Most fresh spice hits us upfront with its textures, and fresh ginger is no different. It provides a **sweet**, **wet** and **astringent** contribution to masala expressed through that sensation of olfactory cleansing. Its aromas are pretty – **candlenut** and **freesia** move through **kaffir lime** and finish in the region of a subtle **garlicky acidity**.

Use in masala

The texture of fresh ginger – on the one hand wet and astringent, and on the other fibrous and earthy – means that in masala it plays a few different roles. Combined with the flavours of South-East Asia – lemongrass, garlic, fresh chilli and fresh kokum or tamarind – ginger escalates acidity and heat, making the masala brighter and higher. When used with dried spices in whole, seed and powdered form, fresh ginger shows aspects of soil and astringency.

Emotive content

I always think of fresh ginger as an aromatic with swag. It's arousing and stimulating, confident.

A tale of two ginger-based remedies

Given the importance of fresh ginger in the Indian householder's kitchen, it feels appropriate to begin with two drinks that, in the regional Indian home, are considered as much tinctures as beverages.

Adrak chai

Makes 2–3 cups (500–750 ml)

- 1 tablespoon chai patti (see note)
- 4 cups (1 litre) water
- 1 × 7.5 cm (3 inch) piece of ginger, peeled and chopped
- 1 tablespoon sugar (optional)
- 1–1½ cups milk (optional)

Boil the chai patti, water and fresh ginger in a medium saucepan. When the water darkens to your desired strength, either remove from the heat for black chai and add the sugar (if desired), or add the milk and bring to a rolling boil, stirring with a whisking action to aerate and thicken the milk. I do this for a few minutes until the chai thickens, adding the sugar during the whisking process. Strain and serve.

Note: Chai patti is Indian tea, normally Assam, in dust or granule form. It looks like instant coffee, only finer, and is malty and strong. If you don't have it, use a strong black leaf tea.

Ginger honey tea

Ginger honey tea has a pungent, hot and sweet post-digestive quality. It's served by the Indian householder to cure the sensory body malaise caused by the common cold. In Ayurvedic thought, it's a tincture that cleans the tongue, improves the voice, treats coughs and reduces the mild inflammation associated with a cold.

Serves 1

Pour about 1 cup (250 ml) cold water into a small saucepan and add an equal volume of unpeeled chopped fresh ginger. Bring to the boil, then put the lid on to reduce evaporation and simmer for at least 10 minutes, or until the water changes colour and becomes a little textured.

Serve hot in a glass, with a little honey stirred through to taste. A squeeze of fresh lemon juice gives the tea a stimulating quality, so add that if you need some energy.

Right: Mug: Adrak chai. Glasses: Ginger honey tea.

Kashmiri Hindu keema

Keema is family-friendly. As a girl, I loved it with dal and rice because it wasn't challenging. The masala is warm and soft, the minced (ground) lamb is silken, and the whole dish feels nourishing and easy to digest. Across the regions of India, traditional minced meat is texturally different from that of a Western butcher – the meat is simultaneously chopped and pounded, and so the fat and protein are emulsified. This cohesion means masala is expressed as a subtler composition of spice. I don't pound my mince because of the time it takes, and I find that pressure cooking the keema results in a similar outcome.

The large volume of fresh ginger in the masala acts as a counterpoint to the richness of the mince. As Hindus, we always use lamb or mutton and never beef.

Build in an extra hour or so to marinate the mince in the yoghurt and masala before cooking.

Serves 4–6 as part of a shared meal

500 g (1 lb 2 oz) minced (ground) lamb
½ cup (130 g) plain yoghurt

Masala

2–3 tablespoons finely grated fresh ginger
3 teaspoons coriander powder
2½ teaspoons cumin powder
2 teaspoons fennel powder
1½ teaspoons fine pink salt
1 teaspoon ginger powder
½–1 teaspoon red chilli powder
½ teaspoon fine white lake salt
scant ½ teaspoon turmeric powder

For pressure cooking

2 tablespoons ghee
¾ cup (185 ml) water

To finish

1 teaspoon garam masala
fresh coriander (cilantro) leaves, to taste

In a large bowl, combine the minced lamb with the yoghurt and all the masala ingredients. Mix thoroughly, then pop in the fridge for at least 30 minutes to marinate. This allows the yoghurt to tenderise the meat, while the fresh ginger will 'slice and dice' into the lamb fat, yoghurt and ghee to give the masala a sharper appearance.

Heat the ghee in a flameproof pressure cooker or large heavy-based saucepan over high heat and add the lamb mince and marinade mixture. Brown off for about 5 minutes to take the edge of 'rawness' out of the meat. Add the water, then set the pressure cooker to high heat. Once it whistles twice, reduce the heat to low and let it putter away for 20–25 minutes. At this point, turn off the heat and let the pressure cooker depressurise on its own.

Alternatively, keep cooking in the saucepan, without the lid on, over medium–high heat for 30 minutes. You will need to watch the pot, stirring occasionally, and add more water as needed so the meat doesn't stick.

Stir the garam masala through the hot lamb for 2–3 minutes. Serve topped with fresh coriander or stir it through just before serving.

FRESH TURMERIC
HALDI

Category: Astringent–sulphurous spices.
Form: Fingered rhizome.
Colour: Beige skin around vibrant orange–umber flesh.

Fresh turmeric is not an aromatic but an ecosystem. If it were categorised, it would fall into the grouping of astringent–sulphurous spices somewhere between hing and fresh ginger. From the fresh rhizome springs a culture – it is the origin of the *haldi* (turmeric paste) applied to the skin at wedding and *puja* ceremonies, and of the powdered turmeric that's almost single-handedly taken the idea of Ayurveda from the region of India to the world. It's the seed of every householder's kitchen medicine cabinet. Fresh turmeric gives birth to the turmeric yellow colour that is as closely associated with the subcontinent as rani pink. It has stained more than one marble benchtop and many open palms.

For the child of the regional Indian householder, the playfulness of *haldi* is the introduction to mythology that establishes the framework for masala. We don't fall in love with the practice of masala because of its efficacy or its philosophy as one might as an adult – we're drawn in by the mystery. It is a presence in our lives from our earliest days: in Haldi doodh (page 38) and in a Ramayana picture book or Panchatantra comic.

Aromatically, fresh turmeric is bright, wet, fresh and a little floral. Its astringent quality is as light as its recessed quality of earth. Similarly, it is functionally gentle. To affect masala, fresh turmeric needs to be used in a far greater quantity than powdered – and even then its effect is not one of structure, but of subtle space creation.

I've had to search a bit for recipes using fresh turmeric because it's never been in the Ganju family canon of masala in any routine sense. And so my friend and colleague Sadaf Hussain was an enormous help. Sadaf's bio includes Indian *MasterChef* finalist, TEDx speaker, author, chef, podcaster and food consultant. But really, Sadaf is a proponent of and believer in the magic of masala, and in the importance of documenting and sharing what that means. His recipe for a turmeric dessert follows, and that for pulao appears on page 305. And his latest book, *Masalamandi*, is itself a brilliant exploration of masala.

Sadaf's Rampur haldi ki halwa

Between Salem and Erode – the two regions of India responsible for growing the bulk of the subcontinent's haldi – Sadaf Hussain (see page 262) nominates Salem-grown turmeric as his favourite. And this turmeric dessert, from the region of Rampur in Uttar Pradesh in India's north, is his favourite way to serve it.

Serves 6–8

- 125 g (4½ oz) fresh turmeric
- 2–3 tablespoons water
- ¾ cup (120 g) whole almonds
- 4 tablespoons ghee

Masala

- 1 cup (150 g) jaggery powder
- 1 cup (120 g) chickpea flour (besan)
- 8–10 green cardamom pods, husks cracked

To finish (optional)

- edible silver leaf or edible flowers
- chopped almonds

Peel and wash the fresh turmeric and let it dry. Cut it into small pieces, then pulse in a blender or food processor with the water until it forms a rough paste. Transfer to a bowl and set aside.

Pulse the almonds in a blender or food processor until finely ground.

Heat the ghee in a medium heavy-based saucepan over medium heat. Reduce the heat to low and add the turmeric paste, stirring and roasting it. When the haldi absorbs the ghee then releases the excess, add the ground almonds, along with all the masala ingredients, and mix well. Keep roasting for 2–3 minutes so none of the ingredients are raw. Remove from the heat but continue to stir for a further 2–3 minutes, to bring the mixture together with an even consistency.

Serve at room temperature, garnished with silver leaf or flowers, and chopped almonds, if you like.

FOREST-FLOOR SPICES

Function in masala: Shifting masala's message by opening the imaginary central space in the upper palate and opening our awareness to different movement patterns in taste.
Emotive quality: Creating ease by giving us more space to be where we are – and to notice new perspectives.
Traditional medicinal purpose: Encouraging appetite and thus aiding digestion.

The topography of the forest-floor spices is unique within the world of masala. Aromatics in this category don't bed in or bed down, they're not particularly concerned with offering a point of contrast or likeness, they won't provide a filter, and they don't establish a tone or voice. They're not even really aromatics that you can over- or under-do. Well of course you *can*, but you'd have to try pretty hard, for two reasons.

Firstly, the visible volume of forest-floor spices instructs us how much to use in a way that dried seeds, pods and powders don't. Because the leafiness of these aromatics makes them look like produce, you can easily *see* how much is too much or not enough. And secondly, though some of these aromatics are quite specific to Indian regional cuisine, the use of fresh and dried leaf spices (i.e. herbs) is well established across most culinary cultures, so even those with only basic kitchen knowledge tend to have an idea of how much to use.

These aromatics – curry leaves, coriander (cilantro) leaves – are typically added at the end of cooking. As such, they carry surface emotive messaging. They're not the tastes we cry over. Instead, what's precious about them is their vibrancy, their colour. As elements of masala they sweep in like the scent of rain through an open door. Thool zamboor (page 164), for example, is one of the densest, earthiest articulations of Kashmiri Hindu masala. But stir through coriander (cilantro) leaves at the finish and what was autumn becomes spring.

Functionally, forest-floor aromatics create movement in the hard-to-reach upper–middle palate. This is the cleft area that fills in between the sixth and ninth weeks of gestation. Aromas of forest-floor spices circulate here and translate as freshness.

As a rule, we tend not to scaffold forest-floor spice, although there is an exception in Methi chicken (page 272), where we scaffold the same spice in a fresh and dried capacity. Otherwise, we use only one spice from this category at a time. When more than one is used, the movement messaging becomes confusing, like tipping white wine into red.

What's in a name

In masala, the largest aromatic weight and significance is taken over by the roots, seeds and barks – the elements of the plants that naturally contain the type of structural information that translates into complex tastes and complex functional uses. But the leaves of the plant are different. For a plant, the leaves are the connection between the sun and the earth. They're the axis that turns solar energy into food, and the filter that absorbs carbon to produce oxygen. They're movement, in other words, a point of contact in a plant where something that *was* ceases, and moves to become something else.

Forest-floor spices perform the same role within masala. They provide the axis point that moves the aromatic structure into a new understanding, emotive resonance and structural appearance. It's why these fresh aromatics are included at the finish – not just because they are aromatically gentle, so long cooking would erase their impact, but also because they are best expressed in terms of their impact upon the whole.

METHI
FENUGREEK LEAVES

Category: Forest-floor spices.
Form: Either fresh leaves that resemble clover, or dried, with small, brittle, squarish leaves bunched in unruly clumps.
Colour: The fresh form is spinach green, the dried dusky khaki green.

If Popeye had known about methi, he'd have swapped his spinach in a heartbeat. Methi is a bitter green leaf with more: more bitterness, more taste, more impact, more presence, more forms, more utility. As fresh leaves it can be used as a spinach. As dried leaves it has a windy aromatic input, picking up bitterness from the floor and recess of the palate and whipping it up into the higher reaches of the mouth space, effectively changing the environment of taste like a dust storm through a forest and exposing structural, brackish and dying elements (see Decay and taste, opposite). Methi moves bitter tastes from the palate borderlands to the centre of town, bringing the attitude of the borderlands with it. It's most commonly used in Northern Indian regional cooking.

Aromatically, it's the heaviest of all forest-floor spices. It sits lower in that imaginary central palate space, a little like an overhanging cloud. Its movement is forceful and its drive impactful. This experience is best tasted in Methi fried flatbreads (page 271).

Emotively, methi has an inherent Indianness that conveys that sense of otherness. It isn't always a taste to connect to as much as it is a point of reference from which we can ascertain proximity or distance from anyone or anything. Ourselves included.

Methi receives the most attention in this section for a couple of reasons. First, it's the only forest-floor spice routinely used in both dried and fresh formats. But it's also the only aromatic in this category that will direct a dish: curry and coriander (cilantro) leaves are additions, not determinants. If you're not sure how to use methi outside Indian cooking, note that the peppery quality of fresh fenugreek leaves makes them a natural match for lamb, chicken and fish; and that dried methi can be used in dishes where basil and oregano would find a natural home, adding an exotic twist without disturbing the known taste profile. Try it in Chicken cacciatore (page 294); any seafood dish served with slow-cooked tomato; or lamb dishes that feature garlic, onion and lemon. If you're not sure about quantity, a few strong pinches in a dish designed to feed four to six people will have an impact.

Tasting notes

In their fresh form, fenugreek leaves are **spinach in a sari**. In their dried form they have an **overripe sweetness** with notes of **pepper** and **sandalwood**, and a lingering and **broadly bitter** finish.

Use in masala

In its fresh form, methi is a spinach-like green that gives depth to chicken or provides a bitter point of reference as a sabji on its own within a thali. In its dried form, methi breaks up heavy textures with movement, and gives a low ceiling to dishes that use fresh aromatics as the main structural body of masala.

Emotive content

Confronting. It hits the sensory body with strong movement, forcing you to know where you stand.

Decay and taste

These aren't two words we're likely to put together very much, but decay has a story to translate in our pots and pans. More than just the decay of muscle and bone, the word is a process most commonly apparent in fermentation – think of kimchi, idli or wine, whose aromatic identity has the breakdown of matter at its heart. This is a very visceral experience of the way decay affects taste. But dried spice displays a subtler element of the process – within the drying process of any spice is an aspect of decay that tucks dark, bitter and brackish tastes into its recessed heart. When methi – particularly dried methi – moves into masala, these aspects are revealed.

1
2
3
4
5
6

Methi fried flatbreads

These are a hybrid bread I first cooked up for Friday-night beers at the Wallcliffe fire shed in Margaret River where I volunteer as a firefighter. Designed as a scoop to dip into the Dal makhani (page 83) and Baingan bharta (page 79) left over from recipe testing for this book, they were delicious enough to eat on their own. I call them 'hybrid' because of the confluence of preparation and cooking techniques. They are prepared like a quick-style paratha and then fried like a poori. This makes them crispy and a little dense, akin to an Italian tostada – if Italian tostada was deliciously weighted with fat, salt and spice.

These breads demonstrate the drive of methi. Even through all of that ghee, flour and frying, the dried leaves are dominant. And while it's not known in Ayurveda as a digestive spice, it will create the aromatic movement required to aid digestion.

Makes 12

Paratha

1 cup (120 g) atta flour (available at Indian grocers)

1 cup (150 g) plain (all-purpose) flour, plus extra for dusting

1 teaspoon fleur de sel

1 teaspoon ghee

generous ½ teaspoon fine pink salt

½ teaspoon bicarbonate of soda (baking soda)

5 large pinches kasoori methi (dried fenugreek leaves)

For rolling

about 6 tablespoons ghee

For deep-frying

2 cups (500 ml) vegetable oil

Combine the paratha ingredients in a large bowl (1). Run a thin stream of hot water and add small amounts to the bowl, mixing with a clean hand until the dough is soft and pliable but not sticky (2–3). If it does become sticky, mix in a little more flour.

Turn the dough out onto a benchtop lightly dusted with extra flour, or keep in the bowl, and knead for 2–3 minutes, until the texture starts to change and soften (4). Divide into six even pieces. Knead each dough ball a little, then set aside for 20 minutes.

If you like, dust the benchtop with extra plain flour – it actually doesn't matter if the paratha sticks a little to the bench, or the shape is off. You will need to dust a rolling pin though, then use it to roll out each dough ball out into a very thin round (5). Spread with a thin layer of ghee. Cut a line from the centre of the paratha outward, along a radius, then roll up the dough from a cut edge into a cone shape and press it down from the wider end into a rose shape. Leave to rest on a plate in the fridge for anywhere between 10 minutes and 1 hour. You can repeat this process with the rolling, spreading with ghee and shaping a second time if you like. Each time will make the paratha more buttery and flakier.

The penultimate step is to roll the paratha out one last time (6). This is the part where we're going to cook them, so try to make them a little pretty. Roll each dough rose out into a round 2–3 mm (1/16–1/8 inch) thick – this will create some of that delicious flaky texture.

Heat the vegetable oil over high heat in a kadai, deep-fryer, stable cast-iron wok or heavy-based frying pan large enough that the oil comes up no more than halfway. Fry the paratha, one at a time, in the hot oil until browned and a little crispy on both sides. Drain on paper towel.

I chop my paratha into triangles then plate them up as part of the boys' after-school snacks, serve them with dips, or eat them whole with dal and channa for a yummy lunchtime thali.

Methi chicken

Methi chicken is a classic Kashmiri combination of spices and produce with a flavour that is soft, strong and striking – another regional culinary characteristic. If you can get fresh fenugreek leaves, do use them instead of frozen. Fresh methi has a quality similar to spinach, though with a little more bitterness and flavour intensity. What you might notice about scaffolding methi is that rather than diminishing its aromatic intensity, as occurs with other aromatics, tiering increases it. There's a beautiful but driving bitterness to the final masala that's unsuited to young or naive palates – something to think about if you're cooking for a family.

Serves 4–6 as part of a shared meal

⅓ cup (80 ml) mustard oil

3 chicken Marylands (leg quarters), chopped into large pieces, bone in and skin on

Masala

⅓ cup (95 g) plain yoghurt, plus extra as needed

2 tablespoons ghee

1 teaspoon fine pink salt

1 teaspoon Kashmiri chilli powder

1 teaspoon fennel seeds

½ teaspoon fenugreek powder

generous ¼ teaspoon fine white pepper

3 dried bay leaves

3 large pinches of kasoori methi (dried fenugreek leaves)

3 cloves

1 whole cassia bark

2 tomatoes (optional), diced

To finish

1 cup (250 ml) water

150 g (5½ oz) frozen or fresh fenugreek leaves

Heat the mustard oil in a large heavy-based flameproof casserole or saucepan over medium–high heat. When hot and sizzling, add the chicken pieces. Leave them to brown on one side then keep turning them over and leaving to cook until they are browned all over. Whenever you turn the chicken, scrape the browned pieces of fat and skin off the bottom of the pan to coat the chicken and to prevent these tasty bits burning. The chicken will be lightly browned after about 15 minutes.

Remove from the heat and take out the chicken pieces, setting them aside, along with the juices and fats, in a large bowl.

Combine all of the masala ingredients except the tomatoes in the same heavy-based saucepan or flameproof casserole and place over medium heat, stirring frequently, until rich and fragrant. Taste it now. It should already be delicious, but if it seems a little too bitter, or if you prefer a less driving masala, add a few tablespoons of extra yoghurt and the diced tomatoes to make it richer and sweeter.

Return the chicken, with its fats and juices, to the pan. Add the water and fenugreek leaves and stir through. Cook, covered, over medium–low heat for about 90 minutes, until tender and richly fragrant. Alternatively, transfer to a pressure cooker and cook for 40 minutes.

Serve with basmati rice or roti, Masoor dal (pages 219, 276) and Simple gobi sabji (page 290).

SECOND TIER FOREST-FLOOR SPICES

It's not so much that the following are second tier, but more that their impact is end-of-dish, reducing the complexity of messaging. The recipes that follow offer further insights.

CURRY LEAVES KADI PATTA

Movement character: Sweet and high.

Emotive content: Not-inappropriate mischief.

Curry leaves are sparky. Their movement in masala is that of the friend who beeps the car horn at the end of your driveway and beckons you for adventure. Part of that attitude is due to their Indianness – the way they instantly shift the cultural frame no matter the origin of the dish. But much of their character is inherent in their light and high movement: of all the aromatics within this category, curry leaves are the brightest.

Taste profile

Curry leaves have a very upfront spike of **pepper** and **basil** that mellows to **almond** and subtle **sesame seed**. Secondary aromas include **cumquat rind** and **white pepper**.

CORIANDER (CILANTRO) LEAVES DHANIA PATTA

Movement character: Grass underfoot.

Emotive content: Upfront and wholesome.

Coriander leaves own significant real estate in the aromatic landscape of chutneys, as in the recipe on page 278. Chutneys are useful in that they translate strong stories simply. Coriander and mint chutneys are Kashmiri Hindu companions to our heavier, richer dishes. Coriander and coconut chutneys are ubiquitous as accompaniments to the dosa and idli of the southern regions of India.

Condiments aside, coriander leaves play an integral role as a finishing aromatic in Kashmiri Hindu dishes. We never ate them growing up because Mum had the gene that makes coriander leaves taste soapy. It's why they're optional in some of my recipes, even though tradition perhaps dictates them as a certainty. That's masala, though: it's based on the household we come from. It's how we know we belong in our family. For other recipes where this spice provides significant movement, see:

- **Thool zamboor** (page 164), where coriander leaves move a dish that speaks of autumn and bring it into spring.
- **Bottle gourd yakhni** (page 133), where coriander leaves move the masala into the tone of a fresh green garden and enunciate the texture of cumin seeds.

Taste profile

Coriander leaves are fresh, with a soft **lemon rind** aroma and a faint kiss of **fine white pepper**.

Masoor dal

Split red lentils, or masoor dal, make a soft style of dal that lacks the structure and integrity of channa (split chickpea) or toor (yellow split pigeon pea) dals. This means we prepare masoor dal differently, creating structure by using spices and produce that give the dal texture and tiers. Poached fenugreek carrot is my go-to to break up the 'glut' of red lentil dal, as is using more water in the initial cooking process. Curry leaf is the power boost to this process – it reinforces movement and adds an additional storey.

Get started at least an hour beforehand, to give the lentils time to soak.

Serves 6–8 as part of a shared meal

- 1½ cups (305 g) masoor dal (split red lentils)
- 3 cups (750 ml) water
- generous 1 teaspoon fine pink salt
- 1 teaspoon fine white sea salt
- scant 1 teaspoon turmeric powder
- 1 × 2 cm (¾ inch) piece of jaggery

Fenugreek carrot

- 2 carrots, cut into 2–3 cm (¾–1¼ inch) pieces
- ½ cup (125 ml) whey or vegetable stock
- 1 teaspoon fine pink salt
- ½ teaspoon red chilli powder
- scant ½ teaspoon fenugreek powder

Curry leaf tadka

- 2 tablespoons mustard oil
- 1½ teaspoons yellow mustard seeds
- 1 teaspoon black mustard seeds
- 2–3 fresh curry leaf sprigs
- 2 garlic cloves, finely chopped

Rinse and drain the lentils repeatedly in a large bowl until the water is clear, then add enough cold water to cover the lentils by about 4 cm (1½ inches). Leave to soak for 1 hour.

Drain the lentils and rinse them one last time. Transfer to a pressure cooker or large heavy-based saucepan and add the water, salts, turmeric powder and jaggery. Pressure-cook for 5 minutes or boil over medium heat for up to 35 minutes, until soft. Set aside and keep warm.

Combine all the fenugreek carrot ingredients in a small saucepan, mix them together and place over medium–low heat. Bring to the boil, then cook for 15–20 minutes, until the carrots are just soft. Remove from the heat and stir into the cooked dal. Taste the dal now to compare with the final taste.

Combine all the tadka ingredients in a small saucepan or frying pan and stir together. Warm through over medium heat, stirring frequently, until the curry leaves and mustard seeds are popping and fragrant but the garlic is not browned – you want it to retain its sweetness. This should take about 5 minutes. Remove from the heat and stir into the cooked dal. Taste the dal again to get a feel for how much movement in taste and weight is created by adding the tadka.

Serve with basmati rice and Kalia (page 292).

Coriander and mint chutney

Chutneys and raitas are an integral part of meals across all regions of India – and their recipes are some of the easiest. This coriander and mint chutney is spicy with green chilli, cool with yoghurt, and well seasoned with salt. It's an ideal match for rich meat dishes, and will freshen up your thali and your palate. But it's also a great accompaniment for souvlaki; grilled, charred and fatty steaks; and slow-cooked pork braises. I love that it's a one-blender, one-step prep. It will bring authenticity, vibrancy and texture to your home-cooked Indian meal with almost no effort at all.

Makes 1 cup (250 ml)

- 2 tablespoons plain yoghurt
- 1 teaspoon fine white sea salt
- 1–2 fresh green chillies (seeding optional)
- 1 large handful of fresh coriander (cilantro) leaves
- 1 large handful of fresh mint leaves
- water, as needed

Combine all the ingredients except the water in a blender or food processor. Gradually add the water, a little at a time, until the chutney has the desired consistency. Use immediately – it will only keep for a day or two in an airtight container in the fridge.

Shivani's namkeen lassi

Like Haldi doodh (page 38) and both Adrak chai and Ginger honey tea (page 258), lassi plays a strong medicinal role in an Indian householder's kitchen. It's proffered as a cure for an unsettled stomach, which is how Shivani offered it to me. The watered-down yoghurt is hydrating. Toasted cumin powder is settling weight. Dried mint leaves subtly shift a tired body into a fresher space.

Serves 1

- 2–3 tablespoons plain yoghurt
- pinch of toasted cumin powder (see page 130)
- a few pinches of crushed dried mint leaves
- salt, to taste
- 1 cup (250 ml) water

Combine all the ingredients except the water in a small bowl, then whisk until they are well mixed and the yoghurt has thinned a little. Add the water and whisk again. Serve as is, or with a little ice.

DRIED MINT LEAVES PUDINA

Movement character:
The rustle of an autumn leaf pile.

Emotive content: Uplifting and bright.

I'd forgotten about dried mint until I arrived at Shivani's house in Bengaluru feeling ill from the travel. She poured me a glass of chaas or Namkeen lassi (page 278), made light and sweet with that dried leaf, and then I remembered. Dried mint is commonly used in Kashmiri Hindu kitchens. As dried leaves, mint acts more like a spice than a herb – its movement is slower and heavier, like walking ankle deep through autumn leaves. Shivani and Bui both grow and dry their own.
To do so, they leave fresh mint leaves to dry on newspaper out of direct sunlight (or they burn). Crushed between the palms and fingers, they have intoxicating presence.

Taste profile
Eaten raw, dried mint leaves have a strong **olfactory impact** and a **chewing gum texture**. Their primary aroma is **spearmint** with a **peppermint tail**, with a recessed character of **candlenut**.

TULSI
HOLY BASIL

Mythology and masala
Turmeric is the religion we experience as children, a spice that ties our young bodies to simple householder wisdoms. Tulsi is the aromatic that gives the sweetness of our nursery understanding a spiritual sophistication.

Before Scott and I married, after we went for Ammi's blessing (see page 49) we had our *varshphals* (see page 94) read at the ashram. Arranged marriages are formed on the basis of these astrological readings, alongside – in traditional circumstances – spousal selection based on caste and culture. Like many modern Indian families, the Ganju clan has moved away from arranged marriages, but the tradition of the *varshphal* reading remains. As part of our reading, Scott was instructed to perform a wedding-day ritual, before dawn, with a Pandit and a tulsi bush. It pertained to an element of security around our joint future: as we get older, life's messages become more complex, and we require different rituals to address that.

Mythologically, the tulsi bush is considered sacred as the embodiment of the goddess Tulsi, an incarnation of Lakshmi, goddess of wealth (see right). She is a good luck plant at entrance ways, and is used in offerings to Vishnu. When I made my commercial Turmeric Masala blend with tulsi and took it home to India to show Dad and Chachi and Mum and Bapu, they let it be known that it was their least favourite of my four blends. Partly because in Kashmiri Hindu tradition haldi (turmeric) is used for its structural quality and bitterness – not as a primary taste. But mainly because tulsi, as a sacred plant, is used in vegetarian food and never with animal proteins, and in the commercial sale of masala there is no way to dictate how others use it. I've kept it on the market, but their reactions stayed with me.

All that said, tulsi is a plant little used in regional Indian masala. It is largely the reserve of ritual, *puja* and temple work. Tulsi tea may be the exception.

The story of goddess Tulsi

The Hindu pantheon – like so much of Indian culture – is layered, complex and interwoven. A god by one name has a thousand others, and many stories. Tulsi is no exception. In one telling of Hindu lore, Tulsi was married to Shankhachuda, who had earned a boon from Lord Brahma that no one could slay him as long as his wife's chastity was retained, and whose taste of power made him demonic.

In a trick of the gods, Vishnu took Shankhachuda's form and slept with Tulsi, corrupting her and allowing Shankhachuda to be slain. Tulsi, devastated, cursed Vishnu to turn to stone – which he did: the Saligram or Shaligram stone is used in Hindu ritual as a symbol of Vishnu to bring prosperity and ward off negative energies. Seeing what she'd done, Tulsi begged Vishnu's forgiveness and was granted the boon of being worshipped alongside him – which is how the tulsi plant has become a sacred symbol of purity and devotion.

Goddess stories are interesting to explore in a climate where women have awoken to the discriminatory idea that we cause harm to men by virtue of our sex and our beauty. All I can suggest on that front is that Hindu mythology is not so much a set story as it is a world open to continual reinterpretation. It's like cultural archaeology – excavating, not keeping things buried, is the way to increase our access to new perspectives and continual re-understanding.

STRUCTURAL SPICES

Function in masala: These are the pillar aromatics, like columns on a portico.
Emotive quality: Strength, obviously, but also support.

The structural spices are the collection of aromatics that are used in their whole, dried form and have an emphatic aromatic impact: star anise, cinnamon sticks, cassia bark, cardamom pods (both black and green).

The distinct expression that structural spices bring to a dish translates functionally as posts of support. What they support within masala depends on both when they are introduced during cooking and the particular aromatic in question.

I've always been of the mind that if these aromatics are to be included in masala, they should be introduced at the beginning. But spending time cooking with Shivani in her Bengaluru kitchen has taught me another approach: that of a last-minute, subcontinental-style bouquet garni. Added like this, in the last stage of cooking, structural aromatics work to encircle and reinforce signature aroma. This technique is used in delicately spiced dishes like Shivani's mutton yakhni (page 107) or Lal paneer (page 212), and in dishes that use water instead of fat as the main vehicle for masala, such as Kalia – Kashmiri lamb stew (page 292) – and Turmeric chaaman (page 45).

For beginners, the easiest way to use these spices in masala is in multiplicity. Cloves, cinnamon stick and green cardamom. Or black cardamom, star anise and cassia bark. What matters is that the strength of one aromatic is mollified by that of the others. Used singularly, these aromatics can become too dominant – like a curry that tastes too much of green cardamom, or a liquid stock that's bombastically star anise. Using multiple structural aromatics seems counterintuitive, but it's actually a failsafe.

STRUCTURE, MOVEMENT AND MASALA

Structural spices are the last in this book, but they're often the first in the pan. With masala there is a sequence of thought and a sequence of action, and the two don't always align. These spices are used at the beginning because of their form – spices with so much structure take longer to disperse their aroma through masala. But they're also used at the beginning because they support movement.

Movement within masala is important. It's how flavour is created – through the dish, bit by bit. The ability of all the moving parts to create deliciousness depends upon the structure that's in place: movement in even a simple dish with little or no structure can taste messy. Structure is doubly important within the context of regional Indian cooking traditions. Without it, the subtlety and nuance of masala, and our ability to enjoy its inherent aromatic contradictions, is diminished.

BLACK CARDAMOM PODS BADI ELAICHI

Category: Structural spices.
Form: Large, wizened black pod.
Colour: Hessian–charcoal.

Black cardamom is strength in smoke. The pod itself is charred in order to develop its unique aroma. The weight of it gives gravitas to Kashmiri garam masala (page 242). It is a rebel yell of an aromatic, reminding me at once of that man on the motorbike and of the no-bullshit filter of Ammi. It's one of the first spices people ask me about, because its aroma is unique and surprising.

There are a few ways to use badi elaichi. A traditional Indian householder employs its sultry overtones of smoke and shadow. Contemporary uses would be in desserts where vanilla, orange, chocolate or chilli feature.

As a signature aroma in Kashmiri Hindu cooking, black cardamom is one structural spice that's given permission to dominate certain regional dishes, Salan walah chawal (page 286) being the prime example.

Tasting notes

There is subtlety in black cardamom, as well as strength. Primary aromas of **smoke** and **char** have companion tones of **camphor** and **warm resin**. A secondary character of **mint** relates black cardamom back to its close spice playmate, green cardamom.

Use in masala

Badi elaichi works in masala like a rudder on a boat: it steers from the bottom. The bottom isn't the bottom palate, but rather the structural basement of masala. The actual aromatic nature of black cardamom makes it an ephemeral palate experience.

Used well, in the right quantity and environment, badi elaichi moves in and around the mouth like smoke. Used badly, it tips into unfixable: like a burned dal, that bitterness and unpleasant char is inescapable. Using it well means erring on the side of less rather than more, and ensuring that its companion spices within the masala will show it off to best effect.

If you're using a traditional regional recipe this is a no-brainer – previous generations have done the work of figuring out what tastes best. But if you'd like to go off-piste, consider pairing it with a portion of subtle acidity, some heat, a balance of warmth and a grounding of earthiness. The smoke tends to work with astringent–sulphurous spices to become acrid in a way that is only delicious if handled with skill.

Emotive content

Confidence and individuality.

Black cardamom vs green cardamom

A little like cassia and cinnamon, black and green cardamom are cousins – belonging to the same botanical family but with different aromatic footprints. They are not interchangeable. Green cardamom is floral. Black cardamom is smoke. Green cardamom is cool. Black cardamom is warm.

Emissary spice: connecting cultures

As Dad got older and had more free time, he branched out in the kitchen. His favourite way of flexing his masala muscle was creating cohesion between his two all-time favourite cuisines – Kashmiri Hindu and classic village French. Mum and Dad bought a house in Bordeaux and I remember how chuffed he was when their French friend and neighbour, a woman of exceptional cooking talent, labelled Dad's the best cassoulet she'd ever eaten.

What he'd done to get to that place was integrate the concept of masala into his kitchen preparations, no matter what the cuisine. Dad hadn't always cooked that way. In the earlier years, when stepping outside the zone of Kashmiri Hindu cooking, his food had been less interesting. But French was different. He felt it. And so he naturally evolved to 'think' masala while cooking French. Black cardamom pods in his cassoulet. Subtle use of chilli in his coq au vin. He was doing all the things, back then, that I now teach: creating aromatic length with hot spices, and infusing subtle dark character with structural spices. In effect, Dad was putting touches of himself in classic French dishes. That's what his French neighbour tasted and loved – his insights.

Eventually these aromatic aha moments reversed, and pieces of France made it back into his traditional Kashmiri Hindu dishes – predominantly the use of whole grapes in his meat-based masalas that, when pressure-cooked, added an indefinable note of sweet complexity. It turns out grapes are just the kind of multipurpose ingredient masala loves.

These emissary spices allow us to pour our personhood into spaces where we can see ourselves anew, and then take those insights home. It's a beautiful way to bring texture to our kitchens, our lives and our relationship to masala.

Salan walah chawal

The patience test with salan walah chawal is the protracted browning process: shortcuts will only spoil the end result, and you don't want to cheat yourself with this incredible dish. Pour a glass of red wine for the operation on a Sunday afternoon – that's what Dad always did. The actual browning stage will take around ninety minutes of standing by the stovetop. It might be a little quicker or a little slower depending on how your pot of choice conducts heat, but there is not a minute of browning that you will regret upon eating what is a very traditional and delicious Kashmiri Hindu dish.

It's important to: cut the lamb as directed; use beautiful rice and complete the soaking process; and pay attention to the visual indicators of the dish – wait until the meat is truly rich and a deep, dark sticky brown before finalising the browning process.

Serves 8

- 2 tablespoons sunflower oil
- 4 tablespoons ghee
- 1½ cups (390 g) plain yoghurt
- pinch of hing (asafoetida) powder or a few drops of hing water
- 500 g (1 lb 2 oz) fat-trimmed lamb shoulder, cut into 4 cm (1½ inch) cubes
- 4–6 lamb bones, cut into 5 cm (2 inch) lengths
- 1 teaspoon fine white sea salt
- 2 cups (400 g) basmati rice, rinsed a few times and soaked in cold water for 1 hour
- 4 cups (1 litre) water

Chilli water

- 2 cups (500 ml) water
- 1 tablespoon plain yoghurt
- 1 teaspoon ginger powder
- ½ teaspoon Kashmiri chilli powder
- pinch of hing (asafoetida) powder or a few drops of hing water

Main masala

- 3 teaspoons cumin seeds
- 2 generous teaspoons coriander powder
- 1 teaspoon fresh ginger paste
- ½ teaspoon red chilli powder
- ½ teaspoon ginger powder
- ½ teaspoon Kashmiri chilli powder
- 8–10 cloves
- 5 black cardamom pods, husks cracked
- 4 dried bay leaves

To finish

- 1 teaspoon sea salt, to taste
- 1 heaped teaspoon Ammi's garam masala (page 156)
- fresh coriander (cilantro) leaves

Heat the sunflower oil and ghee in a flameproof pressure cooker or large heavy-based saucepan over medium–high heat. Add the yoghurt to the hot oil and stir immediately – it should spit and sizzle. Straight away, add the hing and stir through.

Add the lamb shoulder, lamb bones and fine white sea salt. Cook, stirring occasionally with a metal spoon, for 30–40 minutes. You will see the lamb release its water, the fat cook away, the lamb begin to stick, and the oil from the meat split, brown and then clear. Cook this oil down until there is no more than a thin layer on the pot's base. Reduce the heat to medium if the lamb begins to burn.

Meanwhile, make the chilli water by combining all the ingredients in a small bowl and stirring well. Set aside near the stovetop.

Using a metal spoon to move it around, begin browning the lamb in small portions of the chilli water – about 2 tablespoons at a time – over medium–low heat. Wait until each addition of chilli water has cooked down before adding more. Stir the lamb during the browning process to remove the caramelised pieces from the bottom and side of the pan. This process is slow and will take 60–90 minutes. The wider your pot, the faster the lamb will brown.

Once the meat has cooked, add the main masala and cook through for 2–3 minutes.

If using a flameproof pressure cooker, add the drained rice, the water and the finishing salt and garam masala. Alternatively, transfer the lamb to a pressure cooker or keep cooking in the saucepan, adding the rice, water and finishing spices. Pressure-cook for 15 minutes, or until the meat is cooked. If using a saucepan, add enough water to cover the meat and cook over medium–high heat for 7 minutes, then reduce the heat to medium and cook for 35–40 minutes, until the lamb is tender and the rice is cooked and dry.

Remove from the heat and cover with a lid lined inside with a clean tea towel (dish towel) to catch the condensation and help the dish dry out. Place the pot or flameproof pressure cooker on a trivet or simmering pad over very low heat and cook for 13–15 minutes. When done, the rice grains should be separated and the meat tender.

Serve with fresh coriander and a raita.

When what you seek, seeks you

Dad had been gone about a year when I went to make salan walah chawal. To me there's almost nothing that tastes of him more. He had sent me his recipe for salan walah chawal years before, but the computer it had once been stored on was corrupted and I couldn't find it. I looked everywhere – through my sheaves of loose recipes, in digital files. I was getting more and more frantic for a taste of him, and more and more distressed that it seemed I would never locate his recipe.

In the end I decided it would just have to be generic – I would search salan walah chawal online and make the closest approximation I could find. But when I searched, the first story that came up was a recipe from *GOYA*, an online journal in India that specialises in reporting on and preserving regional Indian culinary traditions. The tagline spoke of a salan walah chawal originating in the Kashmiri Pandit community – our community. I clicked the link, burst into tears, and grabbed my phone to dial ...

'Chachu? Chachu, it's me.'

'I knew it would be you, *beta*. I was waiting for you to call.'

Chachu had done an interview with *GOYA* on making the Ganju family salan walah chawal, which was beautifully illustrated, and accompanied by a comprehensive recipe. The article had been published just that morning. He thought I'd known and that's why I was calling. I hadn't, I told him, still crying. But it was exactly what I'd needed to find on the night that I needed to find it.

I posted the story a few days later on Instagram and received a message from a friend: 'What you seek,' she wrote, 'seeks you.'

Simple gobi sabji

Cauliflower (gobi) and badi elaichi are natural aromatic partners – milky and cool when eaten fresh and raw, gobi hides a deep recess of subterranean tastes. The pre-fry in vegetable oil draws out these acrid qualities, plumps the florets with a little caramelised sweetness, and prepares the ultimate landscape around which the smoke of black cardamom can wend its way. It's a simple sabji.

Serves 4 as part of a shared meal

2 cups (500 ml) vegetable oil
1 cauliflower, broken into florets

Masala

1 tablespoon ghee
1 teaspoon cumin seeds
1 teaspoon finely grated fresh ginger (optional)
scant 1 teaspoon fine pink salt
½ teaspoon red chilli powder
scant ½ teaspoon turmeric powder
scant ½ teaspoon amchur
3–4 black cardamom pods, husks cracked

Heat the vegetable oil over high heat in a kadai, stable cast-iron wok or heavy-based saucepan large enough that the oil comes up no more than halfway. Deep-fry the cauliflower florets in small batches until well fried and slightly browned. Drain on paper towel.

Heat the ghee in a large frying pan over medium heat then add the masala. Watch for burning and reduce the heat to medium–low if the masala seems to be sizzling too vigorously. Add the fried florets and toss them through. Reduce the heat to low and cook for about 40 minutes, until the oil has been drawn out of the cauliflower and thickened into the masala itself. Taste. If any residue of oil is slicking the mouth and creating a barrier to flavour, then keep cooking over low heat until the oil slick has gone and the flavour comes through.

This should be served as a dry sabji. Serve with Simple yellow dal (page 39), Rogan josh (page 302), Matar paneer (page 230) and basmati rice.

Deep-frying and salt

One way I've been known to trip myself up is to go a little heavy on the salt in sabji where the vegetable has been deep-fried. Deep-frying produce ensures all sorts of deliciousness in the end dish, but it also guarantees a deeper drive of salt. Easing back a little on what you would normally consider a workable amount of salt is a good way to go: the salt penetrates the oil and is carried into the vegetable, which means that too much is impossible to fix.

GREEN CARDAMOM PODS ELAICHI

Category: Structural spices.
Form: Small pod the shape of a miniature almond.
Colour: Pistachio green.

Dad kept elaichi pods in his *puja*. At the end of special *pujas*, he'd crack one open, and place a few of its seeds in our palms alongside the sugar rock that served as customary *prasad* (food taken after religious offerings). Its taste was biting and strident, so strong that not even the sugar rock could disguise it.

In masala, elaichi has that same strong impact, which is why it needs considerate handling – its rose petal element is boosted by savoury contrasts and can easily overwhelm if mishandled: many a poorly executed masala has been undone by excessive elaichi.

Using green cardamom well requires us to understand its context within a particular masala. Are we using it to create strength and structure as we do in Chicken cacciatore (page 294)? Or are we using it to texture a dish that has already found its structure elsewhere, as is the case with Kalia (page 292)? Once we can answer those questions, we'll know how to apply it, and what kind of masala to build around it.

To see the impact of green cardamom in a dessert, turn to the recipe for Kheer (page 204) and remove the saffron to make elaichi the focus. It's a great example of how dairy-based fats and high-tone sugars pull forward the rose aspect of green cardamom and coddle its savoury impact.

Tasting notes

For such a pretty spice, elaichi has a strong presence. Primary aromatic characters of **rose husk** segue to **mint** and **spring eucalyptus**. Secondary characters of **black pepper** and **warm resin** are evidence of its close ties to black cardamom. Green cardamom is aromatically very complex, making it a spice to use sparingly.

Use in masala

The distinct strength and floral husk of green cardamom makes it a spice prone to aromatic mishaps in overenthusiastic hands: too much of this single spice in a dish will consume subtler tastes. As a structural spice, green cardamom is released through the produce over time and so its overuse is difficult to correct. Err on the side of caution. Green cardamom pods work well with distinctive savoury dishes that have very strong and driving flavour. They form a natural marriage with carrot (*gajar*) in traditional Indian savoury (*gajar sabji*) or sweet (*gajar halwa*) dishes. I love to use this spice as a contrast to richly sticky beef cheek in soy and oyster sauce.

Kalia

There are three distinct points of structure with kalia, which is a Kashmiri lamb or mutton stew. The first is boiling the lamb over high heat. The second is the process of cooking it through with milk and yoghurt. The third is the aromatic integrity created by heavy use of structural spices (see right). Alongside cloves, elaichi (cardamom) comes in at the end to provide an additional tier of structure, filling in the adamant masala with a little movement and flexibility.

I love the contrast between the texture of the meat and the behaviour of the masala.

Serves 6 as part of a shared meal

- 1 kg (2 lb 4 oz) lamb leg, fat trimmed, cut into 5 cm (2 inch) chunks
- 1½ cups (375 ml) water
- ¼ cup (60 ml) milk
- 100 ml (3½ fl oz) plain yoghurt

Masala

- 3 teaspoons fennel powder
- 2¼ teaspoons fine pink salt
- 2 teaspoons ginger powder
- 1 teaspoon turmeric powder
- pinch of hing (asafoetida) powder
- 4 black cardamom pods, husks cracked
- 2 dried bay leaves

Tadka

- 2 tablespoons mustard oil
- 1 teaspoon Ammi's garam masala (page 156)
- 4 green cardamom pods, husks cracked
- 4 cloves

Combine the lamb and water in a large heavy-based saucepan and bring to the boil over high heat. This stage of cooking imparts an edgy textural structure to the lamb. Add the masala ingredients and stir them through, then cover and cook over high heat for about 20 minutes, stirring occasionally. The lamb should look quite tense, so don't worry if it seems a little hard. The next phase will soften it.

Reduce the heat to medium–low and cook, uncovered, for about 10 minutes, until the lamb is tender.

Combine the milk and ¼ cup (60 ml) of the yoghurt in a small bowl and whisk together until smooth. Add to the lamb and cook over low heat, stirring constantly, for about 35 minutes, until the lamb has had the opportunity to relax into this slightly acidic dairy bed and become very tender. It's important to take time here.

Combine the tadka ingredients in a small frying pan and temper the spices in the oil over medium heat for 1–2 minutes or until bubbling slightly and aromatic. Add to the lamb and stir through.

For a richer result, stir the remaining yoghurt through until the lamb is glossy.

The secret of the triangle

Embedding triangular structures in masala provides a strong framework that allows for fluid aromatic movement within that support. The corners of the triangle can vary. In this dish, it is the structure of the boiled lamb, the aromatic pillar of green cardamom, and the density created by adding the milk and yoghurt. The triangle in Dal makhani (page 83), for example, is garam masala, urad dal (black lentils) and the initial pressure cooking. Getting a feel for the triangular support points in any dish you cook – every coherent recipe will have support in that shape – will aid you in building a fluid and intimate relationship with masala.

J&K Headed For Winter Of
It Will Depend On Lt
biggest, smallest
victory margins

Chicken cacciatore

Mum made this all the time when we were growing up. Hunter's chicken stew, it means in Italian. She made it from the recipe in the same *Women's Weekly* cookbook she used to make her Osso buco (page 54). I've reimagined both. This recipe illustrates how the strong umami tastes of chicken fat, olives and slow-cooked tomato muscle up to green cardamom so that it can't dominate.

Serves 4 generously

- 1 cup (125 g) cornflour (cornstarch)
- white sea salt and cracked black pepper, to season
- 3 chicken Marylands (leg quarters), chopped into large pieces, bone in and skin on
- ¼ cup (60 ml) mustard oil

Mirepoix

- 4 garlic cloves
- 4 celery stalks
- 4 carrots
- 1 leek
- 1 small white onion

Main masala

- ½ cup (75 g) pitted kalamata olives
- ¼ cup (50 g) salted capers, rinsed
- 2 tablespoons tomato paste (concentrated purée)
- 1 teaspoon fine pink salt
- ½ teaspoon Kashmiri chilli powder
- 6 green cardamom pods, husks cracked
- 3 dried bay leaves

To finish

- 600 ml (21 fl oz) veal stock
- ½ cup tomato passata (puréed tomatoes)
- sea salt and cracked black pepper (optional), to taste

Pour the cornflour onto a plate, season with salt and pepper and mix through well. Thoroughly coat the chicken pieces in the cornflour mixture.

Heat the mustard oil in a large heavy-based saucepan over high heat until sizzling, then add the chicken and cook until slightly brown, turning to cook on both sides. Remove from the heat and transfer the chicken to paper towel to drain, keeping the remaining oil and chicken fat in the pan.

Finely dice the garlic, celery, carrots, leek and onion to make a mirepoix. Return the pan to medium heat and add the mirepoix. Cook down until the vegetables have softened and the onion is translucent.

Add all the main masala ingredients, stir them through, then cook for 2–3 minutes, until the tomato paste is no longer raw.

Add the veal stock and tomato passata. Top with a little water if extra liquid is needed in the pot. The liquid should come up no further than a third of the way up the chicken. Slow-cook for 3–4 hours over very low heat, or until the chicken begins to fall off the bone. Leave the lid on for the first hour, then remove it for the remaining cooking time, checking from time to time that there is still sufficient liquid in the pan.

Serve with rice, polenta or pasta and a green salad.

Emotive content
Respectful confrontation in a savoury capacity. In sweets, elaichi is the reminder that strength fits snugly within the skin of beauty.

The monarch of mithai

Across the regions of India, one aromatic speaks of mithai and that's green cardamom. Mithai are traditional sweets (see Haldi ki halwa, page 265). Historically, regional mithai are simple, made using besan flour, ghee, jaggery and milk products – Khoya, for example (page 110). They can be decorated with edible silver and gold leaf. Nuts often feature – pistachios, cashews and almonds. Rosewater and saffron appear. But green cardamom – elaichi – is the aromatic pivot.

Mithai approach flavour in an interesting way: they are typically cloyingly sweet. You may, for example, have encountered jalebi, barfi, gulab jamun, Kheer (page 204) or phirin. But the Indian palate demands a savoury connection – a breath of spice. Green cardamom has the aromatic authority to make its presence felt even in a pot of condensed milk.

CINNAMON STICKS DALCHINI & CASSIA BARK JANGLI DALCHINI

Category: Structural spices.
Form: Cinnamon sticks are tightly whorled and papery bark. Cassia bark is rough and open.
Colour: Cinnamon sticks are light tan. Cassia bark is warm terracotta.

The whole forms of cinnamon and cassia are unique. They are the only aromatics used within the broad domain of masala that originate from bark. This makes them the most subtle of the structural spices, as the upright nature of the trunk translates into aromatic profiles that don't flame, seed, anchor or blossom, but retain vertical expression, even through long cooking times and heat.

I'm treating them here together due to the similarity in function that comes from their bark form. Best understood in comparison to each other, the two recipe references that follow detail the differing impact of cassia bark and cinnamon sticks upon masala:

- **Tamarind eggplant** (page 188): A **cinnamon stick** introduced at the same time as the Kashmiri chilli powder water will give the sabji an elegant authority. It holds up the smoke of the eggplant (aubergine), provides more room in the masala bed for the hing (asafoetida) to wend through, and draws up the heat of the whole red chilli to create greater length of flavour for the dish as a whole. **Cassia bark** introduced at the same time instead gives the eggplant a more voluptuous presence. The smoke will intensify, and the end mouthful will be fuller and heavier, with a humid heat and more tropical acidity.
- **Sapna's breakfast channa sabji** (page 102): Used in the initial masala that is fried off in coconut oil, a **cinnamon stick** would draw out the dark aspects of Sapna's aunt's masala – black pepper and fenugreek seeds – and create an earthier dish. **Cassia bark**, however, would sweeten the coconut, let the fresh coriander (cilantro) sing louder, and return some autonomy to the dal. In the recipe as it stands, the channa disappears into the masala and becomes more texture than taste.

Tasting notes

Cinnamon sticks have a subtle **woody** aroma of **baked goods**. On the tongue, raw cinnamon sticks taste of **clove cigarettes** and **subtlety**.

Cassia bark is **woody**, **pungent** and **hot**. The **sugared** notes of cassia powder are recessed deep within the structural form of this whole spice. The bark is much **rougher** and **darker** than that of the finely elegant cinnamon stick.

Use in masala

Cinnamon sticks act as a structural counterpoint to dense powders, a supporter of movement to forest-floor spices, and a counterweight to gullet-opening astringent spices.

Cassia bark has a louder imprint than cinnamon sticks – it's hot blooded. Use it to give structure to a masala that has heavy volume or sultry messaging.

Emotive content

Emotively, cinnamon sticks convey a strong sense of contained beauty and regal restraint.

Cassia bark offers boisterous and blousy authority.

SECOND-TIER STRUCTURAL SPICES

These aromatics are on constant rotation in my masala, but I call them second-tier because they support rather than determine the tone of a dish. You'll find these aromatics in many of the Ganju family recipes, and for the most part, they're an extension of Kashmiri Hindu aromatic tradition.

CLOVES LAUNG

Structural character: Broad and flat, like low verandah posts.

Emotive content: Subterranean – they speak to aspects of ourselves beneath the surface.

Cloves in masala perform a few key functions. Firstly, they work as a backboard for delicate aromatics such as cinnamon powder and cardamom powder. These powdered spices that enter the front palate are drawn back by cloves, and are expressed in the masala with greater force. This is thanks to the pungent quality of cloves, which anchors into the molars and back lower jaw, luring delicate flavour back and holding it down. Secondly, cloves provide structural integrity to masala in the lower jaw. Most other structural aromatics have an upright effect.

Taste profile

Cloves have a distinct and strong, pungent aromatic character that combines **medicinal aniseed** with **hardwood** and **camphor**. There are eager secondary profiles of **bitterness** and **heat**.

STAR ANISE CHAKRI PHOOL

Structural character: Charismatic, like a central feature post.

Emotive content: Bright and sweet or forceful and sweet.

When I looked through my previous book, *The Spice Companion*, to find my tasting notes on star anise, I realised it wasn't actually included. This is a telling oversight: though I do occasionally use star anise as a strong structural component of masala, I'm not enamoured of its aromatic expression. That forceful licorice/hot camphor medley seems more like cacophony than harmony to me. As a spice, it is the most visibly beautiful – its star shape is a jewel in Sadaf's pulao (page 305). The following recipes also contain star anise:

- **Easy skinless chicken thigh burritos** (page 155), where star anise adds penetrative aroma to a skinless and boneless chicken cut
- **Sapna's auntie's ready-made masala** (page 216), where star anise brings a loud sweetness as counterbalance to a masala that has forthright bitterness and heat.

Taste profile

Star anise has a powerful **wooded licorice** character and a **hot sweetness** reminiscent of cloves. Its secondary characters are recessed – because of the power of its primary nature – and veer into the territory of texture as much as taste: think **weight** and **shadow**.

MACE FLOWER JAVITRI

Structural character: Elusive strength.
Emotive content: Aloof beauty.

Mace flower is not actually a flower but instead the outer covering of the nutmeg kernel. It's a visually beautiful spice. When fresh, it's vermilion red. Once dried, it tones down to a peachy apricot – a delicate look that belies the strength of its impact. Newcomers to mace flower, javitri in Hindi, find it naturally challenging to use because it's rarely found outside of regional masala.

Perhaps the easiest way to find a place for it is to think of it as a substitute for nutmeg that brings additional flounce and depth when used in its whole form. The following recipes offer examples of the various impacts that mace flower can have on masala:

- **Ammi's garam masala** (page 156), where mace flower creates a prettier underbelly for a masala that's heavy on earth spices and sterner structural spices
- **Matar khoya** (page 180), where mace flower provides a faceted structure – its flounce is expressed as a pinwheel of strength and order.

Outside the savoury context, whole mace flower could be an interesting inclusion in cooked cream desserts such as panna cotta, or even as a point of aromatic strength and diversity in a white chocolate mousse.

But the main reason I'm giving space here to mace flower is that we need outlier aromatics to maintain the breadth of our vision. One of the underlying messages of Ayurveda and of Hindu mythology is that we're better served by mystery than by certainty (see page 301). It's what keeps curiosity alive.

Taste profile

Much like star anise, the primary characters of mace flower dominate. Its obvious first tastes segue from **menthol** to **orange rind** and through to **saddle leather**. A secondary character is a recessed **anaesthetic quality**.

MASALA, AYURVEDA, AND THE LIMITS OF HOUSEHOLDER UNDERSTANDING

In the beginning, I presumed that every question asked in the kitchen should have a tellable answer. But over the years I've come upon many unanswered questions. Like when I ask Bui why we don't toast spices in our Ganju family kitchens, and she laughs – 'I don't know'. At 75 years old, it's likely she'll never get to know the answer, and so neither will I. The previous keeper of that wisdom has passed away, and so the reason remains tucked into the pleat of some ancestral sari.

Of course, we know there *is* a reason, because there is a reason for every addition, action, technique and contradiction in masala. At this late stage of the book, I can sum up masala as a regional Indian kitchen methodology that serves as a map for how to live a life. But its beauty is that it's not scripture. Religion is owned by the clerics. Traditional Ayurvedic practice is the domain of the healing scholar. Masala is the companion of the Indian householder, replete with the contradictions that level of humanness entails. And so the 'I don't knows' of that householder become the gargoyles guarding against any claims that we could ever know it all.

> 'I've yet to meet any householder who's attained perfect understanding. For as long as we're here, there's always more to learn.'

This guardianship matters because summary understanding murders fascination. When I stand with Bui in the kitchen and she expresses wonder at the raita Ammi would make from fresh curd and flower petals, in those moments we're equals as students. And it's good. Connective. Loving. Fun. An immediate antidote to notions that masala could ever be something that fixes us if we just follow the rules well enough, if we can work out all the reasons why.

Over the years, so many of my students have asked questions I could never answer. I've had questions that I can answer. I've had questions to which the answer I once gave is my answer no longer. Every time I come to the kitchen bench and open my dabbas, I'm starting from scratch. And, sure, my scratch is different from your scratch, but I've yet to meet any householder who's attained perfect understanding. For as long as we're here, there's always more to learn.

Rogan josh

The rogan josh of Indian takeaway is similar to the dish which graces our Ganju tables in name only. Ours is more angular, less red and with dominance given to the masala (as it should be). In this recipe there is no ratan jot (dyer's alkanet) – a root that can be used to give rogan josh its luxurious red sheen.

As a style of cooking, rogan josh tells the tale of low, broad and strong masala. This is why the inclusion of cloves is important: the structural expression of cloves is also low, broad and strong. So seamless is the structural tapestry between cloves and rogan josh that the aroma of the spice is indistinguishable from the experience of the dish.

Starting marinade

- 1 kg (2 lb 4 oz) lamb shoulder
- 1 cup (250 g) plain yoghurt
- 6 cloves
- 4 black cardamom pods
- 2 dried bay leaves
- 1 cinnamon stick

To cook

- ½ cup (100 g) ghee
- 2–3 tablespoons canola or vegetable oil
- 2 teaspoons fine white sea salt
- 3–4 pinches of hing (asafoetida) powder

Main masala

- 1 teaspoon Kashmiri chilli powder
- 2 tablespoons water
- 1 tablespoon fennel powder
- 2 teaspoons ginger powder

To finish

- 2 cups (500 ml) water
- 1 teaspoon garam masala

Start by cutting the lamb shoulder into large cubes, about 5 cm (2 inches). If you prefer a less rich rogan josh, trim some of the excess fat from the lamb as you cut. I leave mine as is.

In a large bowl, combine the lamb chunks with the remaining ingredients for the starting marinade. Mix well and leave to marinate for about 10 minutes.

Meanwhile, heat the ghee and canola or vegetable oil over high heat in a large heavy-based saucepan large enough that the ghee and oil come up no more than halfway. Set the salt and hing by the stovetop, along with a metal spoon and the lid for the saucepan. When the oil is very hot, add the marinated lamb without stirring, taking care to avoid the spatter. Cover immediately with the lid until the spitting subsides, less than 1 minute. Once it quietens, remove the lid, stir the lamb through the oil and add the salt and hing.

Now start the browning process (see page 97 for the technique). Stay at the stove and continue to watch and stir the meat with a metal spoon as it cooks, still over high heat. It will take about 15 minutes for the yoghurt to begin to dry and the oil and yoghurt to separate. Stir in a folding motion, scraping the browning pieces of meat and yoghurt-thickened spice from the bottom and side of the pan.

After a further 10–15 minutes, the yoghurt should have dried almost completely, leaving just the oil. At this point, add a little water once or twice to prolong the browning process. Cook down for another 20–30 minutes, until the oil begins to diminish and the lamb requires constant scraping to prevent it sticking. Reduce the heat to medium–high.

Now to the main masala. In a small bowl, dissolve the Kashmiri chilli powder in the water and add to the lamb. Stir through. Add the fennel and ginger powders and continue to brown and cook over medium–high heat for a further 15–20 minutes.

To finish, add the water and stir the meat as the gravy softens and becomes a little creamy, 5–10 minutes. Add the garam masala and stir through. Reduce heat to medium–low and cook for another 10 minutes.

Serve with paratha, Mum's raita (page 229), and Simple yellow dal (page 39) or with Sadaf's star anise pulao (photographed on page 304).

THE TRUTH OF SPICE STORYTELLING

The premise of this book is the use of specific recipes to illustrate the messaging a spice carries within the framework of capital-'M' masala – masala as the whole expansive concept and everything that entails. Rogan josh tells the story of the impact of cloves. Sadaf Hussain's recipe for pulao (see page 304) showcases star anise. In most recipes I've been deliberate about establishing the link between spice and recipe. I've been repetitive about it because masala by its nature is complex in the way it combines aromatics. There is rarely one clear standout spice, other than in a domestic medicinal application – when a householder might brew up Jeera pani (page 125) or a cup of warm Haldi doodh (page 38).

Because we've reached the end of the book together, I can now tell you a secret ... The recipes I've chosen to illustrate each spice within the context of masala are arbitrary. I could choose any spice from any masala and tell a story. Yes, cloves represent a structural element of rogan josh. But we could also talk about chilli in rogan josh, and the way it lengthens darker aromatic qualities. Or how hing (asafoetida) ensures rogan josh maintains a Kashmiri Hindu voice.

The truth of masala is that it is a vast arena for storytelling through spice, and that any one dish offers multiple conversations. Zeroing in on one specific meaning is a skill to polish – not in order to arrive at a definitive expression of masala, but to develop the tools to see a spice, a dish, an experience or ourselves in fresh ways we might not have considered before.

Sadaf's star anise pulao

When I asked Sadaf Hussain (see page 262) for his favourite spice, I was happy to hear him nominate star anise, chiefly because it's not an aromatic with which I have a particularly close relationship. When we chatted on Zoom about this recipe, I was staying with Shivani in Bengaluru and it turns out this is *her* choice of dish with star anise, too. They both love the look of the spice in the rice: like a jewel, Shivani says.

Serves 4 as part of a shared meal

- 2 tablespoons ghee
- 4 green cardamom pods, husks cracked
- 10 whole black peppercorns
- 1 star anise
- 1 cup (155 g) chopped onion
- 1 cup (200 g) basmati rice, soaked in cold water for 1 hour then rinsed
- 1¼ cups (310 ml) vegetable or chicken stock
- sea salt, to taste
- fresh coriander (cilantro) leaves, to garnish (optional)

Heat the ghee in a stockpot or flameproof rice pot over medium heat until melted and aromatic. Add the cardamom pods, peppercorns and star anise. Stir for 2–3 minutes, until the spices release their aroma, then add the onion and cook for 3–4 minutes, until translucent but not browned – we want to keep the masala light.

Add the rice and stir to coat it with the ghee and spices. Pour in the stock and add the salt. Bring to the boil over medium heat, then reduce the heat to low and simmer, covered, for about 15 minutes or until the liquid has been absorbed and the rice is tender.

Remove from the heat. Fluff up the rice with a fork and adjust the seasoning if necessary. You'll notice in the first taste how the peppercorn has a savoury quality that lets the star anise shine, while the green cardamom is the stage that props both up.

Sadaf recommends chopped coriander leaves as a garnish.

Left: Top: Sadaf's star anise pulao. Bottom: Rogan josh (page 302).

Glossary

aromatic logic: The way tastes have logical natural associations, such as that of chilli to flames, or curry leaves to forest leaves.

ashram: A place akin to a Hindu pastoral retreat and more like a monastery than a temple, where a group of Hindus live with God and where Hindus can go in order to pray. Families are often aligned with single ashrams and the **gurus** that head them for generations.

atta: A stoneground wheat flour with a nutty taste that's used to make chapati, roti, poori and **paratha**.

Ayurveda: The traditional Indian system of medicine that's been used for more than 3000 years, based on the idea that our unique **dosha** (life force) is universally connected to everything around us, and that we can balance our spiritual, emotional and physical bodies through conscious consumption. See also **domestic Ayurveda**.

besan: Chickpea flour (see page 140).

***beta*:** A Hindi term of endearment that's commonly used by parents towards children. *Beta* literally means child. Technically, *beta* means son and *beti* means daughter, but the former is often used in a gender-neutral way.

bhatura: A puffy North Indian deep-fried bread made with leavened dough and commonly served with a spiced chickpea curry (chole). Bhatura is salty, fluffy, a little chewy and deliciously rich.

blueprint tastes: Genetic memories of taste built into us via ancestry and heritage.

Brahman: A caste (*varna*) or social ranking that finds its origin in the now-outlawed caste system. Also spelled Brahmin.

***chatai*:** Eating mat.

chaas: Lassi.

chokhta: A Kashmiri lamb or mutton dish.

***chyawanprash*:** A bitter Ayurvedic medicine, traditionally used to support the health of the gut.

cooling: A term used to denote tastes or aromatics that have a calming, slowing or grounding effect on the **sensory body**.

dabba: In this book, spice tins in which an Indian **householder** keeps commonly used spices (see page 28). See also **masala dabba**.

dahi: The Hindi and Gujarati word for curd or yoghurt.

deep gut: Our metaphysical centre of gravity that contains the sum of who we are. See also **digestion**.

Desi: Used to describe people and cultures from the Indian regions. The word *desi* means country or land in Sanskrit.

dhania: Hindi for coriander in all its forms, including leaves (cilantro).

digestion: Broader than a physical function, the word digestion in the regional Indian tradition encompasses the Ayurvedic idea that our digestive system is the engine that drives the body. See also **deep gut**.

domestic Ayurveda: The casual knowledge of traditional Ayurvedic practice passed down to children within the ordinary day-to-day running of a household. See also **Ayurveda**.

dosha: Ayurvedic body type, used in traditional Indian medicine to determine what foods and treatments are best for an individual (see page 26). See also **vata**, **pitta** and **kapha**.

drive: We talk about drive a lot with **masala**. Drive refers to the push of taste to increase flavour volume, dial up aromatic intensity, or harden or increase the impact of any emotional or **sensory body** messaging.

dum cooking: A traditional method of cooking that uses steam in a pot with a sealed lid (see page 255).

emotional eating: How our emotions are affected by our consumption in ways that can be both productive and unproductive. From the perspective of **masala** and **Ayurveda**, the idea of emotional eating is not necessarily about addiction and/or self-flagellation.

fleur de sel: Salt that's harvested and used as a large flake or a 'salt flower' (the literal translation of the French term).

garam masala: A blend of earthy, warm and pungent aromatics typically comprising bay leaves, cinnamon sticks, black and green cardamom pods, cumin seeds and fennel seeds (among other spices). Recipes vary from region to region and house to house. Garam masala usually refers to the powdered form of this blend but can also refer to the use of the whole aromatics.

gobi: Hindi for cauliflower.

gullet: The space beneath the **palate** that drops down into the throat. Physically, this part of the **sensory body** is activated by astringent and sulphurous tastes. Emotively, it holds difficult-to-access emotions and experiences. Metaphysically, it is our blind spot or the truth of our own behaviours.

guru: A person, man or woman, who serves as a spiritual guide.

haldi: Hindi for turmeric.

haldi doodh: Turmeric milk.

***havan*:** Hindu ceremony or ritual that involves offerings made to a consecrated fire, performed by a **Pandit**. *Havans* are performed to officiate weddings and funerals, and as part of the observance of specific religious rites.

heating: Term used to denote tastes or aromatics that have a stimulating, driving or elevating effect on the **sensory body**.

hing: The word in several Indian languages for asafoetida.

householder: One of the phases of life as defined by Hindu philosophy. The householder is responsible for passing on cultural and faith-specific information to younger generations via domestic or quotidian traditions.

inflammation: A word used within **Ayurveda** for **heating** of the body systems. Ayurvedic thought considers excessive inflammation to be the root cause of disease.

***janampatra*:** The Vedic astrological chart used to map an individual's lifetime.

kadai: A heavy, rounded, wok-like vessel, normally made from cast-iron or stainless steel, used in high-heat, oil-based cooking (see page 27).

kala namak: Indian black salt (page 72).

kapha: One of the three **doshas**. Related to water and earth, kapha is described as steady, consistent and heavy. Kapha-dominant folk are said to be physically solid, with lustrous hair and shining eyes, and to be mentally strong, reliable, protective, thoughtful and calm. See also **pitta** and **vata**.

kasoori methi: Hindi for dried fenugreek leaves.

katori: Small traditional bowls used with **thalis** to serve an Indian meal (see page 28).

***katu* foods:** Foods that bring pungency. They are said to allow increased focus but can be inflammatory and drying when consumed in excess.

kesar: Hindi for saffron.

lal mirch: Hindi for red chilli.

last: How long a taste can be detected by the **palate** and the **sensory body** after consumption indicates its flavour resonance.

length: A vertical pull of flavour.

maida: A refined, finely ground wheat flour used to make naan, **bhatura** and **parotta**.

marron: A freshwater crustacean that is endemic to south-west Western Australia.

masala: A word with many meanings. It can refer to a single spice, a blend of spices, the body of taste of a dish or the cultural messaging within how spices are used.

masala dabba: Typically a round tin with a lid that holds seven smaller bowls in which commonly used spices are stored within easy reach of the stovetop.

masoor dal: Split red lentils.

methi: Hindi for fenugreek leaves.

movement: Deliberate use of certain spices to shift **masala** into specific regional taste frames.

mukhwas: Candy-coated fennel seed, traditionally eaten after dinner to aid **digestion**.

pakora/pakoda: Vegetables that have been stirred through a batter of **besan** flour, spices and a little water and then deep-fried.

palate: General term that encompasses the mouth interior, as well as notional spaces immediately exterior to the mouth affected by aroma – around the neck, the outside of the jaw, the front of the face and just behind the base of the neck. In this book, the palate has sentience in the way of the sensory body. Connecting to the palate spaces enables us to harvest cultural, emotional and physical information from the experience of taste.

Pandit: The term used for a Hindu 'priest', as well as an honorific term offered to a wise person (historically a man) or gifted musician. It is also an alternative to **Brahman**.

paratha: A flaky, unleavened flatbread from North India normally made with **atta** and employing a technique of spreading ghee or oil on the surface of the flatbread during a repeated folding and rolling process, much like making puff pastry. Paratha can also be filled with aloo (spiced potato), paneer, gobi (spiced cauliflower) or keema (a minced/ground lamb, mutton or beef curry) to make a light meal when served with pickles and **dahi**.

parotta: A South Indian flaky and unleavened flatbread similar to **paratha** that is made by rolling the dough, coiling the dough and rolling the dough again. Parotta is made using **maida** or plain flour.

patterning: The way the taste of a spice is experienced throughout the course of a mouthful.

pitta: One of the three **doshas**. Related to fire and water, and described as driving, **heating** and energetic. Pitta-dominant folk are said to be of medium height and ruddy, with a well-developed athletic figure, and a charismatic, fiery and tenacious nature. See also **kapha** and **vata**.

***prasad*:** An edible blessing from God. Strictly speaking, *prasad* refers to offerings of food given at *havans* or *pujas*. But in all Indian regional traditions, all food is considered *prasad* and should be treated with reverence.

primary taste: The first and most obvious tastes we experience when trying individual spices. Primary tastes almost always eat like the spice smells. See also **secondary taste** and **tertiary taste**.

***puja*:** Hindu religious ritual performed both inside the home and at temples and **ashrams**. It is focused on the utterance of specific mantras or prayers to offset certain malefic planetary aspects, or to draw forward particular planetary blessings.

rajma: Hindi for red kidney beans.

sabja: Hindi for the seeds of the holy basil plant.

sabji: A vegetable dish (i.e. one that doesn't contain meat).

safad channa: Hindi for chickpeas.

***sattva*:** Sanskrit for complete, but also vital, clean, conscious, of balanced mind, of balanced state, harmonious, pure, strong and of the essence (see page 200).

***sattvic* food:** A food that is neither **heating** nor **cooling** but instead sits in balance with the body.

scaffolding: Another word for **tiering**.

secondary taste: The aspects of individual spice tastes that help build form and structure. These tastes often reference non-food-related flavours, such as the woody nature of cinnamon powder, or the clay taste of turmeric powder. See also **primary taste** and **tertiary taste**.

sensory body: The natural intelligence of our physical body, and the ways we can learn to decipher physical sensations to gather information about how our consumption affects our physical, emotional and intellectual states. See **three-body state**.

Shaivites: A group of Hindus who worship **Shivji** as their central deity.

Shivji: One of three male gods that form the trinity at the head of the Hindu pantheon. Shivji is the god of destruction to Brahma's creation and Vishnu's preservation.

tadka: Tempered spices added to a dish at the end of cooking.

taste: More than flavour, taste contains **sensory body** information that can be manipulated to achieve better health outcomes across the **three-body state**. See also **primary taste**, **secondary taste** and **tertiary taste**.

tawa: Concave pan, made from iron, cast iron, aluminium or carbon steel, traditionally used to cook Indian flatbreads.

tertiary taste: The most complex part of taste that largely refers to the overall feeling of **movement**, or emotive tone of a particular individual aromatic. See also **primary taste** and **secondary taste**.

texture: The creation of shape and form in **masala**.

thali: Traditional plates used with **katoris** to serve an Indian meal (see page 28). The word *thali* refers to the style of plate, but also to a complete meal.

three-body state: The confluence of meaning created by recognising the interconnectedness between the health of our physical, emotional and spiritual bodies. See also **sensory body**.

tiering: A technique in **masala** that involves using more than one aromatic in the same category to create a textured effect, such as three types of salt. It can be used to exponentially increase masala's complexity. I also refer to it as scaffolding.

tulsi: Hindi for holy basil.

urad dal: Hindi for black lentils, aka black gram (*Vigna mungo*).

***varshphal*:** A yearly reading and interpretation of a Hindu devotee's *janampatra* – their personal Vedic astrological chart.

vata: One of the three **doshas**. Related to air and space, and described as cool, light and dry. Vata-dominant folk are said to be very thin and either small or tall, with a sensitive digestive system, quick movements and creative spark. See also **kapha** and **pitta**.

yakhni: A traditional style of Kashmiri Hindu cooking that uses yoghurt as the primary fat and signature filter for **masala** (see pages 107, 133).

zafran: Urdu for saffron (from Persian).

Top row: New Delhi, 1979. Ammi and Papa with the cousins. (There are more of us now.) That's me, sitting naked on Ammi's lap. Shivani is bottom right. Eeshan is the one with the stripey socks. Cute.

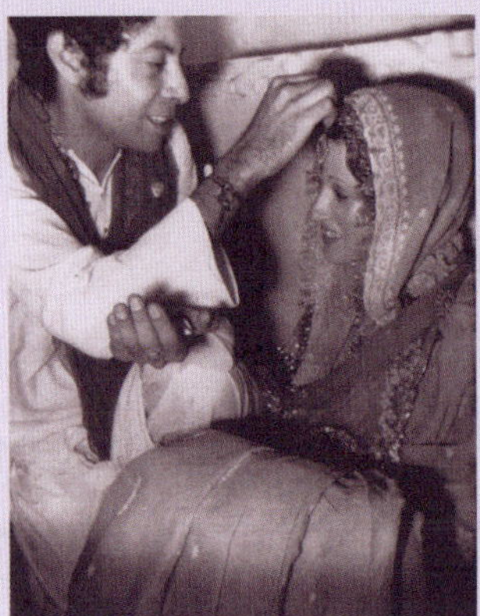

Second row, left to right: Mum and Dad's New Delhi wedding, 1974. Dad, Eeshan and me, 1977. Our kitchen in Jan Juc and Dad at the helm. Diwali, 2013.

Third row: Scott, Cailean, Ashok, Chips and me. Our Margaret River Christmas photo, 2020.

Bottom row: Cailean, Scott and Ash in the UK, 2024. The boys, Chip and me in Margaret River, 2024.

Acknowledgements

Masala is a vessel for wisdom, because no householder lives forever and the culinary traditions of the Indian regions are too vast to be held by any one recipe book. In this way masala is receptacle and source. It's how we honour those who came before and preserve the gift for those to come. Papa. Badi Ammi. Ammi. Dad. Bapu. Mum. Thank you for the time you gave me, and for the pieces left behind. Pranaam.

Bui and Shivani: it was enormous, what you both did for me during the Bengaluru book shoot. But bigger than that are our relationships with and to each other. That's what I'm really grateful for. I wouldn't have wanted to do it without either of you.

Jane Willson: publisher extraordinaire, always asking me to drill down further. You really fought for this. The email exchange that resulted in the title was one of the best ever. You pulled together the dream team for this project. I hope *What We Call Masala* does you proud.

Jen Crescenzo: I got here because of your work with me as development editor during those initial months establishing the frame, voice and looong writing sample for what became this book. Our agreement was no sugar-coated feedback, and you certainly delivered! Cherished friend and whip-cracker, both.

Kirsten Jenkins and Patricia Niven: I had no idea the work that would be involved in styling and shooting the photographs for this book. It still blows my mind that you both did what you did. Rooming in Bengaluru with you guys, drinking epic South Indian kopi, whizzing around in autos, working the kinds of hours unions strike over. And the laughter! Love you both. BFFs.

The rest of the Murdoch Team: thank you! Design manager Sarah Odgers and your creative genius. Editorial manager Justin Wolfers for your thoughtful way and genuine eagerness. Designer Klarissa Pfisterer for the most beautiful book I've ever seen. Editor Nicola Young, you moderated my voice with a light and loving hand, thank you. And Kerryn Burgess for the index of my dreams.

The tireless MB sales teams: Mary-Jane House. Ashleigh Jordan. Eleanor O'Connor. Matt Hoy. Anne Bowman. And the marketing and publicity genius of Sue Bobbermein.

Ridah Zaman: what a gift it was to have you alongside us in Bengaluru, recording every moment.

Lauren Trickett: for the Margaret River images we needed to make the story complete.

To the bit cast: Kaira, Neerav and Sherlock, thank you for letting us steal Shivani and trample your home. Cora for the cuddles. Kamila for your dedication and care.

And to my foundation: Scott, Cailean, Ashok and Chip Dog. Last because you are all the ground that I walk on. I know you've loved watching this come together for me and for us. But I also know you just love me. And that you're all happy when I am. Thank you for choosing to do life with me.

Let's do it all again.

Index

Quick Index of Spices

Including dry and wet spices, salts, and fats and other carriers.

Recipe Index

Subject index

For spice index and recipe index, see page 312.

Published in 2025 by Murdoch Books,
an imprint of Allen & Unwin

Murdoch Books Australia
Cammeraygal Country
83 Alexander Street
Crows Nest NSW 2065
Phone: +61 (0)2 8425 0100
murdochbooks.com.au
info@murdochbooks.com.au

Murdoch Books UK
Ormond House
26–27 Boswell Street
London WC1N 3JZ
Phone: +44 (0) 20 8785 5995
murdochbooks.co.uk
info@murdochbooks.co.uk

For corporate orders and custom publishing, contact our business development team at salesenquiries@murdochbooks.com.au

Publisher: Jane Willson
Editorial manager: Justin Wolfers
Design manager: Sarah Odgers
Design and illustration: Pfisterer + Freeman
Editor: Nicola Young
Photographer: Patricia Niven
Stylist: Kirsten Jenkins
Production manager: Natalie Crouch

Murdoch Books acknowledges the Traditional Owners of the Country on which we live and work. We pay our respects to all Aboriginal and Torres Strait Islander Elders, past and present.

EU Authorised Representative:
Easy Access System Europe,
Mustamäe tee 50, 10621 Tallinn, Estonia,
gpsr.requests@easproject.com

ISBN 9 781 76150 028 2

A catalogue record for this book is available from the National Library of Australia

A catalogue record for this book is available from the British Library

Colour reproduction by Splitting Image Colour Studio Pty Ltd, Wantirna, Victoria

Printed in China by C&C Offset Printing Co., Ltd.

OVEN GUIDE: You may find cooking times vary depending on the oven and oven setting you are using. The recipes in this book were tested using a fan-forced (convection) oven. As a general rule, if using a conventional oven, set the oven temperature to 20°C (25–50°F) higher than indicated in the recipe.

We have used 20 ml (4 teaspoon) tablespoon measures. If you are using a 15 ml (3 teaspoon) tablespoon add an extra teaspoon of the ingredient for each tablespoon specified.

10 9 8 7 6 5 4 3 2 1

Sarina Kamini

Food writer. Author. Hospo worker. Teacher and taste impresario. Sarina is all of those things, but her most important qualification for this book is that of Indian daughter. Spice is an education and masala is a legacy. Sarina's life journey has taken her from homes in New Delhi and Bangalore, to Paris, Southern California and Barcelona. Now living between the extended family home in New Delhi, and on Wadandi Boodja/Margaret River, Sarina opens her family kitchen and her masala masterclasses to share the world she was raised in with curious cooks of all skills and persuasions. Find Sarina online at sarinakamini.com or @sarina_kamini on Instagram.